The Fertilizing Seed
Wagner's Concept of
the Poetic Intent

Studies in Musicology, No. 63

George Buelow, Series Editor

Professor of Musicology
Indiana University

Other Titles in This Series

The Fertilizing Seed
Wagner's Concept of
the Poetic Intent

by
Frank W. Glass

UMI RESEARCH PRESS
Ann Arbor, Michigan

Produced and distributed by
UMI Research Press
an imprint of
University Microfilms International
Ann Arbor, Michigan 48106

Library of Congress Cataloging in Publication Data

Glass, Frank W.
   The fertilizing seed.

   (Studies in musicology ; no. 63)
   Revision of thesis (Ph.D.)–University of North Carolina
at Chapel Hill, 1981.
   Bibliography: p.
   Includes index.
   1. Wagner, Richard, 1813-1883–Aesthetics.   I. Title.
II. Series.

ML410.W19G46 1983   782.1'092'4   82-21813
ISBN 0-8357-1396-2   AACR2

To my mother and the memory of my father

Hans Sachs:

Der Regel Güte daraus man erwägt,
dass sie auch mal'ne Ausnahm' verträgt.

One weighs the value of rules
by letting them occasionally suffer an exception.

Die Meistersinger von Nürnberg, act 3, scene 5

Contents

List of Examples

List of Tables

Acknowledgments

I would like to express my appreciation to all those who by their advice, encouragement, and support have contributed to this study and have helped make it possible for me to complete it:

—at the University of North Carolina at Chapel Hill, Professor William S. Newman, the original advisor for my doctoral studies; Professor James W. Pruett, who kindly consented to become my advisor when Professor Newman retired; and the other members of my doctoral committee: Professors Calvin Bower, Jon Finson, James Haar, and Howard E. Smither;

— at the School of General Studies, Columbia University, my colleagues and friends who have borne with me through numerous revisions of the text; Dean Ward H. Dennis, Associate Dean Frank Wolf, and Joseph M. Kissane, Associate Dean for Student Affairs; and the students of the School, who for the past four years have proven to me daily that one can fulfill the responsibilities of family and job and yet undertake the demands of scholarship if the desire for learning is strong enough.

I owe a debt of gratitude that can never be adequately repaid to three people for their generosity to me throughout the years it has taken me to complete this work: my sister, Sally Boericke, and her husband, Jim; and Archibald McDowell III, whose perceptive and critical reading of this study has contributed so significantly to it.

Example 5.6 is reproduced from the Dover Publications, Inc., edition of *Tristan und Isolde,* itself a reprint of the C.F. Peters edition of about 1911. All other examples from *Tristan und Isolde* and the examples from *Die Meistersinger von Nurnberg* are reprinted courtesy of G. Schirmer, Inc. The examples from *Parsifal* (English translation © 1962 by Stewart Robb; international copyright secured) are reprinted by permission of G. Schirmer, Inc.

1

Introduction

A number of circumstances in the late 1840s conspired to disrupt Richard
Wagner's life and to alter the course his musical activities were taking.
Lohengrin was completed but unperformed; *Tannhäuser*, performed but
largely, to Wagner's way of thinking, misunderstood. Revolution was
smoldering or erupting throughout Germany and Europe; and revolutionary activities were becoming increasingly attractive to Wagner, while his
conducting duties in Dresden were becoming increasingly irksome. Caught
up in the Dresden revolt of 1849; misunderstood in his work by those he
sought to enlighten; with financial obligations mounting, relations with his
wife Minna deteriorating, and new ideas about his art occupying his
thoughts more and more, Wagner stopped composing for a time after he
had completed *Lohengrin* and turned his creative energies instead almost
entirely to essay writing.[1]

The titles of the essays Wagner wrote during this time indicate fairly
clearly the context in which his ideas were developing, as well as, to some
extent, the nature of those ideas. What the titles *Die Kunst und die Revolution, Das Kunstwerk der Zukunft,* "Kunst und Klima," and *Das Judenthum in der Musik* suggest, moreover, the essays themselves confirm:
a resentment against the popular operas of the day, exacerbated by a
growing disaffection with the society that had made those operas popular.[2]
The critical trend revealed in these essays culminated quickly in Wagner's
best-known theoretical work, *Oper und Drama,* completed in February
1851, only four months after it was begun, and published in November of
the same year by J. J. Weber of Leipzig. (See table 1 for an outline of
Wagner's creative activities from 1848 through 1856.)

In later years, Wagner described his state of mind at that earlier
period of time as "abnormal,"[3] implying not that he was mentally un-
balanced but that, as a creative artist, he was working in a field of study—
that is, abstract thinking—to which he was unaccustomed. He explained
that he felt compelled to treat in a theoretical manner what had become
increasingly clear to him in the operation of his artistic intuition. The

Table 1. Wagner's Creative Activities, 1848-1856

Year	Selected Essays	Prose Sketches	Librettos	Compositions
1848		*Götterdämmerung*	*Götterdämmerung*	*Lohengrin* completed
1849	*Die Kunst und die Revolution* *Das Kunstwerk der Zukunft*		*Götterdämmerung* revised	
1850	"*Kunst und Klima*" *Das Judenthum in der Musik* *Oper und Drama* begun			
1851	*Oper und Drama* completed *Eine Mittheilung an meine Freunde*	*Siegfried*	*Siegfried*	
1852		*Das Rheingold* *Die Walküre*	*Die Walküre* *Das Rheingold* *Siegfried* revised *Götterdämmerung* revised	
1853				*Das Rheingold* begun
1854				*Das Rheingold* completed *Die Walküre* begun
1855				*Die Walküre*
1856			*Siegfried* revised *Götterdämmerung* revised	*Die Walküre* completed *Siegfried* begun

results of this compulsion to give the workings of his subconscious mind a concrete, conscious expression (and, incidentally, to make his artistic goals better known to a wider range of the opera-going public) appear most exhaustively in *Oper und Drama*. The treatise includes Wagner's criticisms of the operas of his day, his analyses of the faults that underlay those operas, and his recommendations for artistic strategies to eliminate those faults. Because of both its subject matter and its place in time, *Oper und Drama* has generally been regarded as a significant dividing point in Wagner's creative life. On one side of it lie the operas of his young manhood, from *Die Feen* up through *Lohengrin*; on the other, those of his maturity: the *Ring des Nibelungen*, *Tristan und Isolde*, *Die Meistersinger von Nürnberg*, and *Parsifal*. The size alone of *Oper und Drama* distinguishes it from all Wagner's other writings; and in any discussion of Wagner and opera, it necessarily plays a prominent part.

This study takes its title from a sentence near the end of part 2 of *Oper und Drama*. "The understanding is therefore driven by necessity to wed itself with an element which shall be able to take up into it the poet's aim as a fertilizing seed, and so to nourish and shape this seed by its own, its necessary essence, that it may bring it forth as a realizing and redeeming utterance of feeling."[4] The frankly sexual image evoked here of a seed being taken up into a womb and brought forth again as something different recurs throughout *Oper und Drama*. The image is only reinforced by the two German verbs—*befruchten* and *zeugen*—Wagner borrowed from to describe the principal dramatic attribute of the seed. The English equivalents of both verbs—beget, procreate, generate, engender, fertilize, fructify, fecundate, impregnate, stimulate—offer, moreover, enough sexual implications to make Wagner's intentions and meaning too obvious to be doubted. His view of opera, consequently, was not the traditional one in which poetry and music warred with one another, in a master/servant relationship, for rights of supremacy. As far as Wagner was concerned, between the two arts, questions of dominance and subservience did not arise. Instead, he saw music and poetry uniting in opera in an act of love in which poetry was the masculine partner and music, the feminine. In the procreative act of their union, the poetic intent, or *dichterische Absicht* as it is in German, served as the fertilizing seed which music took up into her womb to bring forth as drama.[5]

It is Wagner's concept of the *dichterische Absicht* that is the subject of this study. The concept is defined at the outset only by a literal translation of the German, so that by *dichterische Absicht* is meant the aim, intention, purpose, or design arising from a poetic text that is to be set to music. (I have throughout the study used "intent" as the translation of *Absicht,* in preference to "aim," which appears in the quotations taken from William Ashton Ellis's translations of Wagner's prose works.) The *dichterische Absicht,* therefore, is considered to be not the equivalent of the poetry in a libretto but the essence of the libretto (as the metaphor "fertilizing seed" suggests)—the word or idea behind the words rather than the words themselves. Put another way, the *dichterische Absicht* is not the operatic text; it is the verbalized design, purpose, or intention of which the text is an elaboration.

In discussing Wagner's concept of the poetic intent, I have tried to do five things: (1) to show how the concept is related to the other ideas advanced in *Oper und Drama;* (2) to trace the appearance of the concept (and its relation to poetry and music) in Wagner's later theoretical writings; (3) to determine whether, in the years after he wrote *Oper und Drama,* Wagner altered the concept or his opinion of its importance in the creation of musical dramas; (4) to suggest ways in which the concept may be seen to operate in three of Wagner's mature operas; and (5) to expand the definition of the concept by relating its theoretical statement to its apparent practical application.

In this study, I have relied principally on the primary sources of Wagner's published essays and operatic compositions; and since I have dealt mainly with material that anyone might have had access to, my approach has been more critical than historical. The essays discussed are those that deal in one way or another with the subject of creating drama in music; and although *Oper und Drama* is chief among these, many written after it also bear significantly on the subject of the poetic intent. (The essays and their chronological relation to Wagner's operas are listed in table 2.) None of the *Ring* operas are discussed in this study, since they are considered to be intimately related (at least in their original conception) to the theories outlined in *Oper und Drama* but not necessarily to those set forth in Wagner's later theoretical writings. Nevertheless, this assumption represents only one point of view. One might also trace the similarities and differences among the *Ring* operas and any interrelationships between the operas and the theoretical writings. I have chosen, however, not to pursue this line of inquiry. Musical examples in the study are drawn instead from the three non-*Ring* operas that come after *Oper und Drama* on the assumption that any changes in Wagner's theories would be more likely to find their practical expression in *Tristan und Isolde, Die Meistersinger von Nürnberg,* and *Parsifal* than in *Das Rheingold, Die Walküre, Siegfried,* or *Götterdämmerung.*

The study is divided into eight chapters. The first introduces the study, states its goals, outlines its approach, and relates it to previous works in the field. The second provides a brief survey of influences affecting Wagner's theory of opera and includes a summary of *Die Kunst und die Revolution, Das Kunstwerk der Zukunft,* and parts 1 and 2 of *Oper und Drama* as works preliminary to the all-important statement of ideas found in part 3 of *Oper und Drama.* The third part of the study examines Wagner's view of the relationship between poetry and music in opera and of the role of the poetic intent in that relationship, as set forth in part 3 of *Oper und Drama.* The fourth part of the study traces the concept of the poetic intent through Wagner's theoretical writings that come after *Oper und Drama.* The fifth, sixth, and seventh parts of the study offer musical illustrations of the poetic intent at work in *Tristan und Isolde, Die Meistersinger von Nürnberg,* and *Parsifal.* The eighth part, which contains the conclusions of the study, relates the musical analyses to the ideas found in Wagner's essays and redefines the concept of the poetic intent in practical musical terms.

No previous studies that I have found deal specifically with Wagner's concept of the poetic intent; but a very large number, of course, deal with the related subject of poetry and music in Wagner's operas and theoretical writings. Of these studies, Jack M. Stein's *Richard Wagner and the Synthesis of the Arts,* published in 1960, has exerted considerable influence on subsequent writers on Wagner. In examining Wagner's early idea of combining all the arts into one complete work of art, the *Gesamtkunstwerk,* Stein concentrated primarily on the arts of poetry and music. He discussed at length the theories of opera that Wagner developed after *Oper und Drama* and drew a correlation between all the theories and Wagner's overall operatic output. The results of Stein's research led him to conclude that Wagner changed completely both his theory and his practice in the years following the completion of *Oper und Drama.*

Stein saw *Oper und Drama* as the embodiment of what he interpreted to be Wagner's conviction that a synthesis of the arts could best come about "by subordinating the music to the total drama, making the latter the point of departure at all times."[6] As Stein interpreted *Oper und Drama,* the words in opera should dominate the music. Stein felt that Wagner, after he started reading Schopenhauer in 1854, later accepted a philosophy and assumed an artistic stance that completely contradicted the theoretical basis of *Oper und Drama.* Since Schopenhauer's philosophy denied the possibility of a synthesis of the arts, Stein saw Wagner's subsequent theoretical problem as involving a need to reconcile his own idea of a union of the arts with Schopenhauer's belief that such a union was impossible. (Stein, incidentally, did not attempt to explain why Wagner should have felt at all compelled to reconcile the ideas in *Oper und Drama* with the philosophy of Schopenhauer.) In the process of reconciliation, Wagner's essay *Zukunftsmusik* was, in Stein's view, an effort to impose Schopenhauer's philosophy on the "curious combination of Romantic

Table 2. Wagner's Creative Activities, 1857-1882

Year	Selected Essays	Prose Sketches	Librettos	Compositions
1857	"Über Franz Liszt's symphonische Dichtungen"	Tristan und Isolde	Tristan und Isolde	Siegfried I completed Siegfried II Tristan und Isolde begun
1858				Tristan und Isolde
1859				Tristan und Isolde completed
1860	Zukunftsmusik			
1861		Die Meistersinger, 2d	Die Meistersinger	
1862				Die Meistersinger begun
1863				Die Meistersinger
1864				Die Meistersinger
1865		Parsifal, 1st		Siegfried II completed Die Meistersinger
1866				Die Meistersinger
1867				Die Meistersinger completed
1868				
1869				Siegfried III begun Götterdämmerung begun

Year			
1870	Beethoven		Siegfried III Götterdämmerung
1871	Über die Bestimmung der Oper		Siegfried III completed Götterdämmerung
1872	Über Schauspieler und Sänger Ein Einblick in das heutige deutsche Opernwesen		Götterdämmerung
1873			Götterdämmerung
1874			Götterdämmerung completed
1875			
1876			
1877	Parsifal, 2d	Parsifal	Parsifal begun
1878			Parsifal
1879	Über das Opern-Dichten und Komponiren im Besonderen Über die Anwendung der Musik auf das Drama		Parsifal
1880	Religion und Kunst		Parsifal
1881			Parsifal
1882			Parsifal completed

ideas, the esthetic rationalism of Lessing, and the materialistic sensation-alism of Ludwig Feuerbach"[7] that formed the philosophical basis of *Oper und Drama*. According to Stein, Wagner later abandoned the old *Oper und Drama* theory completely and, in the essay *Beethoven*, developed a new theory of the dramatic artwork based entirely on Schopenhauer's doctrines. Stein considered Wagner's later essay *Über die Bestimmung der Oper* to contain a variation of the theory set forth in *Beethoven*.

Stein tried to illustrate the process of theoretical reconciliation he saw in Wagner's writings by referring to Wagner's musical compositions. In Stein's view, which was not strictly chronological (see table 2 above), *Tristan und Isolde* was the musical counterpart of *Zukunftsmusik*; *Parsifal,* of *Beethoven*; and *Die Meistersinger von Nürnberg,* of *Über die Bestimmung der Oper.* Stein believed that in Wagner's earlier operas "the word came into its greatest dominance over the other elements of the synthesis,"[8] while in his later operas music gradually assumed an ascendancy over words. Thus, Stein saw Wagner's creative output as representing a musical development from opera toward symphony. In this development, *Parsifal* stood at the farthest extreme from *Lohengrin* and *Das Rheingold*. In the early operas, words played a principal part; but Stein found the dialogue in *Parsifal* to be of less importance than in any of Wagner's other operas—a conclusion based, in part, on Stein's own assessment of the importance of the dialogue in *Parsifal* and, in part, on the observation that the *Parsifal* libretto is one of Wagner's shortest, while the score itself is one of Wagner's longest.

In discussing the music of *Parsifal*, Stein pointed to the increased amount of stage action during which no words were sung as confirmation of his belief that the orchestra had assumed a dominant role in the Wagnerian music drama. Stein felt that the importance of the orchestra was shown additionally by the fact that all the motives but one were generated by the orchestra independent of the vocal line. Only the "Durch Mitleid wissend" motive appeared to Stein to be a true "reminiscence" motive of the old *Oper und Drama* variety—that is, a motive first associated with text in the vocal line and later used in the opera to recall the words sung at its first appearance. Stein considered the other *Parsifal* motives to be generally unrelated to specific verbal concepts. He characterized these motives as primarily symphonic themes which Wagner varied and combined freely with "no slavish attention to the text."[9] Stein found final support for his thesis and "a striking analogy in the fact that Wagner intended, after the completion of *Parsifal,* to turn to a form of pure music and write a symphony."[10]

As excellent as Stein's study is, it is nevertheless marred, in my opinion, by a fundamental misunderstanding of *Oper und Drama* that equates the functions of poetry with the end result of drama; or put more simply, the words in the libretto with the drama itself.[11] The mistake is easy enough to make, since in the spoken play the words do, in the majority of cases, create the drama and since Wagner himself used the word "drama" to mean both the spoken play and the dramatic situation, incident, or mood that results in a heightened emotional state. The equation, which is sufficiently valid in the spoken play to allow "play" and "drama" to be used interchangeably, simply does not stand in opera, however, where music, a powerful emotional stimulant in its own right (more powerful than words, in Wagner's opinion), is one of the components of the artwork. The failure on Stein's part to differentiate between "words" and "drama" as the two terms apply to opera led him to read into the theories of *Oper und Drama* the idea (which I think Wagner never intended to convey) that in opera the words should dominate the music. The mistake invalidates the thesis of Stein's book but does not necessarily invalidate many of his observations. One can profit from Stein's views on how poetry and music combine in Wagner's operas without subscribing to the fallacy those views are intended to support.

The chief merit of Stein's study, as I see it, is that it offers a systematic and extensive discussion of some of the discrepancies that exist between the theories of *Oper und Drama* and Wagner's later theory and practice. Other writers before Stein had noted discrepancies, but almost only in passing. Of the many, the following may serve as examples of the cursory manner in which these discrepancies were noted:

(1)   Cosima Wagner noted in her diary on 23 October 1872 that "a pamphlet has also been sent to us which sets out to prove that *Die Meistersinger* is a backward step in W.'s development."[12]

(2)   The summer of 1876 "marked the beginning of the end of the friendship"[13] between Wagner and Friedrich Nietzsche. For some time before that, Nietzsche had been growing more and more disillusioned with Wagner; eventually he made a complete and public break with the composer. Among Nietzsche's many subsequent writings against Wagner are the following pertinent sentences from the third essay of *Zur Genealogie der Moral,* published in 1887. Nietzsche wrote that Wagner adopted the philosophy of Schopenhauer

> to such an extent that there exists a complete theoretical contradiction between his earlier and his later aesthetic creed—the former set down, for example, in *Opera and Drama,* the latter in the writings he published from 1870 onward. Specifically, he ruthlessly altered . . . his judgment as to the value and status of *music.* . . . He grasped all at once that with the Schopenhauerian theory and innovation *more* could be done . . . with the theory of the *sovereignty* of music as Schopenhauer conceived it: music set apart from all the arts.[14]

(3)   Georges Noufflard, in his *Richard Wagner d'après lui-même* of 1885, maintained that in the composition of *Tristan und Isolde* Wagner turned his back on the theories that underlay *Oper und Drama* and the *Ring* operas and wrote instead, for much of the opera, absolute music accompanied by incoherent words in the vocal parts.[15]

(4)   Houston Stewart Chamberlain, although he did not mention any change of emphasis in Wagner's theories (as perhaps befits so complete a Wagnerian), did not discrepancies between *Oper und Drama* and some of the later operas. Chamberlain accounted for these discrepancies by pointing to the connection between *Oper und Drama* and the *Ring* operas and by attributing the theoretical details found in the former to Wagner's ideas for realizing these operas. "I even think," wrote Chamberlain in 1888, "that this preoccupation with the particular poem that he had in view is a fault in this fine work, . . . and that *The Artwork of the Future,* written at a moment when the *Ring* was less in the forefront of his thought, is in many respects its superior."[16]

(5)   Shortly after the turn of the century, Guido Adler repeated the observation that the theoretical norms in *Oper und Drama* derived from the artistic plan for the *Ring.* In his lectures on Wagner, delivered at the University of Vienna in 1903 and 1904, Adler pointed out that, as far as the relationship between Wagner's poetic and musical forms was concerned, "Wagner gives different explanations and makes different assertions that sometimes contradict one another and do not always correspond with the artistic executions in his succeeding works."[17] Adler, however, considered the discrepancies in Wagner's works to show merely that Wagner as an "artist places himself high above the speculating theoretician."[18]

(6)   In the 1920s, Paul Bekker recognized the inconsistencies in Wagner's writings but tried to show an underlying unity in them. He wrote that the governing factor in Wagner's development, the factor "which lends his philosophy a semblance of consistency, is his truly consistent theory of theatre."[19] Later, Bekker altered his position somewhat and observed that Wagner's "later writings hold fast, though with somewhat different deductions than his youthful essays, to the idea that opera must be sung and that language must render the singing natural."[20]

Of the writers mentioned above who, like Stein, noted the inconsistencies in Wagner's theory and practice and even the inconsistencies among his theories, most offered little more than suggestions to explain what they had observed. Stein went beyond suggestions to develop a theory to account for the inconsistencies and then to test that theory by applying it to portions of Wagner's operas. The importance of Stein's effort can be judged, at least to some extent, by the influence his study has had on writers who have come after him. We see both direct and indirect evidence of his work in the following:

(7)   Robert W. Gutman, in *Richard Wagner: The Man, His Mind, and His Music,* published in 1968, added to Stein's observations his own belief that Wagner, in trying to justify the changes in his compositional technique after *Oper und Drama,* practiced duplicity. Thus, Gutman saw the Wagner of *Beethoven* "no longer pretending," as Gutman felt the Wagner of *Zukunftsmusik* had tried to do, "to restate the Swiss essays in abbreviated form."[21] Gutman tried to show that Wagner hid his new ideas about opera by writing about them in articles that treated a wide variety of other subjects. "He did not appear eager," Gutman wrote, "to make the general public aware of how completely his work and thinking had altered. Quite the contrary, unsure of himself, he added to the confusion."[22] In support of this point, Gutman extracted from Wagner's final essays statements to prove that Wagner could not make up his mind about the roles poetry and music should play in opera and that "to the end of his days he oscillated on this theoretic point."[23]

(8)   Robert Bailey, in the introduction to his dissertation on the sketches and drafts for act 1 of *Tristan,* observed that "any attempt to deal with *Opera and Drama* in connection with [the second and third acts of *Tristan*], or, indeed, with any of the operas after *Tristan,* is both uninformed and futile."[24]

(9)   In *Richard Wagners Musikdramen*, Carl Dahlhaus spoke of the confusion brought about by what appeared to be discrepancies in Wagner's definitions of what the relationship between words and music in opera ought to be. Dahlhaus suggested that the theory of *Oper und Drama* appeared to be reversed by the theory outlined twenty years later in *Beethoven*. In Dahlhaus's interpretation of the problem, Wagner decided in *Beethoven* that it was not music which created drama, but drama which created music. "Obviously," Dahlhaus wrote,

> the aesthetic theory Wagner outlined in *Opera and Drama* was thrown into confusion, on the one hand by his reading of Schopenhauer, from 1854 onwards, and on the other by his experiences in the composition of the *Ring* and *Tristan*. The dogma lost its clear definition.[25]

Echoing Gutman's opinion, Dahlhaus claimed that Wagner's confusion was reflected in the later essays, the texts of which frequently made it difficult to tell exactly what Wagner really thought about the matter.

(10)   In a recent collection of essays on Wagner, Stein's influence is explicitly acknowledged. Richard David notes in "Wagner the Dramatist" that Stein charted well the change of emphasis in Wagner's writings about

opera after *Tristan*. David also recognizes the influence of Schopenhauer on Wagner and, along with Stein, concludes that Wagner finally accepted Schopenhauer's belief in music's supremacy among the arts. Like Stein (and Nietzsche before him), David states that the later essays "allowed music an independence and leading role that quite contradict Wagner's earlier theories."[26]

The preceding selection of writers who have observed discrepancies in Wagner's theory and practice can be divided into two groups: one including those who, like Stein, have considered these discrepancies to be critical indications of a substantial change in Wagner's view of opera; and the other, those who have discounted these discrepancies as relatively unimportant. Against both of these groups can be set a third that affords a completely different point of view. This group includes those writers who have seen no inconsistency in Wagner's theories and no lack of harmony between those theories and Wagner's practice. A prime example of the opinions of this group can be found in the writings of George Bernard Shaw.

Shaw's review of Noufflard's *Richard Wagner d'après lui-même* appeared in 1894. The review was entitled "The Tone Poet," and in it Shaw countered Noufflard's assertion that in *Tristan und Isolde* Wagner had written absolute music without coherent words. Shaw maintained that wordless music was not necessarily absolute music. "Absolute music," he wrote, "is the purely decorative sound pattern: tone poetry is the musical expression of poetic feeling."[27] In illustration of his point, Shaw referred to the shepherd's tune that begins act 3 of *Tristan*: intensely dramatic music, even though wordless. Shaw gave as the reason for this opinion his belief that there was a great deal of feeling that was both highly poetic and highly dramatic and yet incapable of verbal expression. He observed that words were "the counters of thinking, not of feeling,"[28] that music was the best artistic medium for expressing feeling, and that Wagner had recognized this fact. Shaw considered the condensation of language in *Tristan und Isolde* a practical example of what Wagner had recommended in *Oper und Drama*:

> There is a great deal of this reduction of speech to mere ejaculation in Wagner; and it is a reduction directly pointed to in those very pages of *Opera and Drama* which seem to make the words all-important by putting the poem in the first place as the seed of the whole music drama, and yet make a clean sweep of nine-tenths of the dictionary by insisting that it is only the language of feeling that craves for musical expression, or is even susceptible of it.[29]

In support of his argument, Shaw reiterated Wagner's belief, stated in *Oper und Drama,* that feeling is the drama's proper subject and that music is the means by which feeling is most effectively expressed. As long as music in a drama maintains the appropriate level of feeling, Shaw felt that the composer could substitute "even balderdash"[30] for a coherent text and still produce drama. Coherent words were only necessary in drama when a thought "impenetrated with intense feeling"[31] had to be expressed along with the feeling in order to give the feeling meaning. Shaw concluded that Wagner's progress from *Der fliegende Holländer* through *Parsifal* took "a perfectly straight line ahead in theory as well as in artistic execution."[32]

Even in the face of the accumulated weight of evidence from writers like Stein, Shaw's views carry a weight of their own because they are the informed, reasoned, articulate thoughts of a man whose knowledge of drama, in all its manifestations, was considerable and firsthand. The impact of his views, however, is diminished by his being a professional writer rather than a musician; and today the views themselves would probably not be those held by the majority of writers on Wagner. Nevertheless, there are those whose studies lend support to the belief that Wagner's theory and practice after *Oper und Drama* formed stages in a consistent artistic development, the foundation of which was *Oper und Drama*. The following may be considered representatives of this group:

(1) At a time when Wagner's music was generally being criticized as formless, Alfred Lorenz undertook to prove that it was not. He devoted the four volumes of his monumental work on the formal structure of Wagner's music to showing that the musical-dramatic period, mentioned by Wagner in *Oper und Drama,* was the structural basis not only of the *Ring* operas but of *Tristan und Isolde, Die Meistersinger von Nürnberg,* and *Parsifal* as well. In his analyses, Lorenz tried to show that throughout all Wagner's mature operas the theoretical concept of the musical-dramatic period remained constant and that all these later operas were organized into more or less clearly defined musical forms held together by a united poetic and musical content.[33]

(2) In his book *Aspects of Wagner,* Bryan Magee affirmed that *Das Kunstwerk der Zukunft, Oper und Drama,* and *Eine Mittheilung an meine Freunde* "embodied an entirely new theory of opera, which [Wagner] then went on to realize in his remaining works."[34] Magee felt that the ideas in these theoretical essays were confirmed by Wagner's operas and that "over and over again the subsequent practice of Wagner's greatest works is elaborated"[35] in the theory.

(3) In a study that dealt with a small portion of act 2 of *Tristan und Isolde,* Irmtraud Flechsig attempted to prove that there were definite relationships between verbal and musical structures that could be seen throughout the entire opera. In particular, she considered that sequential

structures in both text (where a number of subordinate clauses frequently precede a main clause) and music were absolutely typical of the opera.[36] Flechsig drew the assumption upon which her study was based—that is, the assumption of a unity between text and music in which neither is more important than the other—as much from the evidence of Wagner's theoretical essays as from her own perception of Wagner's compositional practices.

(4) Robert Bailey's dissertation on the sketches and drafts for the first act of *Tristan,* which has been quoted from above to suggest the influence of Stein, can probably be more appropriately used to support conclusions that contradict Stein. In the introduction to the dissertation, Bailey emphasized the difficulty and even the impossibility of trying to determine the "precise nature of the dialogue between the poetic conception and the ultimate musical realization,"[37] since the interrelationship often occurred in ways that Wagner himself did not always understand or seem aware of. Bailey felt, nevertheless, that in the majority of cases it could at least be stated that the text usually preceded the music, even though there were times when the music occurred to Wagner before the text and times when both music and text seemed to occur to him simultaneously. Bailey's research led him to conclude that Wagner's whole compositional procedure was

> quite the reverse of the usual assumption that Wagner thought fundamentally in instrumental terms, that he concocted an elaborate orchestral texture, and that he then—often carelessly—overlaid a vocal part not essential to that texture. Actually the reverse is true, and we can summarize the point by saying that the vocal part is the generating element of the entire texture.[38]

A later study by Bailey, based on his dissertation, describes Wagner's compositional procedure and a change in it that began with *Das Rheingold.* Before that, Wagner had written preliminary drafts from earlier sketches in which he was primarily concerned with setting the text. With *Das Rheingold,* however, he began to work out the music in his early sketches independent of the text and to adapt the music to the text only in the preliminary draft.[39] This change in compositional procedure might perhaps suggest a corresponding change of emphasis in Wagner's opinion of the importance of music in opera; but if it does, then the change of emphasis must be considered to hold good for every opera Wagner wrote after *Oper und Drama,* which is to say that *Oper und Drama* either takes the change into account and applies, like the change, to all the later operas or does not take the change into account and applies to none of them.

(5) In the introduction to a study curtailed by his death, Deryck

Cooke proposed to elucidate Wagner's dramatic intentions throughout the entire *Ring* cycle "by considering the simple overt meaning of each passage of the text as it is given its full and complex symbolic significance by its musical setting."[40] Cooke intended to carry out his study in the belief that "the ultimate meaning of a Wagner 'drama' is achieved through the music, as Wagner himself was perfectly well aware."[41] The successful completion of the study would have shown, consequently, not only the link between words and music in the *Ring* operas but also the determinative role of music in bringing about the full realization of the drama. The proof of the belief upon which the study was to have been based, drawn as it was to have been from the *Ring* operas, would have served, moreover, to invalidate the basis of Stein's study; or it would have shown that the fundamental theory of *Oper und Drama,* as Stein and others have understood it, serves no practical purpose, since it applies to none of the operas Wagner wrote.

The preceding studies that have been loosely grouped under Stein's book and Shaw's review are intended to illustrate two fundamentally different opinions about the role Wagner assigned poetry in *Oper und Drama.* Implied in the difference of opinion about the role of poetry is a corresponding difference of opinion about the role of music, both of which contribute to one basic problem in the treatise. All the studies cited bear on this problem; its components can be stated fairly simply in three questions: What is the relationship of poetry to music that *Oper und Drama* recommends? Do the later theoretical essays support or contradict this recommendation? How do Wagner's later operas reflect the relationship that the theoretical works advocate? The striking differences to be seen in the answers to these question suggest that perhaps the basic problem has not been accurately defined and that a restatement of the problem in different terms might allow for more reliable answers to the questions the problem raises.[42]

The present study states the problem not in terms of poetry's relation to music but in terms of the poetic intent's relation to music. The poetic intent is considered to be related to poetry but different from it. It is from this point of view that the study seeks to answer the questions raised above. The study views the concept of the poetic intent—which is to say, the idea that the poetic intent inspires the musical response and helps bring it forth as drama—as the foundation upon which *Oper und Drama* is built. It traces the concept through *Oper und Drama* and the later theoretical essays and attempts to show its operation in the later operatic compositions. In the dichotomy of opinion set up between Stein and Shaw, the study inclines more toward Shaw than Stein, since it finds the concept of the poetic intent to be a consistently valid aspect of Wagner's theory and practice from *Oper und Drama* on, in spite of the varied views expressed in the later essays and in spite of the different musical ideas realized in the later operas.

2

Influences on Wagner's Theory of Opera

Wagner came to write down his ideas about opera under the influence of a German nationalism that by 1850 had grown to pervade almost every sphere of German intellectual life. The manifestations of this nationalism were not merely political: they were literary, historical, philosophical, musical, artistic, and linguistic as well. To the influence of nationalism in most of these fields, moreover, Wagner responded; and when he declared his intention of creating an artwork of the future, it was a German artwork he had in mind, an artwork rooted in Germany's artistic past, brought to life by Germany's revolutionary present, and supporting a new German cultural future.[1]

In one respect, the growing feeling of national pride in Germany was stimulated by discoveries in the second half of the eighteenth century of several German medieval manuscripts, including a thirteenth-century copy of the *Nibelungenlied*. These newly discovered manuscripts sparked an interest in Germany's literary past that gradually spread throughout the country. As a result, the study of philology assumed a particularly timely applicability to national life as old German legends, folk tales, and myths were unearthed and found new popularity. The research of philologists provided one type of response to Lessing's call for German themes in literature (original contemporary writings, such as Goethe's *Faust,* based on older sources provided another); and works like Herder's *Stimmen der Völker in Liedern* (1778–79) were succeeded by Achim von Arnim and Clemens Brentano's collection of German folk poems, *Des Knaben Wunderhorn* (1805–8), and Friedrich and Jakob Grimm's immensely popular *Kinder- und Hausmärchen* (1812–15) and *Deutsche Mythologie* (1835). These fruits of philology not only glorified the primitive beginnings of the new German literary tradition but also held up as admirable the simple, humble life of earlier times, which was the background and essence of the stories the folk tales and myths related.[2]

Tales like those of the Grimms and those in E. T. A. Hoffmann's *Die Serapionsbrüder* formed part of a literary heritage that Wagner, like most

Germans of his time, knew well. It was not until he went to Paris in 1839, however, that he came to appreciate fully the artistic possibilities inherent in the sources that lay behind the popular tales. In Paris, Wagner met Samuel Lehrs, a German philologist who introduced him to the study of German medieval literature. Through Lehrs, Wagner acquired the beginnings of a knowledge that not only formed one of the foundations of his theory of opera but also provided the principal subject matter for virtually all of his subsequent opera librettos. Lehrs provided Wagner with the initial access to a body of literature that even before Wagner wrote *Oper und Drama* included the following sources: Wolfram von Eschenbach's thirteenth-century epic *Parzival*; Albert von Schaffenburg's *Die jüngere Titurel*; several twelfth- and thirteenth-century variants of the Lohengrin legend; Gottfried von Strassburg's thirteenth-century rendering of the Tristan legend in Hermann Kurz's modern German version; Christoph Wagenseil's *Von der Meistersinger holdseligen Kunst*; the *Volsunga Saga*; the *Nibelungenlied*; and the *Völuspâ* from the *Elder Edda*. Wagner augmented his knowledge of these early works, moreover, by reading contemporary studies on related subjects: Georg Gottfried Gervinus's *Geschichte der poetischen Nationalliteratur der Deutschen* (1826); Jakob Grimm's *Über den altdeutschen Meistergesang* (1811); and Friedrich von der Hagen's *Minnesinger* (1838), which Ernest Newman has called "a mine of information about the German poems of the 12th, 13th and 14th centuries."[3]

Related to the growing national interest in philology was an emphasis on the creation of a new national literature. Lessing had said that Germany needed its own national drama; and together with writers like Herder, Goethe, Schiller, Schelling, Kant, and Hegel, he helped create not only a national drama but a literature that aimed at being truly German as well. The ideas that these writers espoused were not without effect on Wagner, and many of their beliefs find a reiterated expression in *Die Kunst und die Revolution, Das Kunstwerk der Zukunft, and Oper und Drama*. Among the ideas Wagner borrowed and included in these treatises are these: art wells up from its own time; national art is popular art; art should develop from its own necessities, not from antiquated rules; true art is characterized by organic forms; popular art displays the need for myth; true poetry is a natural, primal utterance of man; the theater should be an organ of communal life; drama is the most truly social art.[4] Thus, Wagner's artistic theories developed from a common intellectual stock to which many German thinkers had contributed; and while much in Wagner's theoretical writings was unique, not everything, naturally, was original.

The idea of revolution, an outgrowth of German nationalism in the nineteenth century, also influenced Wagner and colored much of his writ-

ing during the latter half of the 1840s. In reviewing part of Eduard Devrient's *Geschichte des deutschen Schauspielkunst,* for example, Wagner
insisted that the aftermath of the Vienna revolt in March 1848 had shown
that, as far as entertainment was concerned, the German people were no
longer content to accept the ballets, Italian operas, and other varieties of
"theatrical offal"[5] that for so long had made up Germany's standard
theatrical fare. Instead, newly free Germans were demanding wholesome,
uplifting works of art that matched the "resolute, courageous mien"[6] of
the people themselves. Wagner saw in this demand a reflection of the
people's revolutionary interest in the state: the people who wanted responsible government wanted, at the same time, worthwhile theater. He
affirmed that the state, therefore, had a responsibility to the people to
repay their interest in government by supporting the theater, a quid pro
quo that would allow it to be made "independent of every consideration
other than that of invigorating and ennobling the taste and manners of the
people."[7]

Even the unlikely title and subject matter of "Kunst und Klima" did
not prevent Wagner from voicing his revolutionary concerns. Arguing that
art could develop wherever man had mastered his dependence on his
climate, Wagner proceeded to assert that mastery of climate would allow
men to "stride onward also to the mastery of each dependence on those
oppressive tenets which have . . . ruled both the religious and political
conscience of mankind with equal cramping dictates of authority."[8] Wagner maintained that more important to the development of art than climate
was a brotherhood of men living in a freedom that all shared together.
Such a free community of people, however, could only result from love.
Love also made possible the creation of true art. Thus, in Wagner's view,
love—beginning with love between man and wife and going on to encompass love of children, friends, brothers, and all mankind—was the common denominator that linked art and revolution.[9]

Out of this atmosphere of emotionalism and political unrest grew the
statements of operatic reform found in Wagner's writings of 1849 and
1850. In a volatile situation, Wagner assumed the role of an artist-revo-
lutionary who recognized the relation between art and society and built
an artistic revolution on a political one. He saw art as a social product
reflecting the culture from which it comes and realized that a decadent
culture produces decadent art. This is the thesis, in fact, of *Die Kunst
und die Revolution,* an essay in many ways seminal to Wagner's later
operatic theories. In the essay, Wagner wrote as both an artist and a
revolutionary, roundly condemning the theater of his day and the society
that produced and maintained it. He considered that this theater existed
almost entirely for the distraction and amusement of people bored to

Aeschylus,

death by their lives. Consequently, for the sake of humanity, Wagner proposed to abolish the standard fare of plays, ballets, and operas and replace it with dramas that would snatch audiences away from their daily routine and attune them instead to "a reverent reception of the highest and sincerest things the human mind can grasp."[10]

In *Die Kunst und die Revolution,* Wagner held up as a model for the ideal relationship that should exist between the theater and the public the art and society of ancient Athens. In Greek tragedy, he found words, music, and gestures uniting to create dramatic artworks that were open to all and, because they were rooted in the common experience, were understood and appreciated by all as well. Such artworks were, of necessity, dependent on a "mutual intercourse"[11] with society; and when the society that made up the Greek state ceased to exist, Greek drama ceased to exist too. Wagner attributed the dissolution of both the state and the art to a spirit of egoism which grew up and destroyed the spirit of brotherhood and community. At all costs, therefore, egoism had to be avoided in society; and at the end of *Die Kunst und die Revolution,* Wagner, in his role as revolutionary, tried to formulate an organizational basis for society that would eliminate the defects of spirit that had destroyed Athens and would lead, in his time, to a nobler society and a nobler art.

In considering the degree to which revolution may have influenced Wagner's theory of opera, one is confronted by the substantial part revolution seems to have played in Wagner's daily life at the time. His participation in the Dresden revolt of 1849, together with his writings from the time, bespeaks a pervasive interest in and commitment to the business of revolution. Nevertheless, these same writings and the later events of Wagner's life suggest that the motives behind his interest and involvement were not altogether unalloyed. In the whole span of Wagner's life, his attempts to improve society through political agitation played, in general, a very small part; and of his two most publicized interests at mid-century, art and revolution, the first was unquestionably predominant.[12] After all, art was Wagner's profession and his primary concern. The titles of the principal essays from the period—*Die Kunst und die Revolution, Das Kunstwerk der Zukunft,* and *Oper und Drama*—illustrate this. The essays themselves, moreover, although liberally sprinkled with references to art's need for revolution and to the artistic benefits to be derived from revolution, reveal an increasing concentration of interest away from revolution toward art in general, and toward musical-dramatic art in particular. By the time Wagner reached the final chapter of *Oper und Drama,* he was no longer trying to promote the benefits to art that a successful revolution could supply. Instead, he was proclaiming the artwork of the future as the means by which society could be reclaimed. As far as Wagner's theory of opera is concerned, therefore, the influence of the revolution must be considered to have been slight. It was scarcely more than a happy coincidence that offered Wagner a catalyst for his own thoughts on operatic reform and then gave those thoughts a historical context whereby they achieved a timeliness and universality that they would otherwise have lacked completely. _–1848_

In *Die Kunst und die Revolution,* Wagner had attempted to plan for a nobler society and a nobler art; but, not surprisingly, in *Das Kunstwerk der Zukunft,* he developed more extensively his vision of the art. Again discussing Greek tragedy and its dissolution, he proceeded to trace the subsequent development of each art that had contributed to the united artwork. He tried to show that when the arts had been united, they had been able to inspire and teach the public; but when they had become separated, they had turned out to be nothing more than idle diversions for private connoisseurs. Contemporary art, Wagner thought, had become "a mere product of culture and [had] not sprung from life itself."[13] No matter how much the separate arts developed, Wagner asserted that they could never attain the power of expression available to the united artwork. The assertion was based on his belief that each separate art evolved along a line of force which eventually brought the art to the limits of its expressive capability, beyond which it could not go without becoming either unintelligible or absurd. At the boundary of expressivity, however, where one art's powers ended, Wagner believed that another art's powers began and that, at that point, each art reached out for help to another correlated art. This process was, in Wagner's opinion, the artistic fact of life upon which Greek tragedy (and all truly successful drama) was based.

Wagner's view of Greek tragedy, tied as it is to his concept of the artwork of the future, was influenced by an idea common among many German thinkers of the nineteenth century. The idea was that of the *Gesamtkunstwerk,* a complete work of art in which all the arts would be combined to produce an overall effect greater than that of any individual art. The *Gesamtkunstwerk* was a chief artistic goal toward which German nationalism tended: it was seen as an art form that would bind the nation closer together because it would speak through all the arts to all the people. Certain writers developed the idea to almost impossibly farfetched extremes incorporating synesthesia,[14] but Wagner's version of the idea was not improbable or unreasonable. It closely resembled, in fact, the *Gesamtkunstwerk* proposed in the early years of the century by August Wilhelm Schlegel. Schlegel saw the ideal artistic union in

the theatre, where many arts are combined to produce a magical effect, where the most lofty and profound poetry has for its interpreter the most finished action, which is at once eloquence and an animated picture, while architecture contributes her splendid decorations, and painting her perspective illusions, and the aid of music is called in to attune the mind, or to heighten by its strains the emotions which already agitate it.[15]

It has been recently suggested that Wagner never actually practiced the *Gesamtkunstwerk* theory that he espoused,[16] but I think it might be fairer to say that he never seriously espoused the theory. It is true that Wagner tried to follow the tendency toward communality in all the arts, that in *Das Kunstwerk der Zukunft* he discussed architecture, painting, and sculpture as well as poetry, music, and dance. But it is also true that he saw the communal tendency itself most strongly revealed not in the plastic arts but in the arts most directly related to mankind—the living arts of words, tones, and gestures.[17] Wagner's concern for architecture and painting was important, but it was peripheral in that it was directed toward creating an appropriate setting for the drama. The drama itself, which was the focal point of Wagner's interest, was not really a *Gesamtkunstwerk* at all. *Dreikunstwerk,* or even *Zweikunstwerk,* would probably describe Wagner's art form more accurately.

Nevertheless, like the revolution, the concept of the *Gesamtkunstwerk* contributed to the development of Wagner's ideas about opera and allowed those ideas to seem very much in the spirit of the times. But neither the revolution nor the *Gesamtkunstwerk* was essential to Wagner's view of what opera should be. His writings at mid-century show him becoming increasingly concerned with how words, music, and gestures— and more especially how words and music—could be combined to produce concentrated, emotionally satisfying drama. In response to this concern, Wagner narrowed the focus of his artistic vision; and what had been only a general, subconscious urge in his creative processes gradually became more definite—a conscious ideal, in fact. Without waiting for a successful revolution to come to pass, he began giving shape to this ideal. A little over a year after he had finished *Das Kunstwerk der Zukunft,* Wagner started work on the treatise that would lay the foundation upon which the first of the artworks of the future could be built in the present.

The treatise was *Oper und Drama.* When Wagner wrote it in the latter months of 1850, he knew something of the history of opera and of the series of conflicts that had arisen during that history over the proper relationship between words and music in opera. His knowledge of the current operatic repertory and of recent critical literature was considerable; but beyond that, of opera's early history from its beginnings to about the middle of the eighteenth century, he appears to have known little or nothing. The lapses in his knowledge are especially noticeable in part 1 of *Oper und Drama,* which purports to be a historical survey of opera's development. What Wagner did know of opera's early history (indeed, of opera's entire history) he used in a highly subjective manner to support his principal thesis, which was that, throughout its entire history, opera had been based on a fundamental error: Music, as a means of expression, had been made the end to be expressed; while drama, as the end of expression, had been made the means whereby music achieved its end.

In stating this error, Wagner sacrificed clarity for wordplay; but in view of the misunderstandings Wagner's statement has occasioned, I think it better to sacrifice altogether the wordplay for a clear statement of the error. Consequently, I would like to repeat a point made earlier in this study about the ambiguity of the word *drama.* In the sentence "A means of expression (music) has been made the end, while the end of expression (drama) has been made a means,"[18] Wagner used *drama* one time to convey two different meanings: the play or libretto, on the one hand; and the emotionally heightened incident, situation, or mood that is in itself dramatic, on the other. The words *drama* and *play,* however, or *drama* and *libretto,* are not necessarily synonymous or even compatible, any more than are the words *music* and *opera.* One can see how important *drama* is to the wordplay in Wagner's sentence, but also how deceptive it can be, by substituting for it words related to its first meaning—*libretto, poem, play, verse,* or even *words.* Substitutions related to the second meaning work no better. In both cases, as a result of the substitutions, the wordplay ceases to exist and the meaning of the sentence changes radically. Drama can be created by either words or music (or by both acting together), but the mere presence of words or music is no guarantee that drama will result. Consequently, in discussions of Wagner's opera theories, I believe that an expanded statement of the error Wagner perceived might be more useful than the original statement. Certainly it can at least do no harm to clarify the original statement by saying that, in Wagner's view, the libretto had heretofore been used only as a means of achieving opera's erroneous goal, which so far had been the creation of a succession of vocal numbers, rather than in combination with music as the means of achieving opera's correct goal, which should always be the creation of intense, gripping drama.

Part 1 of *Oper und Drama,* which is subtitled "Die Oper und das Wesen der Musik," is primarily critical, as Wagner himself acknowledged to his Dresden friend and supporter, the violinist Theodor Uhlig.[19] In part 1, Wagner was intent on detailing opera's faults rather than its merits. He tried to make the point that opera had never been allowed to become the perfect drama because opera composers had never allowed poetry to assume its proper function in the creative process. Wagner supported this point by trying to show that the history of opera revealed primarily a musical development in which poetry, from the beginning, had been used merely to give a semblance of dramatic cohesion to an almost random assemblage of elements that were only remotely related to one another and, quite simply, did not cohere. As Wagner put it, arias, ballets, and recitatives were joined together in opera "in all the sterile immiscibility of unnatural things."[20]

Wagner believed, nevertheless, that the supremacy of music in its unnatural union with poetry in opera had had a positive artistic result. He felt that the degree of expressiveness instrumental music had attained in his own time was a direct consequence of music's having come into contact with poetry without becoming subservient to it. Wagner's reasoning was that, if poetry had assumed control of opera at its beginning, music would never have been allowed to develop its full expressive powers because the poet, not being a musician himself, would never have realized that there were latent powers in music to be developed. Thus, music's usurping the province of poetry was a necessary part not only of opera's development but of music's development.

Having stated the error on which opera was based and the consequences of this error, Wagner proceeded to divide the history of opera into two separate evolutionary lines. One he called the "earnest" line because it was made up of operas written by composers who consciously tried to ennoble the genre in which they worked; the other he called the "naive" line because its composers, primarily Italian, wrote operas without apparent effort and without a conscious intention of changing or improving the genre. Wagner saw the earnest line as both serious and reflective, the naive as nonreflective and occasionally even frivolous. He felt that both lines had had some influence on opera's development (such as it was), and in each line he selected one composer whom he admired and considered to be mainly responsible for that development. In the earnest line, he chose Gluck; in the naive, Mozart.[21]

In discussing Gluck's contributions to the earnest line, Wagner, an operatic revolutionary himself, did not find it possible to support the contention that Gluck's reform efforts constituted "a complete reversal of the views previously current as to opera's essence."[22] Wagner wrote that Gluck did little more for opera than to curb the vocal extravagances of opera singers by asserting the composer's right to determine how his own music should be heard. At the same time that Wagner tried to minimize Gluck's contributions, however, he pointed out that Gluck's reforms were closely allied to a desire to create warmer, more lifelike characters. Gluck realized this desire, at least in part, by making the musical expression reflect more exactly the emotions indicated in the poetic text. Wagner praised Gluck for being the first composer to assert "with consciousness and firm conviction the fitness and necessity of an expression answering to the text substratum in aria and recitative."[23]

The desire to write more expressive music led Gluck's successors to make changes in opera's musical structure. In the works of Cherubini, Méhul, and Spontini, for example, Wagner found that arias were often given a "wider play of motive; modulations and connecting phrases were themselves drawn into the sphere of expression; the recitative joined onto the aria more smoothly and less waywardly, and, as a necessary mode of expression, it stepped into the aria itself."[24] The structural changes that Gluck's reform inspired, however, were limited by the nature of opera itself; and although the barriers separating arias from recitatives became less clearly defined in serious operas after Gluck, structural divisions remained nonetheless. Wagner believed they would continue to remain as long as opera was primarily a musical event.

It is important to emphasize that, as Wagner saw it, Gluck's reform movement was musical rather than poetic. (Wagner does not even mention the name of Raniero de Calzabigi, Gluck's famous poet-collaborator and partner in reform.) With all the expansion of opera's musical forms and the maturing of music's expressive powers that Gluck either brought about or encouraged, Wagner felt that the position of the poet had not improved in the least. After Gluck, as before, the poet still had to follow the composer's lead, still had to write words that conformed to the musical possibilities pointed out to him by the composer. In this situation, the poet had no opportunity to create human, lifelike dramas because the composer, content with existing musical forms or slight variations of them, required no more than undramatic, stereotyped phrases of rhetoric that could easily be accommodated by those forms. Had the poet written librettos that allowed the characters to "speak in brief and definite terms, surcharged with meaning,"[25] the composer would then have been forced to abandon familiar forms and seek instead alternative musical structures that would meet the poetic needs. Wagner was convinced that opera could not begin to fulfill its dramatic potential until composers let the libretto determine the musical forms that would best meet its needs. So far, however, even opera's most serious composers had been unwilling to cede their sovereignty.

Although Wagner decried music's neglect of poetry, he did acknowledge that in certain instances music could overcome the structural restraints of its forms and speak directly to the heart with little or no aid from poetry.[26] Given Wagner's view of the error that underlay all opera, this recognition of music's power, as the power of anything beautiful, is only natural. Indeed, it is the only power that can logically be ascribed to opera as Wagner perceived it. He felt that composers in the earnest line had had to strive to attain this power of beauty to move the heart, but that those in the naive line had called it forth in their best works almost unconsciously. Mozart alone exhibited it spontaneously and consistently.

Wagner reserved for Mozart a unique place in the history of opera's development. He considered Mozart the best example of what the musician's relationship to the poet ought to be because, in Wagner's view, Mozart never usurped the poet's position and never questioned the poet's right to offer him either a good libretto or a bad one. Mozart was so completely a musician that he was able to set "any and every operatic textbook offered him, almost heedless whether it were a thankful or a thankless task for him as a pure musician."[27] (This, I take it, was Wagner's way of saying that some of Mozart's operas are better dramatically than others.) Wagner felt that Mozart's operas were masterpieces, superior to any of his instrumental works, because he believed that poetry, even inferior poetry, drew from Mozart inspiration that he could not otherwise tap in his nonvocal works.

Wagner asserted that Mozart would undoubtedly have solved opera's fundamental problem if he had only met a poet capable of supplying him with a libretto that could have sustained his musical inspiration. The consequence, however, of Mozart's never having met such a poet was that he was never moved to alter opera's formal structures. In the history of opera, Mozart showed, at most, that it was impossible for poetry to place demands on music that were too great for music's expressive powers to fulfill. The unlimited expressive capability that Mozart revealed in vocal music, however, had no immediate effect on operatic composition. As an opera composer, Mozart had no successors. Only Beethoven realized the possibilities inherent in Mozart's accomplishments; and he at last made it possible for the expressive powers of music to break through the formal constraints that for so long had limited music's dramatic development.

Since Wagner believed that no composer could go further in developing the purely musical content of opera's formal structures than Mozart, he conceived the history of opera after Mozart as nothing more than the history of melody, varied but confined to the same well-worn forms that had served opera since its beginning. As a consequence of this belief, Wagner placed almost all the popular operas after Mozart in the naive line, since that line was characterized by unconscious melodists rather than by conscious formalists. Chief among the composers in the naive line after Mozart, Wagner named Rossini and Weber.

Although Wagner distinguished between the frivolity of Rossini's melodies and the nobility of Weber's, he made no distinction at all in the relation either bore to the texts to which they were set. In both cases, Wagner considered that the relation was nonexistent and that the music of *Der Freischütz,* like the music of *Tancredi,* existed independently of the text. This fact, combined with the popularity of the melodies themselves (and the overwhelming popularity of Rossini's melodies), proved conclusively to Wagner that people went to the opera to hear arias rather than to experience drama. Even in the operas of the earnest line, Wagner was convinced that the audience only appreciated efforts to set the text expressively when the setting turned out to be an "absolute, ear-pleasing tune."[28]

Wagner saw the history of opera after Rossini as not merely the history of operatic melody but the history of fashion in operatic melody as well. He felt that Weber's success with *Der Freischütz,* for example, merely encouraged other composers, desirous of similar success, to exploit in their melodies a folk style that would attract the same audiences that were applauding *Der Freischütz.* When operas based on these folk-nationalistic themes no longer proved profitable, composers either allied them to or replaced them with operas based on historical subjects. As usual, however, in opera, the subject matter of the libretto merely provided the composer with the excuse for writing a predetermined type of music. In all these shifting operatic fashions, the poet's position in relation to the composer remained the same. In historical operas as in folk operas, the composer continued to tell the poet what was required of him and alone held the responsibility for degrading the requirements of every libretto to a "vague and empty *schema.*"[29]

The advances in instrumental music made by Beethoven and Berlioz only increased the composer's sense of power and his resulting demands on the poet for more opportunities to display that power. After Beethoven had shown the endlessly diverse structural possibilities of music and Berlioz had shown the unlimited technical resources of the orchestra, the composer realized that he had an important new musical voice to exploit: the orchestra could now "bear itself dramatically."[30] As a result of this discovery, the composer forced the poet to construct librettos that would serve as an excuse not only for scenery, costumes, characters, arias, and choruses, but for the orchestra's new dramatic role as well. Wagner regarded this point in opera's development as its nadir, since every component in the artwork had at last been pressed into the composer's service—not, however, to create drama but to demonstrate music's power. Wagner singled out Meyerbeer as the composer chiefly responsible for bringing opera to this sorry state; he summed up the typical Meyerbeer libretto as a "monstrous piebald, historico-romantic, diabolico-religious,

fanatico-libidinous, sacro-frivolous, mysterio-criminal, autolyco-senti-
mental dramatic hotch-potch,''[31] all intended as an excuse for using every
trick music had to offer to create musical effects that would be sure of
offering something for everyone.

Wagner concluded part 1 of *Oper und Drama* by stating that operatic
music had, with the operas of Meyerbeer, reached the point of "utter
impotence."[32] He believed that opera could no longer be considered an
art (not even a musical art) because it had become so much an article of
fashion, so much a commercial venture. The only hope he saw for opera
lay in abolishing what he considered to be music's unnatural dominance
in the operatic union and soliciting in its place the energetic participation
of the poet in the creative process. Without a change in the poet's role,
Wagner believed that opera would continue to risk the peril of musical
effects without dramatic causes that formed the standard, artificially dramatic fare of the operas of Meyerbeer. In order to create the true, living
drama, operatic melodies could not be based on fashion or on tricks; they
had to be "fecundated by the poet's thought."[33]

Part 1 of *Oper und Drama* serves as critical background for the rest
of the treatise. In it Wagner is not so much concerned with recording the
actual history of opera as he is with detailing a series of faults that all
come together and culminate in the operatic offenses of Meyerbeer. Without question, though, the principal fault in the series (and the one upon
which all the others depend) is the apparent intractability of music's
forms, brought about by the unwillingness of composers to let the needs
of the drama determine music's formal response. The belief that true,
living drama cannot by conveyed in the parceled-off forms of arias, ballets, recitatives, and instrumental interludes is the foundation of Wagner's
theory of opera. It is the main point he seeks to convey in part 1 of *Oper
und Drama,* and the point that prepares the way for part 2 by raising the
question of what true, living drama really is. Part 2, consequently, "goes
deeper"[34] into the problem; and although its title ("Das Schauspiel und
das Wesen der dramatischen Dichtkunst") is similar to that of part 1, it
is even less a history of drama than part 1 is a history of opera. Part 2
offers, in fact, the requirements that true drama should meet and, in
offering them, describes the nature of the masculine element in the operatic union, the essence of which is to fertilize the musical response.

Wagner placed drama's origin in the union of tone, word, and gesture
that existed in ancient Greek tragedy. When that union dissolved, the play
pursued a solitary development along two distinctly different lines. One
of these lines Wagner characterized as "misunderstood" Greek drama.
This line was made up of plays that preserved the form and unity of Greek
tragedy, according to Aristotle's rules of poetics, but ignored completely

its human content. In the other line, Wagner traced the evolution of the medieval romance as it became drama. Wagner saw the romance as an extremely discursive form that at least dealt with man as he was in the world he lived in. As supreme examples of the two lines, Wagner cited the plays of Racine in the first and those of Shakespeare in the second. He maintained that the history of drama since Racine and Shakespeare had been little more than an aimless alternation between these two extremes (as the plays of Goethe and Schiller demonstrated) that had led modern drama into its current "unnatural, mongrel shape."[35]

Obviously, in setting up his two extremes of dramatic art, Wagner set up a conflict between form and content. On one hand, the formal unity of the plays of Racine was offset by the fact that such plays were stilted and did not deal with human beings in human situations. They were, for this reason, entirely unsuited to the sort of dramatic treatment Wagner had in mind. Romance, on the other hand, although it dealt with human beings in human situations, was severely limited dramatically because, by attempting to encompass too much, it ended up being practically formless. Consequently, despite its "human" merits, the drama of Shakespeare was also unsuitable as the poetic basis for the artwork of the future.

Wagner's view of the romance was especially important to his view of opera and had a profound influence on his artistic creed. While it is true, for example, that Wagner believed man could only be understood in conjunction with his surroundings, he also believed that those surroundings, in historical times, had been determined largely by the church and the state. Through the years, both had conspired to impose a host of legal and dogmatic restraints on man that had varied from time to time and place to place but always inhibited the free expression of man's individuality. As a result of this situation, the romance might claim to present man as the subject of its drama, but it could only do so by hedging him in with an inhuman historical context. In order for man to be understood, his historical situation had to be understood; and in order for that situation to be understood, it had to be explained. The necessities of explanation forced the writer of romances to spend most of his creative energies describing the environment in which his hero lived. Such explanations were, by their very nature, undramatic; they appealed, as Wagner repeatedly stated in *Oper und Drama,* to the intellect rather than the emotions. Therefore, the romance, although it attempted to place man at its center, was unacceptable for true drama, not only because of the discursiveness of its form but also because of the peripheral substance that determined that form.

As Wagner's view of Greek tragedy shows, he believed that artworks, in order to be meaningful, had to be based on a view of life held in common by both the artist and the public for whom he created art. Wagner thought that this condition had come to fruition only in ancient Greece. There the common view was of a universe based on human nature and embodied in myth. Greek myth thus represented the knowledge of the world and of life that all men shared. In myth everything pertained to man and was explained in human terms that all men could understand. Gods, who controlled both nature and man, were given human shapes and attributes. In Wagner's view, it was the very humanity of myth that made it so accessible. By looking at everything in human terms, moreover, the ancient Greeks came to understand not only the forces that controlled their lives but themselves as well. In myth, gods became heroes, and heroes became men. Wagner saw in this transformation "the fulfillment of the longing to know oneself in the likeness of an object of one's love or adoration."[36]

Wagner viewed compression or concentration as essential to the process of making myths: man tried to understand the world by compressing its manifestations into events or lessons that could be conveniently assimilated. When myths were eventually given an artistic form in Greek tragedy, the process of concentration was carried to even greater extremes, giving the realities of life an almost overwhelming dramatic intensity and expression.[37] The effect of this concentration received, at the same time, additional force from the fact that, in drama, the subjects of myths were given an actual physical presence: nature, gods, and heroes became men indeed. In the concentrated physical embodiment that drama afforded, man's ideas (as revealed by his actions) and his character (as revealed by the harmony between his ideas and his actions) gained immeasurably in significance. Wagner considered that Greek drama further intensified its concentration of characters and deeds by revealing a single great idea of far-reaching consequence to man. This idea guided the natural course of the drama. The poet, who shaped the drama, had only to let this idea proceed, without interruption or digression, to its inevitable conclusion.

Wagner found in myth the ideal dramatic vehicle. This choice was made as a direct response to his conviction that standard opera librettos and plays were unsuited to and unworthy of musical treatment. Wagner believed that myth, because it was based on man's knowledge of himself as he existed in nature, was true for all time and inexhaustible in content. The dramatic poet who based his libretto on myth had only one task: to expound the myth by making man in all his individuality the "irremovable center of [the] artwork."[38] Wagner felt that, as long as man was human, a drama based on humanity could not fail to be either timeless or universal. It was just such a drama that Wagner conceived as the artwork of the future.

Part 2 of *Oper und Drama* outlines the requirements for the perfect opera libretto. It should be based on man as he is in nature, not man confined and constrained by politics or religion. Everything not related to man in nature should be stripped away; and the remaining actions should be compressed and strengthened to such a pitch that speech, compressed and strengthened like the actions, is forced to mount to song. With such a libretto, music can properly be allied, since the subject matter and the words that express the subject matter are themselves musical. Thus, the musical means used to accommodate the new dramatic libretto should tower over man's ordinary expressive capability, just as the action of the libretto towers over his daily life. The poetic intent, the essence of the dramatic action, should become, in effect, the fertilizing seed that music takes up in love and brings forth newborn as the "realizing and redeeming utterance of feeling."[39]

At the base of Wagner's view of the history of opera and his long disquisition on the merits of myth as drama is a profound dissatisfaction with two main aspects of opera in his time: stereotyped musical forms, which divided operas up into a succession of arias, ballets, recitatives, and instrumental interludes; and stereotyped opera librettos, the verse structures of which encouraged the formal divisions of music and the subject matter of which prevented the full unfolding of music's expressive powers. Of all the influences that affected Wagner's theory of opera, these two "negative" influences can, I think, be considered primary. In part 1 of *Oper und Drama,* Wagner proposed a new relation of poetry to music as a means of eliminating the traditional formal divisions of music in opera; in part 2, he proposed a new type of drama and a new type of poetry as worthy of engaging in a new relationship with music. In part 3, he offered his opinions on how this poetry and drama could be mated with music to create a perfect musical-dramatic union. Part 3, as he wrote to Uhlig, "is a piece of work which—goes to the bottom of the matter."[40]

3

The Theory of Opera Set Forth in
Oper und Drama

Part 3 of *Oper und Drama* is subtitled "Dichtkunst und Tonkunst im Drama der Zukunft"; in it the dramatic artwork that Wagner had envisioned in *Die Kunst und die Revolution* and *Das Kunstwerk der Zukunft* and that he provided the historical and critical background for in parts 1 and 2 of *Oper und Drama* finally began to assume more than a nebulous outline ("Here now do I first begin,"[1] Wagner wrote to Uhlig). It is in part 3 that we at last find Wagner's suggestions for how poetry and music can be combined to produce drama. One is tempted to say "Wagner's *specific* suggestions for how poetry and music can be combined to produce drama," but that adjective makes the subject matter set forth in part 3 seem far more settled than it actually is. Even though Wagner may have thought he had gone to the root of the matter in part 3, he offered no list of rules there for writing the perfect musical drama. Years later, when Wagner wrote *Zukunftsmusik,* he spoke of the "labyrinth of theoretic speculation"[2] he had been forced to tread in his earlier writings; and *speculation* seems to me to be the word that characterizes most accurately the last part of *Oper und Drama.*

The word *labyrinth* also characterizes much of part 3, where Wagner was not always as lucid as he might have been in presenting his ideas. While there is unquestionably an overall organization to the book, for example, that organization is not always apparent on a page-to-page basis. The difficult aspects of Wagner's prose style, by no means present in all of his writings, are particularly noticeable in part 3, where the arrangement of ideas often resembles the design for a maze. Wagner's thoughts frequently seem to tumble over one another, almost haphazardly, in a stream-of-consciousness fashion, as they bid for prominence and emphasis. Ashton Ellis thought that not even Wagner's music offered a better example of the "polyphonic" nature of his mind than did many of the pages in *Oper und Drama.*[3] Ellis's observation seems especially apt when one considers the interludelike nature of Wagner's digressions and the motivelike appearance of his ideas, which continually crop up and reassert themselves at different times and in different places. Ultimately, of course, the recurring ideas give the treatise its sense of growth as well as its unity, but the immediate effect of such verbal polyphony remains one of confusion.[4]

In the last part of *Oper und Drama,* there are, then, difficulties in both the subject matter and its manner of presentation. I believe that most of the trouble one encounters, however, in deciphering the language that describes how poetry and music can be combined to produce the drama of the future derives from the fact that this drama was still a developing organism. In *Oper und Drama,* Wagner was not always sure of himself: he was often speculating. The idea of the perfect artwork was still being worked out in his mind and was still being seen at a distance. That the final third of *Oper und Drama* was conceived in 1850 as the culmination of Wagner's thoughts on opera, as his "testament"[5] after the writing of which he might as well die, does not alter this situation in the least. Wagner completed *Oper und Drama* at the beginning of 1851 but did not even begin the composition sketches for *Das Rheingold* until almost three years later. By the time he finished the autograph score of *Götterdämmerung,* over twenty years had passed to separate the completion of the *Ring* from the statement of artistic ideas intended to guide its creation.[6] The simple fact of the matter is that *Oper und Drama* could not have been Wagner's testament unless he had died shortly after writing it. As it is, *Oper und Drama* shows only that Wagner had settled on an overall concept for the artwork of the future. The specifics of that concept were far from settled in 1851 and were, in fact, never really fixed.

For all its difficulties and ambiguities, part 3 nevertheless represents an important stage in the development of Wagner's ideas about opera. However, it is important to keep in mind that those ideas, which continued to develop as Wagner wrote *Oper und Drama,* did not stop developing when he had finished it. Because of its importance, part 3 demands a more extended presentation of its contents than any of Wagner's other writings have so far received in this study. The number of ideas involved, however, makes their presentation difficult. One is forced to summarize. Unfortunately, the nature of a summary is concision; and in trying to be concise, one is tempted to omit ideas that seem to be less important in order to shorten the summary and give prominence to ideas that seem to be more important. This temptation is particularly strong when one is dealing with a work as complex as the last part of *Oper und Drama.* But the temptation to cut drastically should, I think, be resisted, not only because it is difficult to ascertain from *Oper und Drama* alone just how important any one idea is, but also because too concise a summary gives an entirely inaccurate picture of the range of subjects Wagner covered in his writing. In the summary that follows, therefore, I have tried to retain as many of Wagner's ideas as possible.[7]

I have also tried to deal with another problem, already mentioned, which is characteristic of part 3 of *Oper und Drama*: the state of mental flux that Wagner was experiencing as he wrote *Oper und Drama* adds to the difficulty of having a number of ideas to present that of trying to present ideas that were only just beginning to form. One's tendency (as mine has been in writing about *Die Kunst und die Revolution, Das Kunstwerk der Zukunft,* and parts 1 and 2 of *Oper und Drama*) is to preface any statement of an idea with a phrase like "Wagner thought," "Wagner felt," or "Wagner believed"; but such phrases convey a misleading air of permanence to ideas that were in embryo. It would be more accurate, of course, to say "At that time, Wagner thought" or "For four months in the late 1840s, Wagner believed"; but in this case, where there are so many ideas to report, the accurate statement is awkward, cumbersome, and virtually unusable. For this reason, I have eschewed a past reportorial tense in the summary and have instead tried to use, as much as possible, the actual verb tenses and numbers that occur in *Oper und Drama*. My intention has been to give all the ideas advanced there the sense of presence, the sense of existing at a particular moment in time, that is essential to their statement.

Having said this much about the length of the summary and its manner of presentation, I must add a warning. Although the summary attempts to present Wagner's ideas as they occur in the last part of *Oper und Drama,* in many cases it only presents my informed opinion of what Wagner's ideas were intended to be. Wagner's meaning is often obscured by the tortuous exposition of his thoughts, a fact that he acknowledged and even seemed pleased with. When he was preparing the second edition of *Oper und Drama* for publication in 1868, he wrote:

> My desire to get completely to the bottom of the matter and to shrink from no detail which, in my view, should render the difficult subject of my aesthetic investigation intelligible to simple intuitive understanding, misled me into adopting in my style that pertinacity which, to the reader out for entertainment and not immediately interested in the subject, will in all likelihood seem perplexing diffuseness. In my present revision of the text I did however decide to make no essential alterations, as in the said difficulty of my book I did, on the other hand, recognize the special quality that would commend it to the serious scholar.[8]

Thus, the writing in *Oper und Drama* is not always straightforward; and in reading the book, one must occasionally interpret Wagner's words as best one can. My own opinion in a doubtful passage, however, is no more than that—my own opinion. It is only as reliable as my understanding is and may serve to inform a reader of *Oper und Drama* but need not bind his own understanding. The frequent footnotes in the summary are intended as points of reference for the reader who wishes to consult *Oper und Drama* itself. The Arabic numbers which occur at the beginnings of sections in the summary mark the seven chapter divisions of part 3.

1.   So far poets have used two different methods in their attempts to give speech an emotional expression capable of addressing the feeling.[9] One of these employs verse-rhythm; the other, end-rhyme.

Poets who use verse-rhythm to heighten the expressive range of speech use rhythmic structures that have been borrowed from ancient Greek models. The metrics of Greek verse, however, were intimately associated with both Greek melody and dance, neither of which have come down through time with Greek meters. And since these meters have no meaning without their corresponding gestures and tones, the attempt to counterfeit Greek verse becomes a poetic contradiction in terms.

Used by themselves, Greek meters show that verse-rhythms created for one language do not always fit another. This can be seen in the simplest of all meters, the iambic, which in German is absolutely incapable of any accurate rhythmic utterance.

> Taken on its own merits, the unloveliness of this meter irks the feeling as soon as it is set before us without a break, as in our spoken plays; but when—as indeed is inevitable—the most grievous violence is done to the live accent of speech, for the sake of this monotonous rhythm, then the hearing of such verses becomes a positive martyrdom.[10]

The peculiarity of a regular accent occurring on syllables that should receive no accent not only hinders the rapid and accurate comprehension of the verse but, because the rhythm of the verse draws such obvious attention to itself as rhythm, also renders the verse itself incapable of arousing the emotions.

A spoken verse based on misunderstood Greek rhythmic structures has never been attempted among Latin peoples. They have instead based their verse on lines, governed by a certain number of syllables that culminate in an end-rhyme. This end-rhymed verse derives from Christian church melody and is characteristic of it. The beginnings of this verse can be seen in the chorale melody itself, which is a melodic chant in a neutral rhythm with a certain number of beats per phrase. The end of the phrase occurs where the singer's breath gives out; it is marked by a rest and the verse's only share in the melody: the end-rhyme itself as concluding punctuation. The verse of a chorale, therefore, has no accent except the terrific and disproportionate one of the final rhyme. This fact became glaringly obvious when the chorale verse was finally separated from the chorale melody. The final rhyme assumed such overpowering importance outside its musical context that all the other syllables of the line appeared merely as preparation for the closing syllable. When set to music again in operatic melody, the whole line of verse preceding the final syllable appeared as a lengthened upstroke for the downbeat of the rhyme.

The insensitivity to syllabic accent that we find in end-rhymed verse is entirely in keeping with the speech of Latin races, a speech that long ago lost all understanding of its primal roots. This insensitivity is directly responsible for any conflict that exists between the content of a phrase and its expression in speaking accents. We may turn from habit to end-rhymes whenever we want to give our speech a heightened emotional expression; but unfortunately, end-rhymes are, by their very nature, unable to address the feeling. They may draw the attention of our hearing (and even give it a certain amount of pleasure) as they entice us into listening captivated for the return of a rhyming period, but they cannot engage the whole power of our feeling because the ear's attention is taken up entirely by the mechanics of the verse. Only when the ear is in a receptive state can it allow sounds to enter that can arouse the feeling to such a pitch that it brings to the understanding an "enriched and sapid food."[11]

Because of their feebleness and incapacity for real emotional expression, verse-meters and end-rhymes have never been able to exert a formative influence on melody. In fact, the falseness and emptiness of modern verse only becomes more apparent when it is brought into contact with music. If, on the one hand, melody tries to conform strictly to such verse, it not only exposes the unnaturalness of the verse's setting and the stultifying dullness of its content but also robs itself of all powers of expression by being subordinated to such poverty-stricken poetic material. On the other hand, if melody remains conscious of its expressive capabilities and fulfills them, it must necessarily ignore the "sensuous setting"[12] of the verse completely and settle instead for a broad expression of the general emotional content. Where melody has tried to retain some bond with the actual content of the verse, as in the operas of Gluck, the bond remains the speaking accent of language. But to strengthen the speaking accent melodically only destroys the verse, since speaking accents have nothing to do with either verse-meters or end-rhymes. Consequently, attempts like those of Gluck only succeed in dissolving the verse into prose;

and unfortunately, because the composer is trying to mirror the verse in music, the melody gets dissolved into prose as well.

The whole dispute over different concepts of poetry and melody has revolved around one question: How should melody be affected by verse? The ready-made melody, the melody derived from the periodic structures of dance, will by no means accommodate itself to the speaking accents of verse, since these accents continually vary, whereas the accents of dance-derived melody do not. And yet, a melody can only make an indelible impression on the hearing if it contains a

> repetition of definite melodic moments in a definite rhythm; if such moments either do not return at all, or make themselves unrecognizable by returning upon parts of the bar which do not rhythmically correspond, then the melody lacks the very bond of union which first makes of it a melody.[13]

The speech-accent of a verse, emphasized according to its sense only, does not fulfill the need for periodic accents that a melody requires. The musician who wants to maintain the integrity of his melody can, therefore, only observe speech-accents where they happen to coincide with melodic accents. Needless to say, an attitude such as this only pays lip service to the idea that verse and melody should be united in opera. Thus, the musician who sets his melody above all else may observe the general emotional contents of a verse, but he can rarely render the verse itself intelligibly.

Had the poet really wanted to raise speech to the "persuasive plentitude of melody,"[14] he would have had to make the speaking accent determine the rhythm of his verse. The symmetrical return of the speaking accent would then have established a "wholesome rhythmos"[15] that would have been as vital to the verse itself as it was to the melody. But we see no evidence of such desire on the part of the poet. How significant it is that we hear certain of Goethe's verses described as too beautiful to be set to music. What could better prove that we have no idea whatsoever of the correct relationship that should exist between verse and music?

2.   Rhythmically accented poetry is so different from everyday speech that its use as a dramatic vehicle can only bewilder the feeling. Therefore, if dramatic poetry is to have any semblance of naturalness, its heightened expression must be derived from the prose of ordinary speech. And yet, our speech uses so many words and phrases, so many circumlocutions to explain itself that to accent only the speech-roots in it would render it virtually unintelligible. In drama, accents must be used sparingly and reserved only for the most important moments in the story. Just as the lesser actions of the plot must be pruned away in order to lend weight to

the chief actions, so must all superfluous words and phrases be eliminated from the text. Everything that stands in the way of feeling and obscures the purely human nature of the characters must be excised so that no words remain which do not reveal the purely human core of the drama.

But how can the poet free modern speech from its "mechanical apparatus of qualifying words?"[16] How can the genuine verbal accents be compressed and made readily accessible to the feeling? Our own natural manner of speaking supplies the answer. We can observe the number of accents we normally give a phrase when we are excited. In honest emotion, we forget our convoluted syntax and try to express ourselves in brief, succinct phrases that are usually completed in one breath. When we are excited, we also employ accents more frequently and give them greater emphasis than when we are relaxed. The number of accents we use in everyday speech is directly related to the degree of excitement expressed: an angry emotion requires more accents per breath than a mournful one does. The poet who wishes to write naturally should, therefore, regulate the number of accents he gives a phrase in accordance with the emotion expressed in that phrase. He should rid his poetry of excessive "auxiliary and explanatory lesser words peculiar to the complicated phrase of literature"[17] so that the performer may devote most of his breath to dwelling on the accents of the main words. An extra number of subsidiary words is never justified unless the main word is specifically enhanced by their employment.

The natural rise and fall of accents in dramatic poetry is intensified when it is translated into musical rhythm. Music, with its infinite variety of rhythmic possibilities, is admirably suited to realizing the subtleties of accent that both our understanding and feeling expect of natural language. In music, for example, there are strong and weak beats within measures, just as there are strong and weak measures within phrases. The relative strength or weakness of these beats and measures is determined by smaller intermediate fractions within the beat. When a verse is set to music, its verbal accents should govern the characteristic relationships among these fractions so that unemphasized words or syllables occur as the "valleys" between the "ridges" of the principal accents. These main accents may be given even more emphasis by increasing the number of preparatory syllables that precede them or by removing altogether all subordinate accents. Not only can the poet use music's rhythm to fix the moment of emphasis exactly, but he can also use rhythm to determine the duration of that emphasis, since words that are sung can be prolonged to a far greater extent than is possible in mere speech.

Music can provide the breath of life to speech's presently defunct organism. The poet, however, must determine the musical beat and not allow it to be thrust on him by chance. He can do this by distributing the stronger and weaker verbal accents so that they form a phrase, or breathing segment, to which a following phrase, "necessarily conditioned by the first,"[18] may correspond. Through these compelling and reassuring repetitions, the chief expressive moments of the poem can be made accessible to the feeling. "The arrangement of stronger and weaker accents is, therefore, what sets the measure for the particular kind of beat and for the rhythmic structure of the period."[19] Music offers speech an inexhaustible variety of rhythmic forms in which to express itself and ultimately makes it possible to bring the "necessary accents of emotional discourse to a rhythm instinctively enthralling to the ear."[20]

The poet must take great care to insure that the verse-accents fall on chief root-syllables, for it is in the root-syllables that we find most clearly expressed the original, purely human content of our speech. Properly accented, root-syllables can provide us not only with an idea of an object but also with a sensation of the feeling aroused in us by the physical presence of that object. This is because root-syllables were invented by man to express his earliest emotional needs, and the root and the need are inextricably linked to our feeling.

The root contains, moreover, an even more basic force in the primal substance of the open vowel sound. In this is embodied man's original inner feeling, and it is the uttering of this feeling through the open vowel sound that arouses the same feeling in the listener. This is why the vowel itself is so important and why it should receive full articulation when it is set to music. It is this fullness of sound that music allows vowels that gives the emotion contained in the vowel a corresponding fullness of expression.

The open vowel sound is delineated by closed sounds called consonants. Consonants serve two chief functions. First, they give the vowel definition by enclosing its "infinitely fluid element."[21] In other words, consonants permit root-syllables to retain the emotional color of the vowel and yet acquire a shape that can be readily distinguished and understood. It is in this capacity that the outwardly defining consonant plays its most important dramatic role by making possible the repetition of sounds that so impress the feeling. Consonants increase the impact of repeated verbal accents by adding to them the possibility of a "uniform mode of expression."[22] This repetition of initial consonantal sounds that link words of kindred emotional quality is called *Stabreim*.[23]

Stabreim is a powerful poetic device that presents the feeling with the threefold emphasis of accent, sound, and meaning. *Stabreim* is generally employed to pair words of similar meaning, but it can also be used to make "a mixed sensation swiftly understandable by the already biased feeling,"[24] which is expecting accented root-syllables to be similar. This aspect of *Stabreim* makes it possible to unite the physical expression of one sensation with another quite different sensation so that the union not only sounds natural but appears related as well. By including the antithesis of a sensation along with the sensation itself, *Stabreim* can draw together what seem to be the most far-removed sensations and present them to the feeling as purely human and related.

The second function of consonants is an inward one. Just as consonants hedge in the vowel sound from without, so they also determine from within the specific nature of the vowel's manifestation by the roughness or smoothness of their inner contact with the vowel. Thus, energetic initial consonants (like *k, r, p,* and *t*) affect vowels differently from strengthened consonants (like *schr, sp, st,* and *pr*) and even weak ones (like *g, l, b, d,* and *w*). Moreover, strengthened terminal rhymes (like *nd, rt, st,* and *ft*), where they are determinative (as in *Hand, hart, Hast,* and *Kraft*), so affect the vowel's nature and duration that they practically demand that the vowel be brisk and brief. Because of the effect these determinative strengthened final consonants have on vowels, they can actually characterize the root-syllable itself and fit it for rhyme as assonance (as in the rhyme *Hand* and *Mund*). Nevertheless, the relation between the inward function of the consonant and the vowel itself is so intimate that an understanding of it depends primarily on an understanding of the function of the vowel. Thus, in any given root-syllable, the vowel not only conditions the consonants but is conditioned by them to such an extent that a wholly indivisible organic unity results.

When the poet has arranged his condensed speech-roots into phrases according to the spoken accents of the roots and has used *Stabreim* to bring these roots "to the feeling's understanding in an easier and more sensuous form,"[25] he can then facilitate this understanding even more by drawing together into rhyme the vowels of the accented root-words, just as earlier he had drawn together the consonants. An understanding of vowels, however, is not based on a mere superficial rhyming of like sounds. Although all vowels are primarily related to one another, a real understanding of their relationship in any given dramatic context only comes when the similarity or difference in their emotional context is revealed. This task, moreover, can only be accomplished by musical tone. Whereas consonants achieve their greatest power over feeling in *Stabreim,* vowels have an emotional range that cannot be expressed in speech. Only when the sounding vowel becomes the sounding tone can the vowel at last engross our feeling and stir it to its highest pitch. The poet's thought is ultimately redeemed by being translated into "tone expanded to the universality of feeling."[26] In this translation and redemption, thought achieves the impossible and becomes an immediate outpouring of feeling. It is the musician's task to show in tones that all vowels are related as offspring of purely human feeling.

3.   The primary distinction between the word-poet and the tone-poet lies in this fact: the word-poet must concentrate scattered actions, sensations, and feelings, which can only be recognized by the understanding, into one moment that is most accessible to the feeling; the tone-poet must take what the word-poet has concentrated and expand upon it until it gradually attains the utmost fullness of its own emotional content and at last arouses the listener's whole emotional faculty. Up to the present day, however, both the poet and the musician have gone about their tasks exactly backwards. The poet, in his effort to reach the feeling through the understanding, has amassed more and more circumstantial details that only perplex the feeling; while the musician, in his attempts to reach the understanding through the feeling, has more and more renounced the fullness of expression music makes available to him. This reversed approach to addressing the understanding and the feeling must be abandoned in the artwork that is to come.

In regulating the tones of a verse, the tone-poet not only has to make known to the feeling the individual emotional content of each particular vowel but also has to show that all the tones of the verse are related to each other as members of the great family of tones. Through the tone-poet's power, every vowel in a poetic phrase (whether the vowel is of greater or lesser importance) becomes a member of this family of tones and, in so doing, receives a tonal accent. This accent varies in accordance with the musical feeling that is being expressed and depends primarily on a given tone's function in its home key.

The family of tones, then, is nothing other than musical harmony, which in its horizontal aspect makes up melody. Through melody, music's general emotional power acquires an even greater power to use words for definite, convincing utterances. Melody becomes, in fact, the means by which "the poet's endlessly conditioned thought"[27] is finally redeemed into the deeper consciousness of emotional freedom. Through the redemption of his verses into melody, moreover, the poet himself is offered the possibility of being initiated into the mysteries of music's nature. Once he has seen music's power, he is then in the position not only of wanting to learn from the musician what music has to offer poetry but also of being able at last to understand music's power and command it.

The bond of kinship that joins tones into a melody and makes them plain to the feeling as a family unit is called the key, or tonality, of the melody. The key prescribes the scale in which the tones of the melody are contained. We have seen already that our feeling only seizes what is homogeneous. We know that this is why the poet must strive to rid his verse of all extraneous elements and to condense both words and actions. By translating verse into melody within a definite tonality, the musician gives verse an even more homogeneous form of expression than words alone can command, since through tonality all tones of a melody are made to reveal their innate kinship.

The key is the most united family member of the whole tone-genus, but it has an instinctive inclination for other families in the genus. This inclination appears as the tendency toward harmonic modulation. In the modulations of a large composition, we can see the inner relationships among all keys revealed in the light of one particular key. Up until the present time, however, the unlimited possibilities of modulation have only served to bewilder the composer. With no fixed purpose to guide him (in either instrumental music or opera) other than antiquated musical forms, he has been forced to chart his harmonic course in an aimless, restless manner. "Before him he saw nothing but an endless surge of possibilities, albeit he was conscious in himself of no definite purpose to which to put those possibilities."[28] In such circumstances, the composer could only lament his boundless power to select his own musical course and long instead for something or someone to guide him.

That the poet can answer the musician's need is proven in Beethoven's Ninth Symphony. There the *Freude* melody does not arise from Schiller's poem; it has been invented apart from the poem and then spread above it and, for all practical purposes, can therefore be considered absolute music. The melody itself bears such a close resemblance to folk song that it needs virtually no harmonic modulation. By this marked simplicity of tonality, Beethoven showed that the musician who wishes to address the feeling intelligibly in such "absolute" music can do so only by limiting severely music's vast expressive powers. Consequently, the subsequent union of music with poetry later in the last movement of the symphony is placed in even greater relief by the simplicity of the *Freude* melody. Passages like the setting of "Seid umschlungen, Millionen" and "Ahnest du den Schöpfer, Welt" show Beethoven building his work ever more boldly both in spirit and in form, not from music alone, as he had previously done, but from the poem itself. The *Freude* melody had to be restricted in its tonality in order to accommodate words to which it was only tenuously related, but the *Seid umschlungen* melody stretches the narrow kinship of one key through an alliance with related keys to encompass the broader overall kinship of all tones. In the union of the *Seid umschlungen* and *Freude* melodies, we see at last the real power of the "melody which grows forth upon the word-verse through the working of the poetic aim."[29]

The key of a melody presents to the feeling the melody's various tones in their immediate family relationship. It is the poetic intent, however, supplied by the condensed verse, that provides the "incitement to widen this narrower bond to a richer, more extended one."[30] This extension of the harmonic base is governed by the expressive character of single principal tones that have themselves been prompted by the verse to move away from their home key. These chief tones are called leading tones because of their tendency to move away from one key and lead the melody into another. Leading tones, by their very nature, disclose the kinship that exists among all keys and serve, because of their nature, as powerful musical elements whereby the changing dramatic elements of a verse can be rendered expressively in melody.

We have seen that *Stabreim* can couple speech-roots of either like or unlike emotional content and present them to the feeling as words that are related. Music, through harmonic modulation, can render this kinship even more perceptible. In a verse with a consistent emotional content, such as "Die Liebe bringt Lust zum Leben," the musician has no incentive to modulate. But in a verse with a mixed emotional content, such as "Die Liebe bringt Lust und Leid," the musician feels a definite need to pass from the original key of the phrase to another key at the point in the verse where the emotional content changes. *Lust,* as the climax of the first part of the verse, leads directly to *Leid;* and therefore the note to which *Lust* is set "would instinctively become the determinant leading tone"[31] and thrust the melody onward to the second key in which *Leid* should be delivered. Thus, the inner relationship between two seemingly different roots, clear as it is in *Stabreim,* becomes even more apparent in the musical kinship of keys revealed through modulation. Moreover, just as modulation makes it possible to lead away from the original key into another, it also allows for a return to the original key or a related one if the verse subsequently brings up the original idea or one related to it. The musician's modulatory procedure, which would seem arbitrary and meaningless without the poet, is thus vindicated by the poetic intent.

Music's ability to show relationships among various emotions is immeasurably great. Once a chief emotion has been characterized by a principal tonality, modulations involving the most diverse keys can express all gradations and blends of other dramatically related emotions that in part corroborate and in part reconcile the chief emotion. Moreover, by dominating the intermediate keys, the main key intensifies the principal emotion to such an extent that it is able to "usurp our whole emotional faculty."[32] Thus, the poetic-musical period is dominated primarily by one emotion and one key. The perfect artwork will unite many such poetic-musical periods so that they appear to grow out of one another naturally and reveal to the feeling the nature of man moving along one principal, decisive line of life.[33]

4. The poetic intent instigates melodic motion, but it is musical harmony that makes this motion possible. Poetry may provide the seed that fertilizes music and leads to its growth, but the fruit that grows after fertilization forms and ripens by music's own individual powers.[34] Melody, which is harmony's horizontal aspect, is conditioned by harmony's vertical aspect. This vertical aspect depends on fundamental notes which, in combination with notes of the melody, determine the chords that support the melody. Since these fundamentals and their chords give melody a characteristic expression, their presence as support for melody is absolutely indispensable to the feeling. The ear, in fact, "imperiously demands"[35] the harmonic realization of melody.

Modern music has evolved out of "naked harmony."[36] Such music is merely an exploration of the endless possibilities offered to music by shifting fundamentals and their resulting chords. It is for this reason that we can say that modern music has been constructed out of harmony. The kind of music-making that must occur in the drama of the future is completely different. The tone-poet will add to a melody, already conditioned by the verse, the other necessary musical elements implicit in that melody. He will add, in other words, the "concurrent harmony,"[37] simply as though to make it obvious. Thus, the poet's verse, in conditioning the melody, will also condition the harmony. It is the musician alone, however, who determines the harmony. By taking advantage of the technical developments of modern music, the composer can create melodies supported by all music's powers that will redeem the poet and "arouse and satisfy his stress."[38]

The composer takes harmony as a thought only and renders it perceptible to the senses as a symphony of voices. The most natural symphonic tone-mass (and the original one) is made up of a large number of human voices and is called a chorus. Up until the present time, the chorus has taken a substantial musical role in opera; but in the drama of the future, that role will have to be reduced. In our drama, there can be no room for characters so subordinate to the dramatic purpose that they can be employed merely to supply a harmonic accompaniment to a melody being sung by a principal character in the drama. The compression of motives, actions, and personalities required by the perfect drama will not permit superfluity of any kind. The chorus that simply speaks en masse must vanish to be replaced by characters that are readily distinguishable as individuals. The poet must make every character he puts on the stage seem necessary.

In other words, the surrounding must so display itself to our feeling that we can attribute to each of its members the capability of motives and actions which, under other circumstances than the precise ones set before us, would captivate our interest to an equal degree.[39]

Even the subordinate actors in the drama must seem like real, lifelike human beings at all times.

This, of course, is the main reason why it is so difficult to employ a chorus in drama for the exclusive purpose of creating lyric moments. Whatever lyric moments there are in the drama of the future must arrive as the natural outcome "of motives pressed together before our very eyes."[40] These lyric moments cannot be dramatically unmotivated. The human surrounding that creates the lyric outpouring must be a "well-distinguished memberhood of self-set individualities"[41] who together mount to the lyric moment by sharing in the action of the drama. A harmonic vocal mass will not do; neither the chorus nor the principals can be used merely to supply harmony to a given vocal melody. Only when all the characters on the stage have been led naturally by the surrounding drama to a joint expression of feeling—only then is there made available to the musician a body of singers that may be used harmonically. Even so, the participants cannot be used for "sheer harmonic bolstering of the melody."[42] The characters concerned must make their individualities known to the audience by making definite melodic utterances.

We see, then, that for dramatic reasons the composer seldom has at his disposal a vocal mass that can be used harmonically. This want, however, is supplied by an organ that can characterize both the harmony and the melody in a way that no vocal mass can. This organ is the orchestra; and through it, harmony becomes a characteristic accessory element in realizing the poetic intent. By condensing members of the vertical chord and displaying their "affinitative inclinations"[43] along a horizontal line, the composer can develop a motivic power that makes the orchestral harmony a real and special agent in the drama.

The instrumental tone-mass is different from the vocal tone-mass, not only in its powers of expression but in the range of its tonal colors as well. Instruments have expressive abilities, but only general ones. Nevertheless, individual tone colors give each instrument a consonant-like character that defines the tone in such a way that similar tones from similar instruments can be considered to be a sort of instrumental *Stabreim*. Thus, just as we can group like and unlike consonants to produce an immediately recognizable influence on the feelings, so we can group like and unlike instrumental tones to produce a similar influence. In this regard, the orchestra is capable of individual powers of speech that have yet to be explored. We must keep in mind, though, that the orchestra's powers of speech are limited in relation to those of song. The vocalized tones of speech and song are capable of infinite shadings and meanings; instrumental tone colors are not. The vocal tone-mass is an infinitely richer expressive organ than the instrumental tone-mass. It is this distinction that determines the correct relationship that should exist between the orchestra and the singing actor.

The orchestra's primary function is to assure the listener that vocal tone, melody, and phrasing "are validly conditioned and vindicated by the inner sphere of musical harmony."[44] The orchestra accomplishes this function by the very difference between its tone and that of the human voice. The orchestra should voluntarily and sympathetically subordinate itself to the singer and never try to mingle its own peculiar, instrumental melody with that of the voice. This latter procedure has been one of the great faults of operatic music down to the present day. Composers have persisted in ignoring the determinative nature of melody based on the poetic intent. They have instead drawn their melodies from the realm of absolute, instrumental music and, by treating both human and instrumental voices the same as far as melody is concerned, have shown their complete lack of concern for the differences in tone color and speech that exist between the two.

The true verse-melody proclaims the emotional content of the text by dissolving vowels into musical tones. In this act, verse-melody unites poetry and music and raises what it has united to a higher level than either poetry's verse or absolute music's melody can achieve. Upheld by both of these conditioning elements but well distinguished from them, the verse-melody achieves its "plastic, independent message."[45] Poetry and music must continually vindicate the verse-melody but never swamp it by the admixture of their own individualities. At the same time, the orchestra must maintain its full expressive capacity by remaining an independent element, distinct from the verse-melody. The orchestra may carry the melody, from a purely musical standpoint, by making the harmony that conditions the melody apparent; but the orchestra best retains its own peculiar and endlessly expressive faculty of speech by avoiding the verse-melody itself.

5.   As a "pure organ of the feeling,"[46] the orchestra unquestionably possesses the ability to speak what words cannot express. The orchestra's primary function in this regard is allied to another dramatic element that cannot be spoken: gesture. Our bodily gestures are determined by inner emotions and are addressed not to another person's understanding but to his corresponding emotions. We may use gestures to accompany words (we know, for example, that a passionate verbal expression practically

demands reinforcement through a concomitant gesture), but we also resort to them when words fail us. The gesture that expresses what words cannot is necessarily addressed to the eye alone. To be fully effective in drama, to round off the expression into one that is completely understandable to the feeling, such a gesture requires an appropriate counterpart that says to the ear what the physical motion says to the eye. Verse-melody cannot supply the counterpart, since it is derived from words. At most, verse-melody can only relate the dramatic events that precede a gesture. The aural vindication must be supplied by an organ that is completely separated from the verse, and this organ is the orchestra.

From music's history, we know that the orchestra is capable of accompanying that most physical of all gestures, the dance gesture. This capability derives from the one thing that orchestral music and dance have in common: rhythm. Herein lies their primary affinity; and what appears to the eye in dance as the setting down of an uplifted foot occurs to the ear in orchestral music as the accented downbeat of the musical measure. The farther gesture departs from dance, however, the less energetic and frequent are the accents associated with it. As gesture attains more diverse and delicate expressional nuances, the instrumental figures that accompany it achieve more subtlety until gesture is associated with a "melodic expression immeasurable in its wealth of idiom."[47] It is an expression that cannot be translated into speech because of its very physicality. All that the musical expression lacks, as far as the drama is concerned, is for the actor to fulfill the eye's requirements by making the gesture that the music demands.

The orchestra has another associative power, which can be characterized as the power of remembrance. Through this power, the orchestra can attach itself to verse just as intimately as it can to gestures; and as a result of this power, orchestral melody can develop into "a messenger of the very thought itself"[48] and can transmit that thought, without words, to the feeling. This action is possible because every thought we have is associated with some feeling; and by recalling the emotion associated with a particular thought, the orchestra can recall that thought. The orchestra recalls the emotion by recalling a particular melody associated with a particular verse that announced a particular thought. Thus, a musical motive can incite the feeling to a function akin to thought if the emotion conveyed by the motive has been "definitely conditioned by a definite object,"[49] either seen or referred to. Without such conditioners, a musical motive (no matter how many times it is repeated) can only appear in an indefinite light. But when the motive is properly conditioned, emotions that are recalled by the orchestra can be associated with new emotions that appear in the melodic verse and can thus illustrate the organic growth of one emotion out of another. This growth is perceived thorugh a faculty higher than thinking, the "instinctive knowledge of a thought made real in emotion."[50]

The orchestra has yet another power. When "gesture lapses into rest and the melodic discourse of the actor hushes,"[51] the orchestra can utter unspoken moods that will influence the future course of the drama. This third faculty of the orchestra is its ability to present a foreboding—that is, something that cannot be spoken because it has not yet been defined and has not been defined because it has not yet been determined through association with an appropriate gesture or object. The power of speech that gesture and remembrance have shaped for the orchestra unite in the power of foreboding and make it possible for the orchestra to announce what has been neither seen nor heard.

Instrumental music is supremely suited to the function of evoking emotional presentiments. No other language is so fitted to expressing the "preparatory repose"[52] that precedes an important dramatic event or to developing that repose into an impatient longing. Heretofore, though, this faculty has been a weakness in instrumental music because composers have had to appeal to the listener's imagination for vindication of the foreboding. But in drama, the composer can appeal directly to the feeling because the poet can supply to the senses the physical object of any vague presentiment. In fact, when orchestral music has aroused our emotions to a "state of strained expectancy,"[53] it is the poet's dramatic duty to reward our eyes and feelings by placing the expected, the foreboded object on the stage at the height of the musical moment. The poet, however, can only succeed in his duty when music has succeeded in its; and for music to be successful in its foreboding function, it must be inspired by the poet and must completely absorb the poetic intent.

6. We have now gathered together all the threads that are needed to make the perfect drama and have only to come to terms with how these threads are to be knit so that they answer to the single substance of the drama as a single form of expression.

The focus of dramatic expression must always be the performer's verse-melody. Absolute orchestral melody may lead toward verse-melody as a foreboding or away from it as a remembrance, but the orchestra itself can never intrude on the verse-melody, never give up its important, though subordinate, role as the harmonic carrier of the verse-melody. The orchestra must continually support and elucidate the drama. It is the "moving matrix of the music,"[54] and in it lies the power to unite into one bond all the expressive elements of drama.

The moments when the orchestra may speak independently must always be those that do not as yet allow the "full ascension of the spoken thought into the musical emotion."[55] Just as the vocal melody is conditioned by the verse and just as that melody is vindicated by something brought to pass organically and necessarily in the presence of our feeling, so the dramatic situation must grow from conditioning moments for which the verse-melody appears as the only fit and necessary emotional expression. Neither the verse, nor the melody, nor the situation can be ready-made. If they are, the drama becomes unintelligible. The artwork must grow organically, from the lower forms of the organism to the higher, until all dramatic moments are bound together into one satisfying moment. By letting these moments grow before our eyes, the poet elicits our own active participation in the artwork.

Our feeling grasps most readily those things that have to do with our ordinary, everyday view of life. Therefore, the poet, in constructing his drama, must first solicit the feeling's participation by revealing to it characters in situations that have a recognizable likeness to situations in which anyone in the audience might have found himself. Only by building on such foundations can the poet mount to those wonderful situations, so removed from everyday life, that show man in the fullness of his power. Just as the situations of the plot must mount from the everyday to the wondrous, so must the expression of these situations "necessarily lift itself by well-found stages"[56] above the language we use in everyday life. The point from which both the dramatic situation and the expression of it must rise is determined by the "expectant will of the hearer."[57]

The poet makes use of this expectancy from the very beginning of the drama. Through the use of orchestral music in the prelude, the poet voices this expectancy and guides the audience's indeterminate feeling more and more toward a desire to know the specific poetic intent of the drama. The power the poet draws on here is the orchestra's foreboding faculty, which works so strongly on our emotions that it finally makes us demand a definite phenomenon to fulfill the expectations it arouses. The foreboding expressed in the prelude is fulfilled at its conclusion by the actual appearance on the stage of a character in the drama who begins to make himself known in the same language that has already aroused our emotions—the language of music. At this point, music takes on verse in order to satisfy the audience's heightened expectancy and to condense their general emotions into a specific sympathy for this one particular character "involved in this particular plight, influenced by this surrounding, ensouled by this will, and engaged in this project."[58] Thus, word-speech, welded to tone-speech, becomes the partner and interpreter of emotion. The very fact that this speech is lifted to musical expression raises the drama from the moment the character begins to sing to a plane above that on which man's daily life is lived. From the beginning of the opera, therefore, the dramatic standpoint is already so lofty that the poet can allow the wondrous and extraordinary to happen because it must. From this point on, the drama can develop toward even more exalted levels of wonder; and the actor's language

> can lift itself from the already tonal word-speech into an actual tone-speech, from which there blooms at the last the melody in answer to the sure and settled feeling, in utterance of the purely human kernel of the sure and settled individuality and situation.[59]

The powers of human expression available to music and poetry on this level of emotional outpouring are unlimited.

The true drama consists of a chain of organically developing moments, such as we have described, which condition, supplement, and support one another. The drama shapes these moments to form an "ever new, an ever newly-shaping body."[60] Although the circumstances that feed the drama's growth are diverse, they are all alike in that they deal solely with man and his purely human affairs. This human subject matter can be treated in ways as diverse as the matter itself. That is why opera, as we know it, with its musical and poetic forms that have been determined in advance, is so unsuited to dealing with this drama. In fact, no other forms are more unfit for genuine drama than traditional operatic structures that proceed with their set divisions of vocal numbers, regardless of the dramatic material involved.[61]

The form that we propose for drama is entirely different from the static operatic form we know. For all its necessary and fundamental ability to grow and change, our form is an essential unity which is the resulting "emanation of a united content."[62] We have seen how the poet goes about unifying the drama. His work can be translated into a unified expression that addresses itself entirely to the feeling if the means of expression chosen possesses a unity of its own that can make possible the rendering of a united content. We define this means of expression as one that can "most fittingly convey to the feeling a widest-reaching aim of the poetic understanding."[63] The means of expression must, moreover, conceal the poetic intent by realizing it. This apparent paradox would be impossible even to word-tone-speech if tone-speech by itself could not also be allied to it. Thus, wherever word-tone-speech is forced to reduce its expression in order to clothe the poetic intent "with an almost diaphonous veil of tone,"[64] there the organ of tone-speech alone, heard in the orchestra, is able to maintain a balance of emotional expression.

The orchestra, therefore, is the compensatory organ that preserves the unity of expression in the drama. Wherever characters must use words to define the dramatic situation, wherever they must speak to the under-standing rather than the feeling, there the orchestra compensates for their diminished level of expression by using the power of music alone to ex-press a recollection or a foreboding. The feeling is thus kept in a con-stantly heightened state and is never allowed to descend to transforming itself into a purely intellectual function. Once the feeling has been aroused, it can never be permitted to subside. It can only be further aroused as the musician seeks to carry out the poetic intent.

The orchestral moments must always be related to the dramatic sit-uation. If they are used merely to embellish "drooping or inchoate situ-ations,"[65] they destroy at once the unity of expression and force the ear to concentrate on music not as an expression but as a thing to be ex-pressed. It is for this reason that the melodic moments of remembrance and foreboding must necessarily grow out of the most important motives of the drama. These are the concentrated, stengthened root-motives of the concentrated, strengthened action that the poet plants as pillars of the whole dramatic structure. In realizing the poetic intent, the musician takes these root-motives, already condensed into melodic moments, and distributes them so deftly and appropriately throughout the drama that "their necessary play of repetition will furnish him quite of itself with the highest unity of musical form."[66] In this way, the dramatic motives and structure plastically determine the musical motives and structure, and the dramatic form becomes the musical form. In such an alliance of music and drama, the "perfect unitarian form"[67] is at last realized in the perfect utterance of a united content.

In the unity of expression that creates perfect drama lies the solution to the problem of the unity of time and space. The human action that is in itself united absorbs all our interest, so that time and space cease to be important. The genuine drama is influenced by nothing that lies outside it; consequently, "both time and space are annihilated through the ac-tuality of the drama."[68]

7.   In the concluding chapter of *Oper und Drama,* Wagner empha-sized that he had discovered nothing new but had merely tried to make others aware of the unconscious continuity that had always existed, no matter how well hidden, in the nature of operatic art. "I have grasped in its continuity," he wrote, "a thing which artists heretofore have taken only in its severance."[69] Wagner maintained that he was not trying to set up some "arbitrarily concocted system,"[70] designed to serve as a model for all future poets and composers. He had drawn instead on his own experience of opera to point out to those who were interested the pos-sibilities of expression open to poets and composers who truly wanted to realize in opera the highest poetic intent.

Wagner was not sanguine about the success of the venture he had proposed. Of the three major European operatic languages, he felt that only German was suited to the kind of drama he envisioned. This view derived from his belief that only German had retained any kinship with its ancient speech-roots, a fact of paramount importance to Wagner's theory, not only because he believed that root-syllables offered the poet a wealth of emotional connotations that could be used to color poetry, but also because he knew that root-syllables would prove to be ideally suited to receive both verbal and musical accents.

Even if he could create the perfect musical drama, Wagner doubted that he could find German singers who could perform the language dramatically. He pointed out that even French and Italian singers pronounced their native languages correctly in song but that German singers had been encouraged practically to ignore their language. They had had to sing poor translations of French and Italian operas for so long that to pronounce clearly in German the foolishness supplied them would have been an embarrassment compounded by a mockery. As a result of the operatic situation in Germany, German singers were not accustomed to rendering vowels and consonants; instead, they merely vocalized their imported operatic melodies and ignored the words. With such a situation in view, Wagner despaired of the dramatic task he had set himself and conjured up visions of operas conditioned by their verse that were condemned to being sung by singers who had no aptitude for language.

Even if performers could be found with the requisite artistic intelligence to carry out the highest dramatic purpose, Wagner felt that the composer and poet would be confronted by still another, practically insuperable stumbling block: the opera-going public. Such an audience, because it wanted merely to be distracted, had no need for dramatic artworks of any kind. The audience was, in fact, the sole reason why opera was no better. If the public had no taste, how could taste be expected from the artists the public paid? In a rather startling opinion for a proclaimed revolutionary, Wagner the pragmatist lamented that there were no longer any aristocrats of taste to encourage artists and support the arts. Even Gluck and Mozart had had patrons who allowed them to create art; but the artists of Wagner's day were forced to seek support from cultural Philistines, "the most domineering, the cruelest and foulest of art's bread givers."[71]

Wagner's revolutionary ideas are kept in check for much of *Oper und Drama,* but they reappear prominently in the final chapter. Wagner felt that society had arrived at such a point of degradation that it could not possibly sink further into the mire. He wrote that an earthquake was imminent which, when it came, would sweep away the "heap of refuse"[72] that life in his time had become. What remained after the catastrophe would be man's true, pure, human nature. Such an outcome to the revolution could only benefit Wagner's dramatic dream; and consequently, in the final pages of *Oper und Drama,* we find him proclaiming the artist of the present as the herald of a new life to come. At the same time, however, we find him also proclaiming the drama of the future as the seed that will fertilize present-day life and make it possible for all men to go forward into a future of human fulfillment: all in all, somewhat paradoxical points of view.

Having summarized Wagner's ideas for creating the perfect dramatic artwork, we can now attempt to evaluate what he managed to achieve in part 3 of *Oper und Drama.* If we were to make a list from the summary of ideas advanced there, many things about those ideas would become readily apparent. In the first place, a list would clearly show the sheer number and variety of ideas about opera Wagner had. A list would also show that, while some of his ideas for the artwork of the future were specific—verbal accents should receive melodic accents, for example— most were not—the musician should let the text guide the music's harmonic course. This particular aspect of a list of ideas in *Oper und Drama* would confirm the tentative, exploratory nature of the book. A list would also show that a clear majority of Wagner's ideas (between 60 and 70 percent, according to my estimate) had to do not with the poet's share in the artwork of the future but with the musician's—a silent and perhaps subconscious witness to the importance Wagner accorded music in the creation of drama. More specific proof of the importance of music is given by Wagner himself in his final advice to the musician and poet:

> Let us tell the musician then that every, even the tiniest moment of his expression in which the poetic aim is not contained, and which is not conditioned "necessarily" by that aim and its realization,—that every such moment is superfluous, disturbing, bad; that each utterance of his is unimpressive if it stays unintelligible, and that it becomes intelligible only by taking into it the poet's aim; that he himself, however, as realizer of the poetic aim, stands infinitely higher than in his arbitrary dealings without that aim,—for, as a conditioned, a "satisfying" message, his own is an even higher one than that of the conditioning, the "needy" aim in itself, albeit the latter is the highest aim man has; that, finally, in the conditionment of his message by this aim, he will be incited to a far richer exhibition of his powers than ever he was while at his lonely post, where—for sake of utmost understandableness—he was obliged to restrain himself, i.e. to hold himself to a function not belonging to him as musician: whereas he now is necessarily challenged to the most unrestrained unfoldment of his powers, precisely because he needs and must be nothing but musician.
> To the poet let us say, that if his aim—in so far as it is to be displayed to the ear— cannot be entirely realized in the expression of his musician ally, then neither is it a

highest poetic aim at all; that wherever his aim is still discernible, he has not completely poetized it; and therefore, that he can only measure the height of poetry to which his aim has reached, by the completeness wherewith it is realizable in the musical expression.[73]

As Wagner indicated, the success of the union of poetry and music could be judged by the simultaneous disappearance of each in the joint musical-poetic expression. It was the poet, however, who had to work under conditions imposed by the nature of music: he had to make sure that the verses he wrote had been compressed and refined enough to be capable of emotional expression in music. When this had been accomplished, the ultimate burden of creating the artwork lay with the musician as the *Verwirklicher der dichterischen Absicht,* the realizer of the poetic intent.

On another level, a list of the ideas in part 3 of *Oper und Drama* would allow us to go beyond the obvious in our observations and to form conclusions that only really become apparent when we compare the list with the preceding summary, or the ideas themselves with Wagner's statement of them in *Oper und Drama,* together with all the surrounding verbal material that he felt it necessary to add in order to explain and support them. A comparison of this sort would be particularly beneficial in the case of *Stabreim,* a subject about which Wagner expatiated almost excessively, partly because he was excited about the musical possibilities of *Stabreim* and partly because he must have taken considerable pleasure in explaining thoroughly what for him and most of his readers was a new, unknown poetic device. Certainly *Stabreim* was the most untried of all Wagner's musical and poetic suggestions for the artwork of the future; and, as a result, the space devoted to *Stabreim* in *Oper und Drama* has always made it seem more important to Wagner's new form of opera than it could ever possibly have been at that point in his creative development. A list of ideas in *Oper und Drama* would make this fact clear; it would put *Stabreim* in perspective: one component out of many that would eventually be brought into play as Wagner began to try to create his operatic dream.

Having said this much about the ideas in *Oper und Drama* and the statement of those ideas, I would like to mention another aspect of the book that affects any discussion of it. Throughout *Oper und Drama,* one finds inconsistencies and contradictions; it is not perhaps surprising that this should be so. For one thing, Wagner wrote the book very hurriedly in an almost unbelievably short space of time and then revised it only partially. For another, he tried to deal with a sizeable amount of historical fact and near-fact in addition to his own numerous, evolving, changing thoughts on opera. More importantly, however, Wagner tried to combine in *Oper und Drama* a great many ideas that were not necessarily compatible: ancient Greek myths, later Germanic ones, recent advances in orchestral techniques, new ideas about formal structures in music, Hegel's philosophy of dialectics, Feuerbach's doctrine of necessity, Schelling's community of consciousness, Schlegel's theater of combined arts, Lessing's praise of Shakespeare and disparagement of Racine—to mention some of the more obvious. This is not to suggest that Wagner's combination of opposites was unusual. It was not. Ronald Gray has pointed out that most German thought from the late 1700s on was concerned with the reconciliation of ambiguities or what he calls "contradictory opposites."[74] What is unusual, though, and what seems to distinguish Wagner from his predecessors and contemporaries is the number of opposites he chose to try to reconcile. A juggler with too many oranges inevitably drops one or more. Small wonder, then, that Wagner was not always successful in accomplishing what he set out to do and that in many places in *Oper und Drama* the contradictions, not the reconciliations, remain as the final result of much of his effort.

The portions of *Oper und Drama* that deal with Gluck and Mozart provide examples of the surface inconsistencies the book displays. In the case of Gluck, Wagner maintained that his reform of opera consisted merely in asserting the composer's right over the singers' to determine how the music he wrote would be heard by the audience. This view of Gluck's reform, however, does not take into account the fact that Wagner also admitted that Gluck had made conscientious efforts to create a musical expression that would answer the underlying expression of the poetic text and that he had tried to make the characters in his later operas warmer and more human. One would think that Wagner, having conceded this much to Gluck's credit, would follow his concessions to their logical conclusion and say that Gluck, as a musician, had, at least to some extent, been influenced by the poetry supplied him by his librettist. This final concession, however, Wagner was unwilling to make. He tried instead to show that Gluck, having found himself successful in asserting his rights over the singers', only became, as a result, more dictatorial in his demands on the poet.

In the case of Mozart, Wagner wrote that he never met the poet who succeeded in calling forth his true musical-dramatic gifts. And yet, Wagner proclaimed Mozart's operas his greatest musical compositions because, according to Wagner, poetry drew forth inspiration from Mozart that he was unable to tap in his purely instrumental compositions. Later, Wagner affirmed that Mozart always spoke correctly in music and instinctively ennobled "all the conventional stage characters presented to him."[75]

This achievement was made possible because a skilled poet, as Wagner wrote in an about-face, presented Mozart with the dramatic material that "prescribed the colors"[76] Mozart worked with. Having arrived at this indefensible position (from the standpoint of his theoretical premises), Wagner then proceeded to make a brazen escape by what was probably the only route open to him at that point in his argument: he concluded that the collaboration between Mozart and da Ponte on *Don Giovanni* and *Le Nozze di Figaro* was "amazingly lucky."[77]

Underneath the surface contradictions and inconsistencies, however, lies a more fundamental problem: the correction *Oper und Drama* recommends for the error on which opera is based is itself an inconsistency in Wagner's reasoning. In this regard, Wagner acknowledged that music was an emotional language that spoke directly, immediately to the feeling; while words addressed first the intellect and, if they were related to the feeling at all, only communicated to it at second hand. The combination of an emotional language with an intellectual one was, thus, the dichotomy that made up the artwork of the future. No amount of verbal camouflage on Wagner's part, no amount of attempted rationalization can alter this fact or make it cease to exist. It is true that Wagner tried to lessen the disparity between the two languages by saying that words used in opera should be only those that have to do with the expression of emotional situations or sentiments; but, of necessity, many of the words in any opera libretto must explain, must address themselves to the intellect first in order to set up the emotional situations or sentiments for the expression of which music is so peculiarly well suited. In this regard, what explains the emotion is not really within the proper sphere of music, while the emotion itself unquestionably is.

In opera, words that convey emotions are considered to be lyrical (or musical) by their very nature, whereas explanatory words generally are not. To make these explanatory words musical may entail imposing musical considerations upon them that may not be appropriate to them. In *Oper und Drama*, Wagner suggested that these explanatory words take a particularly active part in guiding the musical response to which they are set. Unlike lyrical words, declamatory words should not be made more musical; on the contrary, in their presence, the music should itself become more declamatory. Here then is the crux of the inconsistency: at the point where the text becomes most intellectual, music, as an organ of emotional expression, is to be guided most straitly by an element that has little in common with it. Looking at the growth of *Siegfrieds Tod,* consequently, from one poem to the entire *Ring* cycle of poems that sets this one poem in perspective and explains it, one can only regard ironically Wagner's assertion in *Oper und Drama* that historical opera librettos were unfit for musical-dramatic expression because there was so much that was unmusical in them and required explanation before the lyrical part of the opera itself could be reached, expressed, and understood.

What consistency can we find then in *Oper und Drama*? On what can we depend? In discussing the book, I think it is important to remember that everything Wagner had to say about the artwork of the future, every feature of this artwork, grew out of a profound dissatisfaction (a dissatisfaction repeatedly stated in *Oper und Drama,* to say nothing of the works that preceded it) with the musical form of opera as he knew it. Wagner regarded the division of opera into arias, recitatives, instrumental pieces, and ballets as unnatural and, therefore, undramatic. Almost every idea in *Oper und Drama,* consequently, is concerned in one way or another with abolishing this form and creating a new, natural, organic form to replace it. Wagner believed, however, that the new form could only grow out of a mutual understanding and cooperation between poet and composer, an understanding based on the composer's desire to have a new operatic form and the poet's willingness to explore music's dramatic possibilities. Given such an understanding and such a desire to cooperate, Wagner believed that the poet could then write an operatic text that would provide the musician with the framework and material necessary to produce an organic musical form that would move from one moment to the next in the unbroken unity that was the essence of drama. The creation of just such a new operatic form was the principal goal envisioned in *Oper und Drama,* the end toward which every suggestion in the book was directed. Before the musician could create this form, however, the poet had to supply a libretto that would allow the form to be created. In this sense, the new form was the tangible result of music's being fertilized by the poetic intent.

Oper und Drama is not a work for all time; it does not fix permanently the rules for writing musical drama. It contains suggestions only for creating a form that Wagner thought would allow the perfect dramatic artwork to develop. Wagner disclaimed any charge that might be leveled against him of setting up a system for composing opera. He preferred to think that he had simply "indicated possibilities of expression"[78] available to poets and composers who wanted to realize in opera the highest poetic intent. The chronological facts of Wagner's artistic life support his claim and prove that in 1850 he was in no position to lay down to anyone the rules for writing a new sort of opera. At the time *Oper und Drama* was written, *Der fliegende Holländer* was ten years old; *Tannhäuser,* six; and *Lohengrin,* almost three. The prose sketch and first verse libretto for what was eventually to become *Götterdämmerung* were only two years old. Ahead were the three remaining poems of the *Ring* operas, textual revisions for both *Siegfried* and *Götterdämmerung*, the music for all four *Ring* operas, as well as the poems and music for *Tristan und Isolde, Die Meistersinger von Nürnberg*, and *Parsifal*. Simply stated, *Oper und Drama* was based on limited practical experience as far as the sort of opera Wagner envisioned was concerned; the operas that preceded *Oper und Drama* could hardly have provided him with the specific knowledge and information he needed to form an inviolate theory of opera. The weight of experience required for that task (if he ever wished to accomplish it) lay in the future.

4

Wagner's Later Writings on Opera

In the preface to his translation of *Oper und Drama,* Ellis has recorded the series of events that precluded Wagner's making an adequate revision of the final third of *Oper und Drama.* [1] At the time Wagner completed the book, he appears to have been mentally overwrought ("The last pages of this copy I have written in a state of mind which I cannot intelligibly describe to anyone"), [2] unwilling or unable to revise what he had just written, and anxious only "to get the hateful manuscript out of the house." [3] Acknowledging that there would be many faults in the manuscript, he sent the whole thing on to Uhlig to read without revising part 3. Even when a publisher had been found for the book and Wagner was correcting proof sheets, he did not correct part 3. Pleading illness, he sent most of the final third to Uhlig for the correction of printing errors only.

The conclusion that Wagner felt some sort of dissatisfaction with the last part of *Oper und Drama* seems almost inescapable; and although the circumstances surrounding the completion and publication of *Oper und Drama* do not prove that Wagner was entirely displeased with part 3, they do suggest that he wished to be rid of it and the responsibilities of thought it laid upon him. Later, after he had begun to put his written ideas into practice, he expressed "great repugnance . . . against so much as reading through [his] theoretical essays." [4] One might with some justification attribute the reason for such a feeling to a change in Wagner's ideas that had occurred over a period of time. In this case, however, Wagner seems to have had the same feeling of repugnance for *Oper und Drama* (as his handling of its revisions and proofreading indicates) immediately after he had finished writing it. In the essay *Zukunftsmusik,* written in 1860, moreover, Wagner frankly admitted his inability to handle the task he had set for himself in *Oper und Drama*—that of giving his subconscious artistic instincts a concrete verbal expression. Abstract meditation on this point had proven to be beyond him. "Nothing," as he wrote ten years later,

can be more alien and distressful to the artist's nature than such a course of thought, so thoroughly opposed to his customary method. He therefore does not surrender himself to it with the needful coolness, the property of the theorist by profession; rather is he thrust on by a passionate impatience, which prevents him from devoting the requisite time to a careful handling of style; he fain would give entire in every sentence the view that embraces the whole picture of his subject; doubt, as to whether he has succeeded in this, drives him to a constant repetition of the attempt—which fills him at last with a heat and irritation that should be absolute strangers to the theorist. Then he grows alive to all these faults and evils, and freshly harassed by his feeling of them, he hurriedly ends his work with a sigh that after all he will probably be understood by none but those who already share with him the same artistic view.[5]

There is probably no better description of the prose style of *Oper und Drama* than the one here supplied by the author. It emphasizes Wagner's eagerness to explain himself in the book, his ultimate inability to do so, and his frustration at not being able to achieve his goal. The reason offered for this inability—his lack of skill as a systematic thinker—is perhaps not as plausible. Wagner's other writings show that he could be clear enough when he chose. A more likely explanation of the diffuseness in *Oper und Drama* lies, I think, in Wagner's own uncertainty, not about what he wanted to do but about how what he wanted to do could be accomplished. It is no coincidence that the most difficult part of the book to understand is the part that purports to be the most practical.

About six months after he completed *Oper und Drama*, Wagner made another attempt to clarify his thinking by writing as a supplement to *Oper und Drama* an essay entitled *Eine Mittheilung an meine Freunde*. The *Mittheilung* was published in December 1851 (one month after *Oper und Drama*) as the preface to the combined published texts of *Der fliegende Holländer, Tannhäuser,* and *Lohengrin* and was intended to explain the apparent contradictions that critics had found between Wagner's previous operatic compositions and his new views of creating opera.[6]

The *Mittheilung* is an extremely important work in which Wagner emphasized his growth and change as an artist. He pointed out that the supposed contradictions in his work did not exist for people who were accustomed to regarding phenomena as developing in time. How, he wondered, could critics use views that had taken years to develop as standards by which to judge works that preceded those views and were part of the "natural path of evolution"[7] that led to them. Wagner thought it was unnatural and illogical to ignore evolution in discussing an artist's career and to "jumble phases separated by time and well-marked difference into one conglomerate mass."[8] He suggested that critics adopt a more reasonable view and regard his earlier works as distinct from his later ones but as organically connected to them. Wagner believed that the development of his current artistic viewpoint could be explained from his previous works but that the new could not be used to judge the old.

A large part of the *Mittheilung* is devoted to a survey of influences that led Wagner to write his early operas, influences that do not concern us here. At the end of this survey, however, Wagner attempted to describe the effect of what he called his "musical predisposition"[9] on the creation of his operas. The remarks in this part of the *Mittheilung* are particularly relevant to this study, since they indicate that Wagner's poetry, before it was written, was first conditioned by musical thought. The effect of this predisposition did not come into play in the operas up through *Rienzi,* since in those operas Wagner was primarily concerned with writing operas that would gain critical and popular approval; but starting with *Der flie-gende Holländer,* Wagner began to shape the dramatic material himself. From this point on in his development, Wagner the musician became Wagner the poet; only in the complete working out of the poem did he become a musician again.[10]

It is important to realize that at this point in his life Wagner saw his mature creative process—the process with which he was about to begin composing the *Ring*—as proceeding from musician to poet and back to musician, not from poet to musician as one might suppose from reading isolated passages in *Oper und Drama.* Wagner emphasized, moreover, that as a musician-become-poet he had complete knowledge of how the ex-pressive means of music could be used to work out his texts. He repeat-edly maintained that it was his acquisition of facility in musical expression that made him a poet, since this facility gave him the freedom to consider not the method of expression to be used but rather the object to be ex-pressed. Because he was a musician, he knew that

> that which is utterable in the speech of music is limited to feelings and emotions: it expresses, in abundance, that which has been cast adrift from our word-speech at its conversion into a mere organ of the intellect, namely, the emotional contents of purely human speech. What thus remains unutterable in the absolute musical tongue is the exact defining of the object of the feeling and emotion, whereby the latter reach themselves a surer definition.[11]

It was, consequently, Wagner's musical knowledge that allowed him to draft verse that could be set to music in a manner acceptable to him as drama. By realizing that matters were increasingly suited to music as they expanded into the realm of feeling, he was able to lay down for himself an infallible rule for what the poet should utter: "the purely human, freed from every shackle of convention."[12]

Wagner's poetic fashioning, already influenced by his musical ability, subsequently influenced his musical expression and the form that expres-sion took in two significant aspects: his dramatic-musical form in general and his melodic form in particular. As far as the first was concerned,

Wagner explained that he did not set out to overthrow opera's traditional forms. Rather, he was led to omit them by the nature of his dramatic concept and material. As an illustration of the knowledge of musical form he gradually acquired, Wagner offered the increasing continuity evident in his settings of *Der fliegende Holländer, Tannhäuser,* and *Lohengrin.* He began to see opera as having no real divisions except those imposed by acts (where the time or place changed) or by scenes (where the characters changed). The simplicity of mythic material, moreover, allowed him to limit characters and events to such an extent that the motives animating them could be dwelt on "with an exhaustiveness already reckoned for in the original draft."[13] Consequently, by the time Wagner began composing *Lohengrin,* his musical forms were being increasingly determined by the requirements of the dramatic material.

As far as the melodic aspect of his new form was concerned, Wagner felt that his general poetic method also had a specific influence on the shaping of his melodies. In setting words to music, he became more and more concerned not to create a melody but to express emotion. In other words, he felt that poetry should mold the melody to which it is set; the melody should not be thrust, ready-made, on the poetry. Wagner considered that the vocal line should rarely draw attention to itself as sheer melody. It should, instead, attract the listener's attention as the "most expressive vehicle for an emotion already plainly outlined in the words."[14] Wagner felt, however, that imperfections in modern verse-forms hindered him from attaining a natural melodic flow because modern verse completely lacked natural rhythm. Not until he discovered *Stabreim* did he feel that he had found the means whereby he could successfully overcome the rhythmic problem. With that discovery, he felt that he was ready to proceed with his artistic work. He could finally allow the vocal line to rise of itself from the "feeling utterance of the words";[15] he could finally undertake the fashioning of the Siegfried drama.

Wagner's principal object in the *Mittheilung* was to make two points: one, that the poetic material for his operas was derived from his musical abilities and in turn conditioned the musical setting of the material; and the other, that his development as a poet could be traced, consequently, in the increasing musical continuity of his operas and the increasing naturalness of their textual settings. The *Mittheilung* also shows—and it is a significant revelation—that Wagner was aware of just how much he had evolved as an artist; and it tacitly acknowledges that he would continue to develop. It shows unquestionably Wagner's need to evolve at the point it was written, his need to allow each new work of art to proceed from a "new developmental phase in the mind of the artist."[16] Both the *Mittheilung* and *Oper und Drama* attest to the fact that the artwork of the future was to be ever newly born, springing directly from the present into the future. Such an artwork could hardly have been intended to be subject to theoretical ideas that, once put on paper, could not change.

Wagner had begun work in 1848 on the libretto for what was eventually to become *Götterdämmerung*; during 1851 and 1852, he completed the poems for all four *Ring* operas. He began composing *Das Rheingold* in November 1853 and by the end of the following September had completed the full score. (He also finished the preliminary draft for act 1 of *Die Walküre* on 1 September 1854.) It was at this time, somewhere between the beginning and end of September 1854, that Wagner first became acquainted with Arthur Schopenhauer's *Die Welt als Wille und Vorstellung*.[17] From then on, by Wagner's own admission, the book never left his side; and by the summer of 1855, he had reread it four times. There can be little doubt that *Die Welt als Wille und Vorstellung* exerted considerable influence on Wagner, influence that he freely acknowledged in his own writings. (Wagner's estimate in *Mein Leben* was that Schopenhauer's philosophy "exerted a decisive influence on the whole course of my life."[18]) Cosima Wagner's diaries, moreover, contain numerous private references to her husband's reading of Schopenhauer and include Wagner's joking declaration from the final year of his life "that from now on he [would] read only Gobineau, Schopenhauer, and himself."[19] Because of the extent and importance of the influence of Schopenhauer's philosophy on Wagner, I would like to interrupt at this point the survey of Wagner's later theoretical writings in order to present a brief summary of Schopenhauer's philosophy and a preliminary assessment of its effect on Wagner's concept of the poetic intent.

In *Die Welt als Wille und Vorstellung*, Schopenhauer posited the will as the primal force of all being, what Kant had earlier called *das Ding an sich,* the thing in itself. According to Schopenhauer, the world was not only the will that animated it but also representations or simulacrums of the will. That is to say, the world was both the will itself, a force unperceivable and therefore unknowable, and representations or images of the will that could be perceived and known. In Schopenhauer's view, the will was hunger, perceived as teeth, mouths, stomachs; it was sexual desire, perceived in terms of the physical organs through which that desire was consummated; it was gravity, perceived as the falling of a rock. Thus, all forms of mind and matter—all time, space, causality—were mere semblances or objectifications of the will, appearing differently to different individuals. Schopenhauer conceived the will itself as a blind, ruthless, brutal force that expressed itself in all things as the will to live or continue. Divided among countless entities in the universe, this will to live was constantly at war with itself, constantly building up only to destroy. The will was the source of all pain and misery on earth, as well as of all happiness.

Schopenhauer believed that the beginnings of knowledge were achieved when man began to recognize the will in everything, both malignant and benign, constructive as well as destructive. He quoted as the highest wisdom man could attain the Sanskrit saying "Tat tvam asi," "That is you." In other words, the wise man knew that he was merely one manifestation of the universal will and that everything else he perceived was only another manifestation of the same will: each man contained within himself all good and all evil. Each man who experienced this knowledge, since he was himself part of the will, helped make the universal will self-aware. At the point where complete self-awareness was reached, however, the will could make one of two choices: it could either affirm itself or deny itself. If it affirmed itself, then it continued as before, refusing to allow its knowledge of the realities of life to destroy its mastering will to live. If, on the other hand, the will denied itself, then it destroyed the will to live by becoming utterly passive in the face of life's joys and sorrows. Schopenhauer believed that the second decision was the greater moral choice and that by denying the will each man could do his part to help end suffering in the world simply by ceasing to strive or to contend. Schopenhauer's final moral deduction, therefore, was summed up in the concept of *Mitleid*, suffering together. By suffering with all men, one renounced his own individuality and thereby helped break down the walls of individuality dividing men from one another.[20]

With this brief introduction to some of the main points of Schopenhauer's philosophy as background, I would like now to turn to Wagner's own account in *Mein Leben*, recollected over a decade later, of his first reading of *Die Welt als Wille und Vorstellung*:

Like every man who is passionately thrilled with life, I too sought first for the conclusions of Schopenhauer's system. With its aesthetic side I was perfectly content, and was especially astonished at his noble conception of music. But, on the other hand, the final summing-up regarding morals alarmed me, as, indeed, it would have startled anyone in my mood; for here the annihilation of the will and complete abnegation are represented as the sole true and final deliverance from those bonds of individual limitations in estimating and facing the world, which are now clearly felt for the first time. For those who hoped to find some philosophical justification for political and social agitation on behalf of so-called "individual freedom" there was certainly no support to be found here, where all that was demanded was absolute renunciation of all such methods of satisfying the claims of personality. At first I naturally found his ideas by no means palatable, and felt I could not readily abandon that so-called "cheerful" Greek aspect of the world, with which I had looked out upon life in my *Kunstwerk der Zukunft*. As a matter of fact, it was Herwegh who at last, by a well-timed explanation, brought me to a calmer frame of mind about my

own sensitive feelings. It is from this perception of the nullity of the visible world—
so he said—that all tragedy is derived, and such a perception must necessarily have
dwelt as an intuition in every great poet, and even in every great man. On looking
afresh into my *Nibelungen* poem I recognised with surprise that the very things that
now so embarrassed me theoretically had long been familiar to me in my own poetical
conception. Now at last I could understand my Wotan.[21]

As this account makes clear, Wagner was more interested in Schopenhauer's moral philosophy than his views on esthetics; and in this regard, he found much in Schopenhauer's writing that he had already
subconsciously incorporated into the *Ring* poems. Later, he incorporated
other aspects of the philosophy into both *Tristan* and *Parsifal,* but not as
textbook examples of Schopenhauer. In constructing his librettos, Wagner
was selective and took from the philosophy only what fitted in with his
own dramatic needs.[22] This was a different procedure from the one he
followed in the realm of politics. There Schopenhauer's concept of resignation from life furnished Wagner with the perfect excuse for withdraw-
ing with honor from political involvement; and he appears, consequently,
to have followed Schopenhauer to the letter in applying Schopenhauer's
philosophy to this sphere of his activities. (Needless to say, Wagner could
hardly have been thinking of Schopenhauerian resignation when he was
working so energetically to secure production and acceptance of his own
works.)

The main points of *Die Kunst und die Revolution, Das Kunstwerk der
Zukunft,* and *Oper und Drama* support Wagner's statement in *Mein Leben*
that he was perfectly content with the esthetic side of Schopenhauer's
philosophy. Schopenhauer considered that all the arts stood in some relationship to the will as objectifications of it. Most arts, however, in Schopenhauer's view, only objectified the will indirectly by means of ideas and
were, therefore, at least once removed from the will because they spoke
through intermediaries. Music, on the other hand, was a direct objecti-
fication of the will: it was not a copy of ideas that tried to mirror the will
but was, instead, a copy of the will itself. Through music, consequently,
all individuals had direct access to the will. Schopenhauer tried to explain,
in part, his view of music and its power by equating the four voices in
four-part harmony to the four levels of existence, so that the bass voice
corresponded to the mineral kingdom; the tenor, to the plant kingdom;
the alto, to the animal kingdom; and the soprano, to man. Schopenhauer
accounted for greatness in music by the closeness of the analogy of melody, rhythm, and harmony to the inner spirit of the will concerned.[23]

Because music was directly related to the will, Schopenhauer considered it the most powerful of all the arts, able to attain its own ends
without any help from the others. He declared that music did not need
words or actions to be effective and, in support of this statement, singled

out Rossini's operatic music, which, in Schopenhauer's opinion, existed independently of words and made just as satisfying an effect without them as with them. (Wagner had made this same point in a different context in part 1 of *Oper und Drama*.) Schopenhauer maintained that, if words were joined to music, they remained "a foreign extra of secondary value"[24] that must occupy a subordinate position in relation to music and entirely adapt themselves to it.

In fairness to Schopenhauer's theories about music, it must be pointed out that his view of the union of poetry and music in song and opera was more balanced and better rounded than the statements in the preceding paragraph suggest. In volume 1 of *Die Welt als Wille und Vorstellung,* for example, Schopenhauer condemned as "a great misconception and an utter absurdity"[25] the idea that music should be a mere means of expressing a text. But in volume 2, written over a period of twenty-five years following the first publication of volume 1 as a commentary on it, Schopenhauer not only mitigated his earlier statements but amplified and clarified them. Thus, in volume 2 Schopenhauer observed that, distinct from situations in which poetry is joined with music, an opposite relationship exists when music is subsequently added to poetry that has already been written (and Schopenhauer included opera librettos in this category). "For in these [cases]," Schopenhauer wrote,

the musical art at once shows its power and superior capacity, since it gives the most profound, ultimate, and secret information on the feeling expressed in the words, or the action presented in the opera. It expresses their real and true nature, and makes us acquainted with the innermost soul of the events and occurrences, the mere cloak and body of which are presented on the stage. With regard to this superiority of music, and in so far as it stands to the text and the action in the relation of universal to particular, of rule to example, it might perhaps appear more suitable for the text to be written for the music than for the music to be composed for the text. With the usual method, however, the words and actions of the text lead the composer to the affections of the will that underlie them, and call up in him the feelings to be expressed; consequently they act as a means for exciting his musical imagination. Moreover, that the addition of poetry to music is so welcome, and a song with intelligible words gives such profound joy, is due to the fact that our most direct and most indirect methods of knowledge are here stimulated simultaneously and in union. Thus the most direct is that for which music expresses the stirrings of the will itself, but the most indirect that of the concepts denoted by words. With the language of the feelings, our faculty of reason does not willingly sit in complete idleness. From its own resources, music is certainly able to express every movement of the will, every feeling; but through the addition of the words, we receive also their objects, the motives that give rise to that feeling. The music of an opera, as presented in the score, has a wholly independent, separate, and as it were abstract existence by itself, to which the incidents and characters of the piece are foreign, and which follows its own unchangeable rules; it can therefore be completely effective even without the text. But as this music was composed with respect to the drama, it is, so to speak, the soul of this, since, in its connexion with the incidents, characters, and words, it becomes the expression of the inner significance of all those incidents, and of their ultimate and secret necessity that rests on this significance.[26]

I have quoted Schopenhauer's remarks here at length because they seem to me to bear witness to the remarkable similarity that exists between Wagner's and Schopenhauer's views on the power of music and on how words can be used to call that power forth and give its specificity. On the evidence of the above quotation, it cannot be doubted that, in parts of *Die Welt als Wille und Vorstellung* at least, Wagner found reassuring support for much of his theory of opera.

With all of Schopenhauer's ideas on music, however, Wagner could not have agreed, any more than he agreed with all of Schopenhauer's ideas on morals or on life. Schopenhauer's praise of Rossini, for example, together with the reasons for that praise might have seemed to Wagner perhaps musically and certainly dramatically naive. The equation of the voices in four-part harmony to the various kingdoms might also have been difficult for Wagner to accept wholeheartedly, as would, undoubtedly, the ranking of music alone above the combination of words and music in musical drama. In this regard, the following sentences from Cosima's diary for 15 February 1881 seem pertinent:

> But we soon go back to the topics that concern us and to Schopenhauer, who, in R.'s estimation, would probably have gone along with him as far as *Loh.* and *T.*, but certainly not from then on. Regarding his errors in the application of his theories, so right in themselves, R. says, "It makes one feel that an artist can be a philosopher, but not a philosopher an artist."[27]

If the statement in this entry is to be believed, then Wagner agreed with Schopenhauer's theories but disagreed with some of Schopenhauer's applications of this theories. Wagner could readily have accepted in Schopenhauer what he already knew to be true when he wrote *Die Kunst und die Revolution, Das Kunstwerk der Zukunft,* and *Oper und Drama*—namely, that music's powers of emotional expression were boundless because music spoke what was true, communicating what it spoke, without intermediary, directly to the feeling; words were barred from this immediacy of expression because they addressed first the intellect and only gradually, if at all, affected the feeling. Beyond this, however, Wagner probably would not have gone. Had he accepted Schopenhauer's entire view of music as wholeheartedly as he did Schopenhauer's advocacy of quiet resignation in the face of life's obstacles, then, without doubt, Wagner would have adopted instrumental composition in the style of the classical symphonists with as much alacrity as he suspended political agitation. But Wagner did nothing of the kind. After reading Schopenhauer, as before, he continued to write operas; he continued to use words to set up dramatic situations that called forth from the music he wrote emotional responses, at once general and specific.

Wagner completed the full score of *Die Walküre* in March 1856. Almost a year later, in February 1857, while he was engaged in the composition of the first two acts of *Siegfried,* he wrote down his views on Liszt's orchestral compositions in a letter to Carolyne Sayn-Wittgenstein's daughter Marie. This letter, written with a view to wider than private circulation, was published two months later in the *Neue Zeitschrift für Musik* of 10 April 1857 and appears in the *Gesammelte Schriften* as the essay "Über Franz Liszt's symphonische Dichtungen." Although Wagner's ostensible subject in the essay is instrumental music, he deals with the subject of the poetic intent in drama as well.

Wagner said that he found it difficult to write about Liszt's tone poems because he believed that true instrumental music existed in a realm removed from words. As he saw it, instrumental music was the "fittest medium for the thought that cannot be conveyed by speech";[28] and the proper reaction to instrumental music was, consequently, emotional, not verbal. With the content of Liszt's tone poems an impossible subject, Wagner turned to the only aspect of the compositions that he felt could be discussed: their form. The Liszt essay is, therefore, yet one more examination by Wagner of musical form and the factors that contribute to its creation.

Wagner maintained that, developmentally, instrumental forms had, for the most part, been based on dance movements and that the development of a dramatic idea conflicted directly with such a formal structure. Wagner considered that in the conflict of a dramatic idea with an instrumental form, either the form or the idea had to be sacrificed. If composers decided to sacrifice the dance form for the development of an idea, then the form intended to accommodate the idea had to be dictated by the idea itself and by the natural development of the idea. The form, in other words, had to be determined by a poetic motive. This determination of musical form by a poetic idea did not mean, however, that music would or should lose its expressive powers. On the contrary, it simply meant that the poetic idea would guide those expressive powers to a greater realization of this potential.

Wagner believed that music, far from being made subservient to other arts with which it came into contact, ennobled those arts; and in "Über Franz Liszt's symphonische Dichtungen" he offered the following statement of this belief as his artistic creed:

> Music can never and in no possible alliance cease to be the highest, the redeeming art. It is of her nature, that what all the other arts but hint at, through her and in her becomes the most undoubtable of certainties, the most direct and definite of truths.[29]

The creed here stated is obviously related to Schopenhauer's view of music, but at the same time it is different. Wagner, contrary to Schopenhauer, felt that nothing was less absolute, less independent of associative meanings, than music. Even music that appeared to be absolute had, in his view, to borrow its formal structures from life—either from dance or from words, from either "bodily motion or spoken verse";[30] and of the two choices, Wagner felt that the poetic was the nobler.

What had heretofore degraded program music, in Wagner's opinion, was the composer's lack of understanding of form and the proper contents of form. The composer had, first, chosen ideas unworthy of musical treatment and, then, forced those ideas into a "traditional, but arbitrarily mangled dance form."[31] The problem thus lay not in music's capabilities but in the composer's. Did he have the necessary musical-poetic gift to be able to see in any given poetic subject its essence, which could subsequently be used to mold intelligible musical forms? Wagner believed that Liszt had this gift beyond dispute and that it was just this gift that distinguished his tone poems from other composers' program symphonies.

That Wagner was thinking of Berlioz as the low-water mark by which Liszt's advances were judged is made obvious by direct reference. Wagner wrote that Berlioz's program music failed because he had mistaken the dramatist's role for the musician's. As Wagner perceived the two, the dramatist

> stands much nearer to the life of everyday and is intelligible solely when the idea with which he presents us is clothed in an action whose various component "moments" so closely resemble some incident of that life that each spectator fancies he is also living through it. The musician, on the contrary, looks quite away from the incidents of ordinary life, entirely upheaves its details and its accidentals, and sublimates whatever lies within it to its quintessence of emotional content to which alone music can give a voice, and music only.[32]

This statement as to what music can fittingly utter in drama is closely related to ideas advanced in *Oper und Drama*. Applied to Berlioz, it is used to show that, in the context of symphonic poems, Berlioz had not chosen as a poet who had to do with music should have chosen; instead, he had chosen as a poet who had to do with words. That was why, in Wagner's view, the love scene in Berlioz's *Roméo et Juliette* did not succeed: it was too literal for music and not literal enough for spoken drama. Liszt had avoided this trap. He had extracted from the verses he dealt with what could not be expressed by words—that is to say, he had extracted the verse's emotional content—and had presented this dramatic essence through music in a manner "uniquely clear, distinct, compact, and unmistakable."[33]

In the decade from 1850 to 1859, Wagner finished composing *Das*

Rheingold, Die Walküre, acts 1 and 2 of *Siegfried,* and *Tristan und Isolde.* With the exception of the essay on Liszt's tone poems, no important theoretical works were written during this period; but on the eve of the production of *Tannhäuser* at the Paris Opéra, a French friend, Frédéric Villot, asked Wagner to write a new statement of the theories he had advanced in *Oper und Drama.* Villot thought that such a statement would greatly enhance the Parisian public's enjoyment of the opera they were about to see by giving them an understanding of the theoretical bases that underlay Wagner's work. It is surprising that Wagner agreed to Villot's suggestion, since the idea that *Oper und Drama* could explain works that preceded it was the same sort of reverse reasoning Wagner had tried to correct in *Eine Mittheilung an meine Freunde.* But Wagner did agree, on the condition that he be allowed not to retrace old speculations but to place before the public the "concrete substance"[34] of his theories. He took the opportunity of prefacing the French prose translations of *Der fliegende Holländer, Tannhäuser, Lohengrin,* and *Tristan und Isolde* with an important new statement of his ideas. The essay, published in September 1860, was *Zukunftsmusik*; and Wagner began it, as he had begun the *Mittheilung,* by emphasizing the importance of the part evolution plays in an artist's creative life.

In *Zukunftsmusik,* Wagner again underlined the fact that poets, in writing opera librettos, had been handicapped by being expected to write poetry for set musical forms. Musicians, who alone could alter these forms, felt no inclination to do so because the old forms were the forms they knew. To ask a poet to supply poetry for some form that did not exist, which neither the musician nor the poet had clearly visualized, would have been unthinkable. The only solution to this problem, as far as Wagner could see, lay in completely altering the poet's role in the creation of opera. The poet had to acquire new knowledge, a musician's knowledge, that would allow him to write poetry that would be musical and yet would develop organically. With such knowledge, the poet could at last become the masculine, fertilizing partner in the union of poetry and music. In response to poetry's new role, music could then become the feminine partner in the union, not merely receiving the poetic seed but, more importantly, bearing it as well. Thus, reiterated in *Zukunftsmusik* is the basic premise of *Oper und Drama.*

Also repeated in *Zukunftsmusik* is Wagner's belief that music's ability to assume her true function in relation to poetry had been made possible by recent advances in instrumental composition. Wagner again praised German instrumental composers for their contributions to the development of music's expressive powers and to the expansion of music's forms. He praised particularly, as usual, Beethoven and his symphonies, in which

instruments speak a language whereof the world at no previous time had any knowledge; for here, with a hitherto unknown persistence, the purely musical expression
enchains the hearer in an inconceivably varied mesh of nuances; rouses his inmost
being to a degree unreachable by any other art; and in all its changefulness reveals an
ordering principle so free and bold, that we can but deem it more forcible than any
logic, yet without the laws of logic entering into it in the slightest—nay rather, the
reasoning march of thought, with its track of causes and effects, here finds no sort of
foothold. . . . Beethoven's music thrusts home with the most overwhelming conviction, and guides our feeling with such a sureness that the logic-mongering reason is
completely routed and disarmed thereby.[35]

Wagner believed that poetry could attain an inner blending with music
such as Beethoven had shown it possible to create and could thereby
contribute to music what music alone could never attain: fulfillment of
man's inevitable desire to know the answer to the question "Why?" All
that the poet had to do to meet this music's need and to create the perfect
drama was to be completely aware of the expressive possibilities that lay
within music's power. With this knowledge, the poet could then write
poetry that no longer described events but instead portrayed emotions.
Such poetry, Wagner felt, would penetrate every fiber of the musical tissue
and allow the spoken thought to dissolve entirely into feeling.

The growing popularity of Wagner's earlier operas (as shown by their
increasing frequency of performance) convinced him that the evolutionary path on which he had started in them and which had led him through
Oper und Drama to the *Ring* poems and the majority of their composition
had been the correct one. "I had set out," he said,

with a right instinct when I deemed it possible for an equal interpenetration of poetry
and music to bring about an artwork that should produce an irresistably convincing
impression at the moment of its stage performance, an impression such as to resolve
all arbitrary reflection into purely human feeling. That I saw this attained in part
. . . inspired me with even bolder views of music's all-ennabling efficacy.[36]

These "even bolder views" were those suggested in *Die Kunst und die
Revolution,* outlined in *Das Kunstwerk der Zukunft,* and finally expanded
in substance and detail in *Oper und Drama.* The views were intimately
associated, moreover, with the Nibelungen drama, which Wagner, at the
time he wrote down most of his theoretical ideas, was carrying around
in his head. The drama matured there in such a way that Wagner described
his theories as "nothing but an abstract expression of the productive
process going on within me."[37]

Tristan und Isolde, however, was another and quite different matter.
One could with justification assume that this opera departed significantly
from the theories of *Oper und Drama,* but Wagner felt differently about
the matter and consented in *Zukunftsmusik* to having imposed on his

latest opera "the severest claims deducible from my theoretic premises: not because I formed it on my system, for every theory was clean forgotten by me, but since here I moved with fullest freedom and the most utter disregard for every theoretic scruple."[38] This quotation is somewhat paradoxical, but I think Wagner clearly meant to imply by it that *Tristan* was based on his earlier theories, that it had grown out of them, but that it had not been confined by them: *Tristan,* in other words, had evolved organically. Wagner himself said that during the composition of *Tristan* he became aware of just how far beyond his system he had gone. He compared his theories to the counterpoint exercises his teacher used to make him write, not because he would ever necessarily write a fugue in his compositions but because the ability to write a fugue and the knowledge that he could write a fugue would give him technical sureness and self-reliance.

In discussing *Tristan und Isolde* in *Zukunftsmusik,* Wagner asserted that the opera's verse continued to determine the vocal line's melodic structure. (This was in accordance with the recommendations of *Oper und Drama.*) The fact that music's form was determined by poetry did not mean, however, that poetry was accorded an ascendancy over music that limited music's freedom of movement and development. On the contrary, Wagner felt that the poem gave the musician a fixed point around which to build his work; that the poem defined the action, but that music explained the emotions. This view appears as a repetition of a principal point in *Oper und Drama*—namely, that the poet condenses moments of action to points that are most readily accessible to the feeling and the musician then expands those moments in a language that the feeling immediately comprehends. Wagner expressed this same idea in *Zukunftsmusik* by saying that the poet's greatness lies mainly in what he leaves unsaid. In this sense, *Tristan* is truly the preeminent example of an opera that meets this requirement: the words of the libretto, condensed at times almost to the point of incomprehensibility, are nevertheless pregnant with emotional potential and ripe, consequently, for musical expansion. Wagner felt that, with such poetry, melody could encompass the whole dramatic structure and, by so doing, give the artwork a total, continuous musical form.

Ten years after writing *Zukunftsmusik,* Wagner again discussed in print the relationship between poet and musician. He had finished *Die Meistersinger von Nürnberg* and the third act of *Siegfried* and had begun the composition of *Götterdämmerung* when, in the autumn of 1870, he wrote the essay *Beethoven,* ostensibly to celebrate the one hundredth anniversary of the composer's birth. In the essay, he invoked the philosophy of Schopenhauer to illustrate the fundamental difference between the poet and the musician and to provide what he considered to be the necessary basis for judging Beethoven's achievements as a musician.

Wagner applied to Beethoven Schopenhauer's statement on the musician in general: "He speaks the highest wisdom in a tongue his reason does not understand."[39] Wagner construed "reason" to apply in Beethoven's case to the formal structures in which his music had been cast. This "reason" was the same as that which underlay all operatic arias and was no more than the concept of musical form that had been handed down since the 1600s. How little Beethoven had to do with this "reason," how little he understood it, however, Wagner felt could be shown by the fact that Beethoven never tried consciously to change or overthrow the outward forms of music. Beethoven's true genius lay in his ability to provide for an "exuberant unfolding"[40] of music that could not be restrained by its set forms. As an example of this genius, Wagner pointed to the Fifth Symphony, where

> lyric pathos already verges on the definitely dramatic, in an ideal sense; and though it might be doubted whether the purity of musical conception would not ultimately suffer by the pursuance of this path, through its leading to the dragging in of fancies altogether foreign to the spirit of music, yet it cannot be denied that the master was . . . prompted . . . by an ideal instinct sprung from music's ownest realm.[41]

The allusion to the program symphony is obvious. Wagner had previously pointed out the general unsuitability of the genre for either dramatic or musical expression. Beethoven approached the program form but did not embrace it.

With the Ninth Symphony, however, Wagner saw an obvious attempt on Beethoven's part to expand the province of absolute music. Wagner likened the introduction of vocal utterance into this symphony to the "anguished cry of one awaking from a nightmare":[42] leaping up in despair, Beethoven had invoked upon his music the comforting effect of the word and had thereby entered a "new world of light."[43] Wagner understood this new world to be the realm of drama which Beethoven, although striving for, did not attain. Even in the final movement of the Ninth Symphony, Wagner felt that Beethoven remained still in the world of music, since what affected the listener in that movement was not the words so much as it was the human voice itself used as an orchestral instrument. This symphonic use of voices was an important advance for Beethoven and one that he used to even greater effect in the *Missa solemnis,* where Wagner saw the text serving merely as a vehicle for singing and having "no disturbing effect on our musical impressions for the simple reason that it starts no train of inductive thought."[44]

As Wagner saw it, Beethoven was the perfect musician to set such unspecific texts as Schiller's *Ode* and the Catholic mass because Beethoven's principal contribution to music consisted of raising melody from all influences of fashion to an eternally human type. Such music had great power in itself, and Beethoven developed it to an almost overwhelming extent. But that power had always been inherent in music. Wagner tried to prove this by pointing out that a piece of music loses none of its character even when the most diverse texts are laid beneath it.[45] Opera, especially, had shown that the mood set by the composer had more power to impress the feelings than the poet's words did; and in this regard, opera proved that the union of poetry and music always ended in the subordination of poetry to music. Nevertheless, Wagner felt that poets continued to be attracted to opera (even in the face of evidence showing music's supremacy over poetry) because they saw that music could give the poetic intent "a more precise expression and a more searching operation."[46]

In *Beethoven* Wagner returned to a matter he had treated many years earlier: what sort of poetry is suitable for musical-dramatic treatment? Wagner felt that poets who wrote ordinary operas could well fear that, no matter how serious their poems, those poems might not be noticed at all when joined with music. The nature of the operatic idiom often made audiences attach more interest to what was happening on the stage than to the poetic thought that explained the action. Wagner thought that traditional opera attracted primarily the attention of hearing and sight; and

> that a perfect esthetic satisfaction was not to be gained for either one receptive faculty or the other is fully accounted for by the circumstance . . . that opera-music did not attune us to that devotional state—the only one in keeping with music—in which vision is so far reduced in power that the eye no longer sees with the wonted intensity.[47]

Wagner considered that even *Fidelio* contained so much that was foreign to music and unassimilable by it that the overture to the opera was far more dramatic than the opera itself. Wagner felt that this single example proved that "music includes within itself the consummate drama."[48] In order to be applied successfully to music, therefore, Wagner reasoned that poetry had to supply a dramatic basis in words that was proportionate to the drama that music could reveal and assimilate. What the poet represented in drama had to be "foreordained by those inner laws of music"[49] operating unconsciously in the poet's mind. This unconscious knowledge, of course, was the same as that which Wagner had required of the poet in *Oper und Drama* and had described himself as having acquired in *Eine Mittheilung an meine Freunde*.

Wagner believed that in the final movement of the Ninth Symphony Beethoven had shown how music could be used to beget the perfect drama. Wagner described the leap in that movement from instrumental music to vocal music as a "certain overcharge, a vast compulsion to unload without."[50] Wagner's implication was that Beethoven had reached the point in his musical development where instrumental music alone simply could not handle the dramatic demands placed upon it. The consequent union of music and words in the Ninth Symphony revealed mutual benefits for both elements: music could be given greater definition and poetry could be given greater emotional range. The success of the union, moreover, could be judged by the degree to which each component merited and complemented the other. (Wagner had said in *Oper und Drama* that, in the perfect union of words and music, both components disappeared as individual entities.) It was this mutual suitability that provided the true basis for perfect drama.

Wagner was careful to point out that the verses of the average poet could not determine music's course. He declared that the progress of music in drama could only be determined by drama itself—"not the dramatic poem," as he said, "but the drama that moves before our very eyes, the visible counterpart of the music, where word and speech belong no more to the poet's thought, but solely to the action."[51] The idea expressed here has been cited as a direct contravention of the theory of poetry described in *Oper und Drama*,[52] but cited incorrectly I think. In the first place, the quotation shows that Wagner had at last made a distinction (which he had failed to do in *Oper und Drama*) between the two meanings of the word *drama*. In the second place, far from contradicting *Oper und Drama*, the quotation seems to me to confirm a basic idea advanced there: not all poetry is susceptible to musical treatment; only the poet who has first become a musician is in a position to know what sort of poetry to write for the composer to set. Every theory in *Oper und Drama* rests on the assumption that the nature of music conditions the type of poetry written to be allied with it. The idea is repeated, in fact, in the closing pages of *Beethoven*, where Wagner declares that the ancient Greek drama succeeded because in it "everywhere we see the inner law, only conceivable as sprung from the spirit of music, prescribe the outer law that regulates the world of sight."[53]

In 1869 Wagner was elected a member of the Royal Academy of Arts in Berlin. In the spring of 1871, shortly after he had finished *Beethoven* and while he was still working on *Götterdämmerung*, he wrote *Über die Bestimmung der Oper* as the thesis for his Academy installation. Wagner stated in the preface to this essay that there was complete agreement between it and *Oper und Drama*, as far as the character and importance ascribed to the musically conceived drama was concerned, but that the essay offered new points of view that made certain details in *Oper und Drama* "necessarily assume another aspect."[54] *Über die Bestimmung der Oper* affords, then, yet another exploration of the relationship between words and music in opera, an exploration that differs from *Oper und Drama* only in details, not essentials.

In developing the theme of the essay, Wagner instituted a comparison between the spoken play and traditional opera. He felt that the play, as far as its outward effect on the public was concerned, could boast of at least one advantage over opera: the play had to have an intelligible, well-motivated plot; traditional opera did not. This advantage, however, was not sufficient to allow the play to fulfill the ideal scope of drama, since the expressive means of the spoken word were too limited. As Wagner put it, there was a "certain insufficiency in the poetic nature"[55] because words dealt principally with abstract concepts that addressed the reason. Music bypassed the reason and appealed directly, immediately to the feeling. It was for this reason that music's dramatic power was greater than poetry's. To illustrate music's power to transport even inferior poetry to an ideal sphere of drama, Wagner pointed to Gluck's *Iphigénie en Tauride* and Mozart's *Don Giovanni,* operas with commonplace librettos that were transformed through music into unquestionably great drama. Wagner suggested that, because these two operas were completely destitute of poetic thought or diction, serious poets could be led to think that opera, as a dramatic genre, belonged solely to the musician.

If music in traditional operas had, then, such dramatic power, what of the poet? What power could he have? Wagner answered this question indirectly by referring to Shakespeare as an artist distinct from and higher than what is commonly considered to be a poet. Wagner found in Shakespeare's plays "such drastic individuality, that it often seemed like unaccountable caprice, whose sense we never really fathomed until we closed the book and saw the living drama move before our eyes."[56] Obviously, Wagner borrowed from Schopenhauer's concept of a dream world in this attempt to give the verbal drama an emotional immediacy such as music had but words alone did not. At the same time, however, the quotation also recalls a point made many years earlier in *Oper und Drama*: the true actor does little more than show by gestures and words life as it really is; a poet, by extension, cannot become truly great until he has first become a mime. This was another way of saying that the poet achieved greatness by making the people and actions he placed on the stage seem always natural and true to life. Shakespeare was an example of this poet who was more than a poet. He was what Wagner was by this time calling the "poet-mime," the artist who, by absorbing the improvising spirit of the mime and developing the plan of his dramas entirely in keeping with that spirit, raised the mime's individuality into the poet's higher reasoning faculty. Following this line of thought, Wagner consequently defined the Shakespearean drama as a "fixed mimetic improvisation of the highest poetic worth."[57]

Wagner thought that Shakespeare could serve as an example of how
the dramatic poet should approach music, since Wagner saw Shakespeare
as being very much like Beethoven, the power of dramatic effect in both
being "different at once and equal."[58] The common tie between the two
lay in the directness of the presentation: Shakespeare, as the poet-mime,
and Beethoven, as the musician, both directly molded the actual artwork.
The poet, as such, only drafted the plan for the artwork. This pronounce-
ment has created a stumbling block in Wagner's later writings because it
makes the poet seem to be less important to Wagner's artwork than formerly. One needs to remember, though, that Wagner had at first made a
distinction among three creative individuals—the musician, the poet, and
the mime—to which he later, in *Über die Bestimmung der Oper,* added
a fourth, solely to account more satisfactorily (in his view) for Shakespeare's unparalleled ability to create drama in words. The fourth individual was, as we have seen, the poet-mime, who combined qualities of
both the poet and the mime to produce an artist of greater power than
either. It was as a separate entity that the poet merely drafted the plan
for the drama; together with the mime, the poet's power became infinitely
greater and complemented, in fact, the musician's. Of these two powers,
the musician's was inherent in the nature of music itself; the poet-mime's,
in his ability to translate his perception of life into words that could
subsequently call the life originally perceived by him back into motion,
sound, and being.

Wagner thought that the dramatic power Shakespeare had shown to
be possible in the play found no counterpart in music until Beethoven
began to experiment with musical form. The formal structures of music
up through the eighteenth century simply could not accommodate the
dramatic demands of the "sublime irregularity"[59] found in Shakespeare's
plays. Beethoven, however, realized that music did not have to maintain
its conventional, symmetrical structures but could be allowed to grow
and develop with the utmost freedom. Wagner believed that such music
as Beethoven had shown to be possible could, when applied to the essence
of Shakespearean drama, create musical drama that would appear as a
work of nature rather than as a piece of architecture. The very adapta-
bility of music's new forms rendered it eminently susceptible to dramatic
treatment.

Far from trying to diminish the importance of words in opera in *Über
die Bestimmung der Oper,* Wagner reemphasized the role he had assigned
them in *Oper und Drama,* that of instigating music's dramatic response,
giving meaning to that response, and guiding that response's subsequent
dramatic development. The importance Wagner continued to ascribe to
words is confirmed in *Über die Bestimmung der Oper* by his choosing
Shakespeare as the preeminent example of the dramatic poet (or poet-

mime) for operatic poets to emulate. I have said that Wagner defined the Shakespearean drama as a "fixed mimetic improvisation of the highest poetic worth."[60] Obviously, what fixed the improvisation, what made its worth lasting, was Shakespeare's use of words. Without them, of course, Shakespearean drama could not exist; neither could Wagnerian opera. One has only to imagine silent actors gesturing their way through *King Lear* or silent singers gesturing their way through *Tristan und Isolde* to appreciate the full ludicrousness of any point of view which holds that Wagner, after he came to know the philosophy of Schopenhauer, abandoned his concept of the dramatic power of words in favor of that of gesture and music, acting either alone or together.

In the summer of 1872, a little over a year after he had written *Über die Bestimmung der Oper*, Wagner again tried to clarify his concept of drama by showing how words, music, and gestures could be combined to produce the perfect dramatic artwork. The essay, written shortly after the laying of the foundation stone of the *Festspielhaus* at Bayreuth, was *Über Schauspieler und Sänger*. In discussing the actor's art, Wagner again had occasion to observe that the great actor could make even inferior plays and operas seem dramatic by the power of his art.[61] Wagner attributed the effect of this power to the fact that the illusions created onstage by the actor were derived from a natural imitation of life. In this regard, the actor's gestures were like music's tones: neither had to depend (as words did) on auxiliary illusions or on reason. Both gestures and tones had the ability to be immediately understandable to the feeling without the intervention of reason.[62]

Wagner declared that the opera orchestra alone was capable of exploring to its fullest the range over which the mime's individuality could be conceived as extending. The orchestra accomplished this feat by permeating the whole dramatic performance so that music itself was responsible for raising the drama to "that ideal sphere for which the costliest poetic diction had proved inadequate."[63] Here again in a late theoretical essay is a recollection of *Oper und Drama,* the whole point of which was that neither traditional operas nor spoken plays had been able by themselves to attain the perfect drama. What followed from this point was that poetry should be suitable for musical expression and that, being suitable, it could then act as the fertilizing seed which music would take up into its womb and bring forth again as drama. In *Über Schauspieler und Sänger,* Wagner repeated his description of music as the feminine, the motherly element of drama, which manifested itself through two organs: "here the infinitely potent orchestra, there the dramatic mime; here the mother-womb of the ideal drama, there its issue born on every hand by sound."[64] Perhaps one cannot overemphasize the obvious point made at the conclusion of this quotation: singers accomplished their part in the ideal drama through sound.

That Wagner had not ceased to regard the contributions of words to drama is borne out in this essay by the length at which he dwelt on the necessity of having the words clearly understood by the audience. He condemned, for example, singers who tried to sing German as if it were Italian and ended up producing a "jumble of inarticulate vowels and consonants, which simply hinder and distort the singing without being understood as speech."[65] Wagner believed that lack of care in enunciation of words had even more deleterious effects on the dramatic performance of opera: "As our singers do not articulate properly, neither for the most part do they know the meaning of their speeches, and thus the character of any role entrusted to them strikes their minds in none but general hazy outlines."[66] Thus, Wagner continued to regard words in drama as determinative, even at a time when he had completed all of his operas but one. He insisted in *Über Schauspieler und Sänger* that the melodic line in performance always be given its "rightful motion, through accent, rise and fall, according to the verbal sense."[67]

The main problem Wagner saw in operas like *Die Zauberflöte, Fidelio,* and *Der Freischütz* was dialogue that could not be completely set to music. It was the same problem of parceled-off forms he had complained of in *Oper und Drama.* The problem, as he repeated in *Über Schauspieler und Sänger,* could only be solved by abandoning music's outmoded forms and replacing them with new forms that would allow the "full unveiling of the orchestra's gigantic power."[68] In Wagner's opinion, however, the German musician, so willing and able to use the orchestra's power in instrumental works, was at a loss to know how to apply that power to opera. Confused by the lyric and dramatic elements in opera, he did not know how to integrate the two into a unified whole. He, like the Italians, could only set opera's lyric elements; the dramatic were beyond him. As an example of this opinion, Wagner singled out the scene in *Der Freischütz* where Kaspar enlists Max through the loan of a magic bullet. Weber, because he was unequal to the dramatic demands of the scene, was compelled to leave it to spoken dialogue. Wagner declared that his own development as a composer stemmed from his instinctive desire "to seek out the possibilities which here lay concealed from Weber."[69] That is to say, Wagner was unconsciously led to set to music both the dramatic and the lyric elements in opera and to render, thereby, the entire work a drama in music, from beginning to end. He felt that the degree of success he had achieved was shown by the fact that although his poems, when read, appeared to be nothing more than spoken plays, they exhibited, when set to music, a "ceaseless flow of music as yet unknown."[70] It was a flow initiated at its source and guided in its channels by the poet.

Toward the end of *Über Schauspieler und Sänger,* Wagner referred to Goethe's use in *Faust* of the old rhyming meters taken primarily from the "rugged art of our old folk poet, Hans Sachs."[71] Wagner posed the question of whether even this so-called *Knittelvers,* or doggerel, might not be matter for musical setting, perhaps even in Italianate vocal lines. In view of the verse and melodies of *Die Meistersinger,* the question was not an idle one. Wagner knew that an important discovery lay at its root— "namely, a singing tongue wherein an ideal naturalism should take the place of the unnatural affectation of our actors ruined by un-German rhetoric."[72] This continuing preoccupation with verse structures in so late a theoretical work seems particularly relevant in light of Wagner's infrequent use of *Stabreim* and his return to end-rhyme after the *Ring* operas. By 1872 Wagner felt, it seems, that even doggerel could be set to music dramatically so long as the underlying thoughts were human and natural and appropriate to the matter at hand. This was a change indeed from the emphasis on *Stabreim* in preference to end-rhyme that we find in *Oper und Drama,* but it was a change that Wagner felt was justified. By the time he wrote *Über Schauspieler und Sänger,* he had finished both *Tristan und Isolde* and *Die Meistersinger von Nürnberg* and knew all too well that *Stabreim* was not indispensable to the creation of drama. He had, in fact, practical experience that music offered the composer "a melismus pulsing with exhaustless rhythm, whereby to fix beyond all doubt an infinitely varied life of discourse."[73]

The major theoretical writings from Wagner's later years have now been examined, but Wagner's later shorter writings also have insights to yield concerning his opinions about music and drama. Thus, in *Ein Einblick in das heutige deutsche Opernwesen,* written in December 1872 after he had made a tour of the country in search of promising talent for Bayreuth, Wagner was not solely concerned with assessing the state of opera in Germany. In addition to commenting on the operas of other composers and their performances in Germany, he pointed out, in comparison, that his own chief concern as a composer had been increasingly to build up the dialogue in opera to a point of primary dramatic and musical importance and interest. He said that he had devoted his whole musical art to this purpose; and, as a result, he felt that in his own operas he could say that "nothing tells but what is understood in due connection with the whole; what remains unclear in this sense leaves the audience uninterested."[74] In connection with this statement, Wagner related his experience at a performance of *Die Meistersinger* in Bremen. The opera was so badly and so extensively cut that he hardly recognized it as his own and what had never seemed too long to him before appeared, because of the cutting, to be unending. Wagner attributed this impression to the cuts that made the story incomprehensible and therefore tedious. Wagner concluded that a spectator, confronted by a story he does not understand, lets his attention wander; and no amount of lovely or appealing music can reclaim it. Music, therefore, was not enough to make a good opera or even a passable drama. In order for any drama to make its intended impression, the words, since they defined the emotions and gave meaning to the music, had to be understood.

The subject of the importance of words in opera came up again in February 1873 in the "Einleitung zu einer Vorlesung der *Götterdämmerung* vor einem ausgewählten Zuhörerkreise im Berlin." Wagner's purpose in this essay was to make his audience better acquainted with the poem of a work that had attracted attention chiefly as a work of music.[75] In his "Einleitung," Wagner repeated and underscored what he considered to be his principal contribution to opera. In referring to the innovations attributed to him, he said he felt

> conscious of having, if not achieved, at least deliberately striven for this one advantage, the raising of the dramatic dialogue itself to the main subject of the musical treatment; whereas in opera proper the moments of lyrical delay, and mostly violent arrest of the action, had hitherto been deemed the only ones of possible service to the musical composition.[76]

One can hardly discount at this point in Wagner's life his own perception of the main contribution he had made to opera. As a significant dramatic change in opera's form, it was the goal toward which he had been striving consciously ever since he first propounded it in the theories of the late 1840s and early 1850s. At the same time, however, one must recognize that the essence of the contribution lay in the importance the composer attached to the words of the dramatic dialogue. It was that which made the words worthy of musical treatment in the first place.

Wagner declared in the "Einleitung" that he had longed to "raise the opera to the dignity of the genuine drama."[77] He felt that the development of instrumental music in the recent past had given him the potential to fulfill this longing. Wagner realized that music could reveal the inner motives of the action together with all the varying ramifications of those motives and, by so doing, could relieve poetry of much of the burden it had previously borne in spoken drama. As a result of music's power, characters would no longer have to explain their impulses in words. That music could do; and dialogue could, consequently, gain "the naive pointedness which constitutes the very life of drama."[78] Restated here again is the idea that the poet should condense the action to the point most readily accessible to the feeling and the musician should then expand that point into pure feeling; here again a fundamental concept of *Oper und*

Drama is repeated and confirmed in Wagner's later writings about opera.

Wagner had always known that music's expressive powers were greater than those of poetry. For that reason, if for no other, he must likewise have realized that, in any given union of poetry and music, music would possess the greater power for drama. He confirmed this fact in "Über die Benennung 'Musikdrama,' " written for the *Musikalisches Wochenblatt* and published in October 1872. In the article, Wagner spoke of the difficulty of finding an appropriate label for his later dramatic works:

> Twist and turn it as one might, music remained the real encumbrance to the naming, though everybody dimly felt that it was the chief concern in spite of all appearances, and more so when that music was invited to develop and put forth its amplest powers through its association with the actual drama.[79]

As Wagner pointed out, the greatest difficulty in labeling his works lay in placing music in a proper relation to drama. The difficulty was inherent in the whole concept of opera. Music, after all, was what distinguished opera from the spoken play. Wagner recognized that in discussing music and poetry in opera the temptation was to place music in a position of rivalry with poetry: music had to be either greater or less than poetry. Wagner, however, concluded that such an attitude was not only wrong but also harmful. In *Oper und Drama,* he had employed the sexual image of male and female uniting in mutual surrender to conceive and produce offspring; in this view, there was no question of rivalry or of supremacy. In "Über die Benennung 'Musikdrama,' " he reiterated his earlier position: music was the "very mother-womb of drama."[80] As a particularly apt illustration of his point, Wagner referred to the second act of *Tristan,* where "there passes little more than music,"[81] and yet there is drama.

Wagner began working on the composition sketches for *Parsifal* in September 1877. He finished them at the end of April 1879. In June of that year, he wrote the first of three articles on words and music that were intended for publication in the *Bayreuther Blätter.* The introductory article, *Über das Dichten und Komponiren,* did little more than serve as a prologue to the series and a complaint on the state of the literary and musical world.[82] The second article, *Über das Opern-Dichten und Komponiren im Besonderen,* written in August 1879, addressed a more specific problem. In this article, Wagner expressed his belief that German audiences generally learned nothing of what the poet intended by his libretto because composers so mishandled the words of the libretto. Wagner considered the "criminal vagueness"[83] with which German composers set texts to music to be the principal fault in German opera; to support his belief, he drew examples from many of the popular German operas of the day. Wagner concluded that, even more than French and Italian opera,

German opera was the result of "bungler's work."[84] Nowhere did he find fulfilled the ideal musical-poetic relationship that produced true musical drama with its "requirements that should necessarily be met by a drama on the one hand and an independent piece of music on the other."[85]

Toward the end of *Über das Opern-Dichten und Komponiren im Besonderen,* Wagner repeated the fundamental principle of *Oper und Drama*: in creating the united artwork, the poet's contribution is the masculine element; the composer's, the feminine. As a means of attaining the perfect drama, Wagner recommended that dramatic composers "never think of adopting a text before they see in it a plot and characters to carry out this plot, that inspire the musician with a lively interest on some account or other."[86] The recommendation was Wagner's idea of a good joke, of course, but it also underscores his view of poetry's role in the creation of musical drama. Wagner repeated his belief (earlier stated in *Oper und Drama*) that the supply of pretty melodies like those of Rossini was exhausted and that the composer who wanted to be creative melodically had to be constantly on the lookout for new ideas. Wagner's advice to the composer, therefore, was "to keep a keen eye on his text, his plot, and his characters for inspiration"[87]—the point being, that the dramatic composer could not rely on music for dramatic inspiration; that had to come from the text.

The third article, *Über die Anwendung der Musik auf das Drama,* was published in the *Bayreuther Blätter* for November 1879. In this final article of the series, Wagner differentiated between the musical style of a dramatic composition and that of a purely musical one. He advanced the opinion that dramatic pathos was excluded from the symphony because the symphony was based solely on dance movements. Therefore, the most intricate combinations of thematic motives in a symphonic movement could not be explained by any analogy to dramatic action. Motivic combinations in a symphony merely represented to Wagner the "mazes of an ideal dance without a suspicion of rhetorical dialectics."[88] Since there was no dramatic problem stated in the dance, there could be no problem stated in the symphony; consequently, there was no need to advance a musical solution or conclusion to what did not exist.

Composers such as Berlioz and Liszt, however, had tried to enlarge the formal boundaries of the symphony by invoking a dramatic incident that could be rendered in music. "Under the guidance of a dramatic synopsis,"[89] these men proved that instrumental music could expand not only its formal structures but its expressive powers as well. The program music of Berlioz and Liszt strove so much to realize a poetic shape that it eventually became melodrama, complete with instrumental recitatives and imaginary action. It finally reached such a point of development that musical drama was the only natural outcome of its growth and the only result that could save it from falling into "boundless follies, threatening serious damage to the spirit of music."[90]

What program music lacked, Wagner believed, was an overall unity, that aspect of music which "moves us to unbroken interest and keeps the broad impression ever present."[91] Wagner knew that the play could supply this unity, that it could draw on music's expressive abilities and give them the impetus to expand to their fullest and thereby make musical drama the perfect artwork. Wagner realized, moreover, that this artwork could achieve its unity in the same way a symphonic movement did—by the statement and restatement of themes. The fundamental difference in the symphony and the musical drama lay in what governed the presentation of thematic relationships. In the symphony, it was the musical structure derived from dance; in the musical drama, it was the play itself. Wagner stated the problem in this way:

> The new form of dramatic music must have the unity of the symphonic movement; and this it attains by spreading itself over the whole drama, in the most intimate cohesion therewith, not merely over single smaller, arbitrarily selected parts. So that this unity consists in a tissue of root themes pervading all the drama, themes which contrast, complete, re-shape, divorce, and intertwine with one another as in the symphonic movement; only that here the needs of the dramatic action dictate the laws of parting and combining, which were originally borrowed from the motions of the dance.[92]

The view Wagner expressed here could just as easily have appeared over thirty years earlier in the last part of *Oper und Drama.* It is a final restatement of his early belief that the poetic drama governs the course and development of the musical drama.

Wagner advised those who wanted to try their hand at this dramatic genre in music "not to aim at harmonic and instrumental effects but to await sufficient cause for any effect of the kind, as otherwise they [would] not come off."[93] Here again, Wagner's later view paralleled his earlier one. He had long ago pointed out that the fault with composers like Meyerbeer was that they reversed the dramatist's proper creative process. Instead of allowing music to explain the play, they used the play to explain music. The result was dramatic effect without dramatic cause. Wagner pointed to examples of what might seem to be harmonic effects in his own operas: the openings of *Das Rheingold, Die Walküre,* and *Siegfried;* but he made it clear that drama, not music, had determined the creation of these "effects." Although music made the effects possible, Wagner felt that it was poetry that had called the music into being. As he said, in each of the three instances the drama's poem demanded from him music that would "gradually quicken into life."[94]

As further examples of how the dramatic style differed from the symphonic, Wagner singled out the variety of motives in the *Ring* and their mutations "in closest sympathy with the rising passions of the plot,"[95] which, more than Wotan's words, gave a picture of the god's fear, depression, and suffering. Again, such an opinion may appear to some as a complete reversal of Wagner's earlier theories; but it is not. Again, the *Oper und Drama* view was that the poet condensed all the words in the story to the point most readily accessible to the feeling; from that point, music's powers expanded, giving to words emotional connotations that alone they could never achieve.

Wagner had always acknowledged that music's expressive power was greater than that of words. For him, music had always been the art that was immediately perceptible to the feeling, the expressive range of which poetry only guided. *Über die Anwendung der Musik auf das Drama* repeated this opinion and restated Wagner's belief that motives in opera should develop, not from music, but from music's relation to the text of the drama. It was this text-incited development of music that formed the "characteristic distinction between the dramatic and symphonic use and working out of motives."[96]

Wagner felt that true dramatic art could transform a theme more naturally and present it with more varied expression than symphonic art could. As an example, he pointed to the closing phrases of Elsa's "Einsam in trüben Tagen" in the first act of *Lohengrin,* a passage of music that, in a symphony, would have appeared as a "piece of eccentric modulation"[97] but, in a musical drama, seemed to be perfectly understandable and well motivated. If, however, the phrases had not arisen from the dramatic situation, they would have been no more than a "far-fetched effect."[98] As it was, they provided drama of a high order.

The essay *Religion und Kunst,* written in the summer of 1880, has little to do with Wagner's theory of words and music functioning in opera to create drama; but since it has been cited as an example of how Wagner reversed his ideas on opera in his later years,[99] perhaps a word should be said about it in conclusion. The essay is one of Wagner's last and comes from the time when he was much involved with *Parsifal.* Its only major successors among the theoretical writings are its supplements: "Was nützt diese Erkenntniss," "Erkenne dich selbst," and "Heldenthum und Christenthum."

In *Religion und Kunst,* Wagner dealt briefly with the lyric aspect of music (as opposed to the dramatic aspect). What he had to say in this regard derived from a discussion of how dogmas of the Catholic Church affected musicians' setting of religious poetry that embodied those dogmas. Wagner pointed out that the poetry, because it was church poetry, had to "retain the conceptual form of the dogma inviolate in every point."[100] But Wagner also pointed out that dogma, by its very nature, was not fit for musical expression; and consequently, the musician, confronted by poems based on dogma, had to decide how to treat the dogma in his musical setting. Wagner said that musicians instinctively realized that poetry was suitable for musical expression only where it rose to a lyrical outpouring of emotion brought about by a state of "rapturous worship."[101] At this point, even though the poem remained faithful to the dogma, the lyric, emotional aspect of its expression could be poured into music which would exalt the emotion behind the dogma without attempting to explicate the abstract terms of the dogma itself. Wagner concluded that the effect of music's power on the words of dogma was to deemphasize them and, in fact, dissolve them and the ideas they represented so that nothing remained in the artistic expression but the purely human emotional content behind the words.

No one who keeps in mind the whole view of *Oper und Drama* and Wagner's later theoretical writings can misinterpret Wagner's meaning at this point in *Religion und Kunst.* In the first place, Wagner was not speaking about drama at all; nor was he discussing the dramatic setting of text. He was speaking solely about the setting of lyric religious poetry. In the second place, the words he was discussing were meaningless in themselves. Like the text of the mass mentioned in *Beethoven,* the words of this Christian poetry were nothing more than religious formulas that had no ability on their own to inspire a musical response. What the early musicians chose to set, therefore, was not the words but the emotional undercurrent that welled up from beneath the words.

In the revolutionary period that brought forth *Die Kunst und die Revolution, Das Kunstwerk der Zukunft,* and *Oper und Drama,* Wagner had singled out the church and the state as the two confining, restricting forces acting on man's life to thwart it. Both institutions were built on aspects of society that were unnatural and inhuman and were, consequently, unacceptable for musical treatment. Wagner's statements about religious poetry in *Religion und Kunst* do no more than reaffirm his earlier views. They reaffirm as well his mistrust of words as expressions of the intellect rather than the feeling. As Wagner had attempted to show in *Oper und Drama,* words could be used either to enhance man's nature or to subvert it; but music, as the language of the feeling, could only speak what was human, natural, and true for all time. The truth in man's emotions could prevail over the falsehood of words meant to deny those emotions. It was thus that music dissolved the words of early Christian poetry and revealed the core of purely human emotion underneath them.

Music's power of emotional response was, in this regard, greater than the power of words to confine that response.

We have now reviewed Wagner's later theoretical writings that are concerned with his ideas about how words and music combine to produce drama. Is there a consistency among them that supports the ideas advanced in *Oper und Drama,* or do Wagner's later writings contradict his earlier ones? It would be astonishing if over the thirty years that separate *Die Kunst und die Revolution* and *Religion und Kunst* there were no changes at all in Wagner's thinking, especially since Wagner believed so strongly in evolution and growth as signs of artistic life and vitality. He realized, moreover, that time and experience had given him new insights into musical drama. He tried repeatedly over the years to put these insights into words. The number of essays alone in which he tried to clarify his thinking about words and music in opera speaks significantly to the fact that *Oper und Drama* was not Wagner's final word on the subject.

Wagner wrote in *Über die Bestimmung der Oper* that there was complete agreement between that essay and *Oper und Drama* as far as the character and importance of the musically conceived artwork was concerned but that *Über die Bestimmung der Oper* offered new points of view in light of which certain details relating to that artwork necessarily assumed another aspect.[102] Robert Gutman has suggested that this statement of Wagner's was sophistical,[103] but I suggest that it was true and that Wagner meant just what he said—namely, that the assumptions underlying the concept of musical drama had not changed but that details of those assumptions had. An obvious detail that had changed, for example, was *Stabreim*; Wagner found that he could do without it. Another was ensemble singing; Wagner found that he could use it to greater dramatic advantage than he had at first believed. There were other details, both forbidden and allowed, about which Wagner changed his mind. Consequently, Wagner's later view of opera was more balanced, more practical. In that view, the emphases may have changed, but not the fundamental relationship between words and music. The basic *Oper und Drama* premise about what constitutes musical drama remained constant. In the operas that came during and after the *Ring,* as in the *Ring* itself, there appears on every hand evidence of the poetic intent at work, instigating the musical response and bringing forth in combination with it what Wagner considered to be the perfect dramatic artwork.

In the chapters that follow—" 'Music and the Inner Movements of the Soul': *Tristan und Isolde*"; " 'Ideal Naturalism and the Singing Tongue': *Die Meistersinger von Nürnberg*"; and " 'Music Divorced from the Reasoned Word': *Parsifal*"[104]—I shall offer from three of Wagner's mature operas musical examples that seem to me to confirm the view of the poetic intent stated above. I should add, however, that there is little documentary evidence in Wagner's writings to support the individual musical analyses in these chapters; in most cases, they represent my views, not Wagner's. For this reason, I have chosen the most obvious examples of the effect of the poetic intent on the musical realization of the text. Because the examples are so obvious, they seem to me to be the least likely to require documentary support and the most useful, consequently, from which to draw broad-scale conclusions about the relationship between Wagner's concept in theory and in practice.

5

"Music and the Inner Movements of the Soul": *Tristan und Isolde*

By the end of March 1856, Wagner had finished the autograph scores of both *Das Rheingold* and *Die Walküre*. In the summer of the same year, he began work on the composition sketches for *Siegfried*; but by the beginning of the following year, ideas for *Tristan und Isolde* were beginning to occupy more and more of his creative thought. He nevertheless completed the autograph of act 1 of *Siegfried* on 31 March 1857 and continued work on the opera despite his increasing preoccupation with *Tristan*. Sometime around the middle of June, however, he finally decided to discontinue work on the *Ring* altogether, at least for the time being. He had at first thought he would not be able to finish even the second act of *Siegfried*; but, changing his mind, he worked on through July and managed to complete the sketches for the act on 9 August. Wagner then put the *Ring* aside for many years and began work almost immediately on *Tristan und Isolde*.[1] He started the prose sketch on 28 August 1857; by 18 September, he had finished the entire verse libretto. The autograph score was completed two years later in August 1859.

As the first non-*Ring* opera Wagner wrote after *Oper und Drama*, *Tristan und Isolde* plays an important and practical part in helping define and delimit ideas in *Oper und Drama* that arose as specific artistic responses to challenges the nascent *Ring* drama posed. Wagner's opinions on the usefulness of *Stabreim* provide an obvious case in point. Although Wagner had implied in *Oper und Drama* that *Stabreim* was superior to end-rhyme and better suited for operatic verse, he made it clear in *Eine Mittheilung an meine Freunde* that the idea of *Stabreim* was intimately and primarily related to his conception of the *Ring* and the Germanic and Norse myths and sagas that lay behind it:

> When I sketched my *Siegfried*—for the moment leaving altogether out of count its form of musical completion—I felt the impossibility, or at least the utter unsuitability,

of carrying out that poem in modern verse. . . . I must straightway have let my *Siegfried* go, could I have dressed it only in such verse. Thus I must needs bethink me of a speech melody quite other. And yet, in truth, I had not to bethink, but merely to resolve me; for at the primal mythic spring where I had found the fair young Siegfried man, I also lit, led by his hand, upon the physically perfect mode of utterance wherein alone that man could speak his feelings.[2]

The association between *Stabreim* and the *Ring* is confirmed, moreover, by the libretto of *Tristan und Isolde,* which contains not only *Stabreim* but end-rhyme as well. Even a cursory examination of the libretto forces the conclusion that, whatever Wagner's opinions on the subject of *Stabreim* may have been in 1850, he either did not speak his mind completely at that time or else later changed it. In either case, *Tristan und Isolde* offers practical proof (as do *Die Meistersinger* and *Parsifal*) that Wagner either did not go far enough in *Oper und Drama* in the specifics of his theorizing or else made a mistake in those specifics. The presence of end-rhyme in *Tristan* is the artistic reality that places Wagner's remarks on *Stabreim* in perspective.

Unlike *Stabreim,* the concept of the poetic intent is, I believe, a more constant aspect of Wagner's theory of opera. We can see this in the first twenty or so measures of act 1 of *Tristan,* where, in the song the sailor sings as the curtain rises, *Stabreim,* assonance, and end-rhyme combine:

> Westwärts
> schweift der Blick;
> ostwärts
> streicht das Schiff.
> Frisch weht der Wind
> der Heimat zu:
> mein irisch Kind,
> wo weilest du?
> Sind's deiner Seufzer Wehen,
> die mir die Segel blähen?
> Wehe, wehe, du Wind!
> Weh', ach wehe, mein Kind!
> Irische Maid,
> du wilde, minnige Maid!

If the music of the prelude has fulfilled the dramatic task assigned it in *Oper und Drama,* then, at its conclusion, the audience has been brought to a point of expectancy that makes it eager to know what the opera is about. This the sailor's song sets out to do to a limited extent. The words are clear enough, as far as they go. They establish that the ship is sailing from west to east; that there is a young Irish woman on board; that she is being taken away from her home; and that she is fierce, lovely, and very unhappy. But aside from this rather meager information, the words do not reveal much about the opera's story. As exposition, they raise at least as many questions as they answer. Who, for example, is the woman? Why is she on the ship? Where is she being taken? Where is she coming from? Why is she unhappy? What is her relationship to the others on board? What is the sailor's attitude towards her? The words of the song thus serve a dual dramatic function: they partially satisfy the vague longing for knowledge that the prelude has aroused but, at the same time, demand additional, more specific information. Because they both answer and raise questions, the words are ambiguous; and it is this aspect of the words that serves, I believe, as the basis for the operation of the poetic intent. Ambiguity becomes the verbal point of departure from which the musical realization is made.

The musical setting that the words of the song evoke adds to them another dimension of the poetic intent that clarifies the dramatic situation to some extent. The music helps establish the sailor's attitude toward Isolde and, by so doing, provides the basis for allowing the audience to establish its attitude toward her. The first four lines of the poem contain two parallel phrases of five syllables each. The parallelism, which assonance and *Stabreim* emphasize, is deceptive, however. Clearly, there is contrast between the direction in which the ship is sailing and the direction in which Isolde is gazing, but the significance of the contrast only becomes apparent in the music (see example 5.1). The first phrase of the song reflects Isolde's confusion at being torn away from her home; and, appropriately enough, the notes of the phrase repeat exactly the intervals of the ascending minor sixth and descending minor second that begin the prelude. In these three notes, the song not only recalls the prelude but also relates it (and whatever meaning it has) to Isolde's dramatic situation at the beginning of the opera. Her longing for home, which "Westwärts" suggests, is thus associated with an ascending minor sixth. From the *e-flat* to which this interval ascends, the melody, in a descending minor-third "sigh" ("schweift"), encircles c ("der") only to leap up an augmented fourth to *f-sharp* for a musically surprising setting of "Blick."[3] The "tonality" of the whole first phrase is a somewhat ambiguous C minor, the uncertainty of which answers well to Isolde's position in the drama at this point.

In complete contrast, the second phrase of the song reflects the sailor's eagerness to return home. The melody is firmly planted in the relative major and, after defining its dominant with a descending fifth ("ostwärts"), takes the straightest possible three-note path to a tonic *e-flat*. The vigorous dotted rhythm which leads to the tonic note is emphasized by *Stabreim,* which links the second half of the line to the first but

Example 5.1 *Tristan und Isolde*: "Westwärts schweift der Blick" (p. 6)

Scene I.

A marquee, richly hung with rugs, on the forward deck of a sailing-ship, at first entirely closed at the back; on one side a narrow companion-way leads to the cabin below.

Isolda on a couch, her head buried in the cushions. Brangæna, holding back a curtain, looks out over the side of the ship.

points up rhythmically, rather than harmonically, the differences of mood that characterize the two halves. The tonality of the first four measures—minor and ambiguous on the one hand and stalwartly major on the other—helps characterize Isolde from the start by contrasting her with the "common" man before we hear her utter a word.

The next four lines of the poem introduce a new element: the wind that is driving the ship forward, carrying the sailor toward his home and Isolde away from hers. The poetic lines are set to two practically identical musical phrases that continue the vigorous rhythmic motion of the second phrase of the song and serve throughout the act as the motive which suggests the sea and the ship's progress through it. The melodic similarity of the third and fourth phrases points up the fact that one agent, the wind, is responsible for one motion that affects the people on the ship in contradictory ways. A slackening of speed (*nachlassend*) in the fourth phrase is the only concession the sailor and the song make to Isolde's desire to linger at home in Ireland ("Wo weilest du?").

The ninth and tenth lines of the poem provide a verbal parenthesis that is characterized musically by a change of meter, a continuation of the ritard, and a shift in tonality from E-flat major to C minor. At this point in the poem, the sailor wonders if Isolde is trying to fill the sails with her sighs; and again, an element of contradiction and uncertainty enters the poem in the suggestion that Isolde's sorrow might be thwarting her desire. The musical phrases—in their beginnings, middles, and ends—outline again the opening motive of the prelude and, thus recalling it, once again relate it to Isolde's position. At the same time, however, the appoggiaturas that now appear in the melody seem to mock Isolde's unhappiness and add to her sorrow the sailor's flippant disregard.

At the conclusion of the parenthesis, the sailor moves abruptly to the tonality in which the song will end—B-flat major. He calls on the wind to blow in the seventh phrase and on Isolde to sigh in the eighth. The seventh phrase, *forte* and clearly in B-flat major, is a virile, sailorlike call; but the eighth phrase displays a change of mood that reflects Isolde's distraught state of mind. The dynamic level subsides to *piano* and, although the rhythmic pattern remains the same, the underlying harmony again becomes ambiguous. Has the sailor still not made up his mind about Isolde? The phrase that follows his call to the wind shows an awareness of the double meaning of "wehe" as it applies to Isolde. The melody veers sympathetically toward G minor, the relative minor of B-flat major; but it remains ambiguous. The sailor, having arrived at the leading tone to G minor, effects a gradual crescendo on that note that makes his final shift of sympathy away from Isolde particularly abrupt and disconcerting. At the height of the crescendo, the sailor apparently abandons both his musical and dramatic intentions and, following the *f-sharp* with an *f-natural*, wrenches the melody away from G minor and back to B-flat major. He delivers the last, insulting line of the song *feurig* (as the directions in the score indicate) with a rhythmic reference to the jaunty, dotted sailing figure.

There are several ways that the musical setting of the words in the sailor's song can be seen to reflect a poetic intent of ambiguity and ambivalence. In the first place, the song is tonally ambiguous (is it in C minor, E-flat major, G phrygian, G minor, or B-flat major?), and its shifting possible tonal centers are only emphasized by the brevity of the song and by its melody, sung throughout without accompaniment. (Even later in the act, when the song is repeated in part, its tonality is merely suggested by pedal tones in the low strings.) In the second place, the song is metrically and rhythmically ambiguous: metrically ambiguous not only because of its shifts from 3/4 to 4/4 to 3/4 but also because, due to the lack of measure-defining accompaniment, the coronas and notes tied across bar-lines distort what little feeling of meter the song does succeed in establishing; rhythmically ambiguous because the song alternates between phrases dominated by half notes and triplet figures and those dominated by quarter notes and dotted-eighth-and-sixteenth-note figures. In the third place, the song is dynamically and expressively ambiguous as well and in both cases alternates between extremes (*forte, piano*; *kräftig, nachlassend, etwas gedehnt, feurig*). In all these musical aspects, the song, by juxtaposing the sailor's state of mind with suggestions of Isolde's, appears to contradict itself repeatedly. Like the words that answer questions only to raise questions, the music makes statements only to deny them.[4]

There is a considerable amount of *Stabreim* in the verses of the sailor's song, but the primary function of this *Stabreim* is rhythmic rather than harmonic. The *Stabreim* emphasizes by its presence the strong beats of the measures in which it occurs. What harmonic coloring there is in the song has little, if anything, to do with *Stabreim*. It is reserved instead for references to Isolde and her plight. For the rest, for the ship and the sea and the men who sail, clearly defined major tonalities reign. In this separation of tonal functions, rhyming structures play a very small part, since the tonal functions have been assigned by Wagner to a more general level of meaning than that encompassed by specific words. Thus, the distinction between tonality and tonal ambiguity is a result, not of the poetic text, but of a consciously realized poetic intent, which both *Stabreim* and end-rhyme serve in its musical realization. During the course of the opera, the meaning of this distinction becomes increasingly important and apparent.

Like the sailor, Kurwenal belongs to the outside world that intrudes upon the lovers. As Kurwenal becomes aware of Tristan's involvement with Isolde, however, he is brought into greater conflict with the world he himself lives in. By act 3 of the opera, he appears to have resolved his conflicts, but in act 1 those conflicts are still evident. Such conflict can be seen in Kurwenal's reply to the message Brangäne delivers to Tristan from Isolde. Isolde has commanded Tristan to appear before her; and Kurwenal, with little regard for the feelings of either woman, tells his master the sort of reply he ought to make to the request:

> Herr Morold zog
> zu Meere her,
> in Kornwall Zins zu haben;
> ein Eiland schwimmt
> auf ödem Meer,
> da liegt er nun begraben!
> Sein Haupt doch hängt
> in Irenland,
> als Zins gezahlt
> von Engeland:
> hei! unser Held Tristan,
> wie der Zins zahlen kann!

The words are brutal enough, certainly, describing as they do Tristan's slaying of Morold, Isolde's betrothed, for his presumption in trying to collect Irish taxes in England; and the melody to which the words are set does nothing to soften their impact. If anything, it intensifies that impact.

Kurwenal's song (see example 5.2, measures 19–44), is little more than a sailor's ditty, melodically and rhythmically as straightforward as the words. The tonal base underneath the melody, however, vacillates. The song begins confidently in what, to judge from the first cadence, sounds like D major; but it becomes apparent almost immediately that the key is D minor. As the song progresses, however, secondary dominants and cadences on the submediant, the mediant, and the minor dominant (a deceptive cadence) suggest how difficult it is for Kurwenal to maintain a simple, folklike harmonic setting for what should be a simple, folklike song. When his difficulties in this regard are finally resolved, it is with curiously ambivalent results. In the ninth and tenth lines (measures 30–32), Kurwenal manages to establish a tonality clearly, but it is neither D minor nor its parallel major: it is B-flat major, the submediant, which is confirmed as the song ends.

This interpretation of the poetic intent influencing the setting of Kurwenal's song is not meant to imply that Kurwenal is necessarily aware of his own ambivalent feelings toward Isolde; he is not. Nor does it imply that the words of the song indicate the contradictory forces acting on

Example 5.2 *Tristan und Isolde*: "Herr Morold zog zu Meere her" (pp. 25–27)

(While Tristan by gestures tries to silence him, and Brangæna, offended, turns to go away. Kurvenal, as she moves slowly away. sings after her at the top of his voice)

Example 5.2 *Continued*

Kornwall Zins zu ha - - ben; ein Eiland schwimmt auf ö - dem Meer, da liegt er nun be -
Mo - rold once was fer - ried; 'mid tussocks damp, in dis-mal swamp, his bod-y now lies

gra - - - ben! Sein Haupt doch hängt im I - ren - land, als
bur - - - ied! His head, tho', went to I - rish lands, as

Zins gezahlt von En - ge - land. Hei! unser Held Tri - stan, wie der Zins zah - len
tax - es sent by English hands. Here's to my lord Tris - tan! For a tax, he's the

(Kurvenal, driven away by Tristan, goes below to the cabin; Brangæna, much disturbed, comes back to Isolda, and closes the curtains behind her while the whole crew is heard singing without)

kann!"
man!"
Tenor.

Noch etwas beschleunigend
Ancora più mosso

All the Men. „Sein Haupt doch hängt im I - ren - land, als Zins gezahlt von
Bass. His head, tho', went to I - rish lands, as tax - es sent by

Example 5.2 *Continued*

Kurwenal; they do not. That is what makes the harmony of the song so interesting; the words do not account for it. The explosive Zs that make up the majority of the *Stabreim* in the song deny that Kurwenal is experiencing any other emotion than scorn for Isolde and her dead lover. Nevertheless, I believe that there is already an underlying, subconscious conflict in Kurwenal's feelings in act 1, a conflict recognized neither by the words of the libretto nor by Kurwenal himself but recognized, all the same, by Wagner's poetic intent and realized, consequently, in music. Unlike Kurwenal, the sailors have no outside influences affecting their loyalties. No sooner has Kurwenal sung his last *B-flat* than they take up the song in four parts and, without harmonic excursions, repeat the whole last half in D major, a key that Kurwenal could only briefly suggest in the first measure of his song.

As a group, the sailors in act 1 represent the world from which Tristan and Isolde will soon long to escape. The sailors are the visual personification and tonal embodiment of this aspect of the poetic intent. One sailor begins the act; all of them end it. When Isolde is suffocating with rage and Brangäne opens the curtains to let in fresh air, Brangäne admits, along with the air, the taunting voice of a sailor. The sailors echo Kurwenal's song on the death of Morold and, just as callously, provide the gruesome aural background for Isolde's preparation for murder and suicide. When Isolde chooses the death potion, when Brangäne presumably prepares it, the sailors are there, singing "Ho! he! ha! he!" and hauling on the sails. During the lovers' decisive confrontation, however, the sailors remain silent. For over a hundred measures, they do not sing a note; the world they come from does not intrude upon Tristan and Isolde as they pledge themselves to what they think is death. When the lovers do not die and the true properties of the potion become apparent, the sailors' gaucherie comes as a rude interruption of the phrases from the prelude that here become associated with Tristan and Isolde's love. As the ship fills with people, the real dramatic conflict in the lovers' unhappy situation is reflected musically by the juxtaposition of the C-major trumpet fanfares of the king's retinue (which the sailors have helped prepare for musically) and the chromatic motive representing the lovers, which strains upward in the orchestra by half steps (see example 5.3). Although each motive possesses a rhythmic vitality all its own, the struggle between the two is brief and ultimately futile as far as the lovers' music is concerned. As the curtain falls, it is the king's theme and the king's trumpets that predominate.

In act 2, the working of the poetic intent results in a continued juxtaposition of diatonicism and chromaticism that symbolizes the contrast between the ordinary, settled, everyday world of reality and the restless, insatiable yearning of the lovers who cannot live in that world. In a trans-

Example 5.3 *Tristan und Isolde*: Conclusion of Act 1 (p. 104)

feral of orchestral symbols from act 1, the king's trumpets become his hunting horns, marking the course of the midnight hunt arranged by Melot. The ostensible purpose of the hunt is to remove the king from the vicinity of the castle so that the lovers can be alone; but the real purpose, of course, is to entrap them. During the course of the hunt, the musical realization of the poetic intent here makes Melot's treachery obvious.

Like the trumpets at the end of act 1, the horns are royal instruments of power; and as the curtain rises on act 2, they sound forth bravely (see example 5.4, measures 1–20). The sound of the horns has barely ceased, however, when the orchestra establishes a second, contrasting dramatic mood: the strings and woodwinds take up two motives that alternately and simultaneously rise and fall by half steps (see example 5.4, measures 27–31). The restraint under which Isolde is chafing, her longing and impatience are graphically limned by the contradictory motion of these two motives.

Seven measures after the horns have ceased, Isolde declares that she can no longer hear them. The hunt, nevertheless, is still nearby; and the horns, intruding on Isolde's mood, establish their presence (and the king's) unmistakably. As Isolde listens, tremolo strings reflect her attempt to concentrate on the B-flat major of the horns; but Isolde has no ear for horns (or for major tonalities, for that matter). She quickly loses interest in them; and as her mind returns to her longing for Tristan, the strings lose their grip on B-flat major (see example 5.4, measures 37–59). They slide from the subdominant chord, to the mediant, to a dominant-seventh on E. A chromatic melody played by the clarinet rises out of the string tremolos only to fall back to the B-flat that leads directly to the horns' characteristic dominant-ninth on F.

The horns again sound, distinctly but farther away, as Isolde accuses Brangäne of trying to deceive her: what Brangäne hears is only the rustling of leaves, Isolde says. And, indeed, the rustling is there in the tremolos of the strings, but the horns are there as well. Their distant sound finally dissolves into muted string and clarinet triplets that represent the soft rippling spring that Isolde insists is the only sound she hears. The strings and clarinets maintain B-flat major briefly, but soon that tonality gives way to D minor, as Isolde dismisses the king and his hunt from her mind and lets her thoughts turn again to Tristan.

As the scene between Isolde and Brangäne progresses, the shifting tremolos come to signify more than wind in the trees, or water in a brook, or Isolde's wandering thoughts: they accompany Brangäne as she tells Isolde her doubts about Melot's loyalty. When Isolde defends Melot as Tristan's truest friend, the tremolos vanish only to return to add emphasis to Brangäne's response: that is why I mistrust him. The tremolos dissolve

Example 5.4 *Tristan und Isolde*: Beginning of Act 2
(pp. 108–10)

Scene I.

(A garden with high trees before the chamber of Isolda, which lies at one side and is approached by steps. Bright and inviting summer night. A torch burns by the open door. A hunter's horn is heard. Brangæna, standing on the steps, is watching the retreating hunt, which can still be heard)

(Horns on the Stage.)

(Brangæna looks anxiously into the chamber where she sees Isolda coming)

Example 5.4 *Continued*

Example 5.4 *Continued*

into the hunting theme itself as Brangäne warns Isolde that Melot is sowing the seeds of evil in Mark's heart (see example 5.5, measures 12–19). The lovers are the game the king hunts, declares Brangäne; it is for them that the hunting horns sound. Isolde is unwilling or unable to believe the truth, however; and, as her passion-clouded brain converts Brangäne's loyalty to jealousy and Melot's jealousy to loyalty, the hunting theme itself is converted to Isolde's own impatient chromatic lines (see example 5.5, measures 26–37).

Isolde begs Brangäne to give the signal for Tristan to come by extinguishing the torch that keeps him away. She insists that all is quiet, that night has spilled silence over the sleeping world and has filled her heart with rapture and awe. Isolde's vocal line attempts to support her claim (see example 5.6): the tessitura falls; note-values increase; phrases lengthen; and chromaticism virtually disappears. But Isolde's claim is false, her calm is only pretense. Her vocal line, consequently, is a lie intended to convince a recalcitrant Brangäne that the hunt has passed and all cause for alarm has been removed. The orchestra, however, reveals the truth behind the lie. It shows, in the first place, that Isolde's longing has only been suppressed, not extinguished: the motive associated with that longing sounds in the orchestra with a ritarded rhythmic and harmonic motion that gradually increases as Isolde again becomes more and more impatient. In the second place, the orchestra shows that Isolde is wrong in her assessment of Melot: beneath the calm of her melodic line, beneath the stilled orchestral statement of her longing, the hunting horns continue to sound, softly but inexorably, to contradict her misplaced trust. The hunting calls will sound once again before the act is over; and when they do, it will be to signal the arrival of the hunters, the quarry tracked to its lair, and daylight's discovery of the love that heretofore night had hidden.

Throughout the scene that begins act 2, Wagner's poetic intent makes striking use of music to inform the dramatic situation. It is a use that is not tied particularly to individual words, however, as is normally the case when music is used to intensify poetic declamation. Instead, it is a use that is tied to the expression of broad, text-related concepts that are in direct opposition: truth and falsehood, loyalty and betrayal, patience and impatience. At times, such a use of music may make the poetic intent seem to be little more than a musical road map, charting the course of the libretto. But that, after all, is one of the meanings of *Absicht*: plan. And one of the functions the *dichterische Absicht* serves in Wagner's operas is to help determine the form of the music. Certainly, this aspect of the poetic intent can be seen in the succession of contrasting moods found in act 2 of *Tristan und Isolde,* where the ideas in the libretto provide

Example 5.5 *Tristan und Isolde*: "Von Tristan zu
Marke ist Melots Weg" (pp. 116–17)

Example 5.5 *Continued*

Example 5.6 *Tristan und Isolde*: "Schon goss sie ihr
          Schweigen durch Hain und Haus"
          (pp. 235–36)

Example 5.6   *Continued*

the stimulus for the musical realization of the moods and the ordering of that realization. The general musical means that Wagner employs here to achieve a musical equivalent of the drama's moods is a juxtaposition of diatonicism and chromaticism within a specific dramatic context. But he uses other means as well that are hardly less important: contrasting instrumental colors (brass for the king and his hunt; strings and woodwinds for Isolde and her longing) and contrasting rhythmic patterns (straightforward, insistent dotted notes and triplets for the king; syncopations, rhythmically ambiguous tremolos, and running eighth notes for Isolde) are two. Once the meaning of these musical contrasts has been established in general dramatic terms, then it is possible for the music to serve more specific purposes of the poetic intent: it may then be used, for example, to inform the meaning of individual verses and words (as in the association of string tremolos with Melot's treachery and horn calls with Isolde's calm); but this ability depends, at least in this sense, on Wagner's first establishing a symbolic relationship between contrasting elements of music and broad, contradictory aspects of the poetic text.

The poetic intent may function to draw drama from music even before words or situations have given the music dramatic meaning. Wagner called this function of music in drama the "foreboding" function, and an example of its operation can be seen in the prelude to act 3. This prelude is made up of three musical ideas, the alternation of which gives the music its form. This form can be described in musical terms that constitute the prelude's "map." The first musical idea (see example 5.7), played by the strings in six parts, is a supertonic/suspended-tonic progression in F minor that is repeated three times. *Forte* to start with, it swells even louder the second time it is played, and then subsides to *piano* on the final repetition. Out of the ascending melodic line of the first idea, the second emerges. Slowly, stretching out the ascent (*gedehnt,* as the score says), the violins rise in two parts to e^2 and g^2 (heard as a dominant tonality) and sustain these pitches *pianissimo* for four beats. This is the longest sustained sound in the prelude so far; it is followed by the third idea, which is introduced by the horns and violoncellos. Over an A-flat major triad, the melody descends sequentially in an intertwining line that moves down at first in three successive whole steps and then chromatically. Underneath, the harmony gradually attains a suspended dominant-seventh on C that announces the return of F minor.

In the second section, the strings again repeat the supertonic/suspended-tonic progressions but at a lower dynamic level. The violins again rise but this time to f^2 and *a-flat*^{2}, which is heard as a tonic harmony but which, in fact, soon becomes D-flat major, the key in which the third idea is now reiterated. This second section of the prelude

Example 5.7   *Tristan und Isolde*: Prelude to Act 3
(p. 216)

Act III.

leads into the third in an organic linking of the prelude's third idea with its first.

In the third section, the ascending suspended figures in the strings are once again repeated, but this time they begin at a higher pitch level and their number of repetitions is increased. As a result, the figures sound more intense, more desperate. The dynamic level swells from *piano* to *fortissimo* but subsides again to *piano*; throughout this dynamic arch, the pull to F minor continues. Three times a diminished-seventh on E-natural (the raised mediant of C minor and the leading tone of F minor) resolves to a dominant-ninth on G. The same progression is then repeated three more times in F minor—a diminished-seventh on A-natural leading directly to a dominant-ninth on C. As the violins try to rise one last time, the dynamic level drops to *pianissimo*. The violins reach the e^2 and g^2 of their first ascent, but they are drawn relentlessly down from those pitches by the first descending intervals to occur in the prelude's second musical idea. Even as the violins descend in fits and starts, chromatic alterations in the notes they play serve as attempts to negate the attraction of F minor. But the pull of the key is too strong. In a double suspension, marked *morendo* in the score, the violins succumb to the tonic chord.

Does the music in the prelude to act 3 have a dramatic purpose beyond its purely musical ground plan? I think so. Even without knowing what dramatic course the rest of the act will take, we get a sense of its direction from the alternation of musical ideas in the prelude. When, however, we learn the outcome of the opera, then the poetic intent animating the prelude becomes so much a certainty that we can definitely isolate it. Even at the risk of appearing overly imaginative, we can say that the prelude is a tone-picture that forebodes Tristan's struggles to escape the world (musical ideas one and two) and Isolde's intervention in those struggles to call him back to her (musical idea three). This is not to say that the prelude is pictorial music (although there are certainly pictorial elements in it associated with the height and depth of musical pitch); but it is to say that the musical plan for the work and the musical realization of that plan are derived from a dramatic plan—based on the ideas of struggle, release, and recall—that is closely related to the events in the libretto of the opera. The libretto, moreover, confirms such an interpretation and supports the contention that Wagner's musical plans were often extensions of his dramatic plans. Kurwenal's first speech in act 3 and the music that accompanies it link Tristan's coma with the first and second musical ideas and Isolde's healing presence with the third.[5]

Out of the F-minor chord into which the violins finally resolve at the end of the prelude, the shepherd's plaintive tune that calls Tristan back to consciousness and accountability emerges dramatically. Ernest New-

man called this tune "one of the strangest and most poignant ever imag-
ined by man."[6] Thirty years later, we might be more willing to agree with
Newman on the tune's poignancy than on its strangeness; but the tune
does have peculiarities, most of which are rhythmic (see example 5.8).
The number of tied notes, for example, makes it difficult for the listener
to perceive any underlying meter in the unaccompanied melody. (The
rhythmic ambiguity of the tune recalls that of the sailor's song and the
prelude to the opera.) The introduction of triplets, often tied to longer
preceding note-values, also renders the tune's rhythmic base ambiguous.
The harmonic position, however, is far from ambiguous and emphasizes
F minor exclusively, even obsessively.[7]

As the tune begins, the melody rises in half notes from the tonic to
the dominant degrees of the scale. As in the prelude to act 3, the music
seems to be trying to escape the attractions of F minor; but again, as in
the prelude, the attempt fails. The rise to *e-flat*[1] lasts only for an eighth
of a beat and precipitates a simple melodic descent to *d-flat*[1], *c*[1], and *b-
flat* that, because of the ascending fourths beneath, takes on a curious
limping quality. The reappearance of half notes in the melody at first
slows down the descent, but the subsequent introduction of triplets only
accelerates the melodic fall from *b-flat*, the subdominant, through *a-flat*
and *g-natural* to *g-flat*, the flatted supertonic. The attempt to maintain the
flatted supertonic is prolonged and dynamically intense, but it is in vain.
The melody returns to the tonic only to start the whole struggle over
again.

The second time around, the battle is of more extended proportions.
In the descent from *e-flat*[1], the melody holds on longer to each step of
the way and yields ground in the supporting descending fourths only by
half steps. The melody now falls below the tonic to *d-flat*, and even briefly
to *B-flat*, but halts its descent at *c*. From there it begins the laborious
process of raising itself again. At first in these attempts, extended note-
values on recurring *c*s keep the melody weighted down; but before long,
the extended note-values shift and transfer the melodic center of gravity
to an alternation between *g* and *g-flat*. In triplet and duplet rhythms, the
melody circles around the supertonic and flatted supertonic in a struggle
that gradually yields a whole-note *g-natural* as the victor. From there, in
a crescendo to *fortissimo*, the melody leaps with every appearance of
triumph to a whole-note dominant *c*[1].

Once again, however, in the rise from *c*[1] to *e-flat*[1], the process of
descent is already at work. The *e-flat*[1] is maintained this time for two full
beats, but this achievement only emphasizes the precipitateness of a descent that is marked almost entirely by triplet rhythms. The melody makes
a stand at the supertonic, at which point the dominant pulls on it from

Example 5.8 *Tristan und Isolde*: The shepherd's first tune (p. 217)

Scene I.

(The garden of a castle. At one side are high turrets, on the other a low breastwork broken by a watch-tower; at back the castle-gate. The situation is supposed to be on rocky cliffs; through openings one looks over a wide sea to the horizon. The whole scene gives an impression of being ownerless, badly kept, here and there delapidated and overgrown.

In the foreground inside lies Tristan sleeping on a couch, under the shade of a great lime-tree, extended as if lifeless. At his head sits Kurvenal, bending over him in grief, and anxiously listening to his breath-ing. From without comes the sound of a Shepherd's pipe)

both above and below. The supertonic yields eventually to the flatted supertonic, and the triplet rhythms encircle the notes that successively dominate the struggle until its end—*g-flat, f,* and *e-natural.* The effect of this continued alternation of flatted supertonic, tonic, and leading tone is an almost claustrophobic insistence on the tonic. Struggle as it will, the melody cannot escape F minor. Neither can Tristan. When he wakes into consciousness, both the shepherd's tune and this tonality will harass him until he comes to terms with himself. The struggles of the melody presage Tristan's own struggles.

The tune the shepherd plays at the beginning of act 3 is an unusual one in Wagner's mature works in that it is offered complete at its first appearance. Wagner's usual procedure was to present fragments of a melody as motives that were eventually combined to produce the longer original melody.[8] The effect of this procedure in the operas was, thus, that of fragments being joined together to create a melody rather than the actual compositional process of a melody being broken up to create fragments. In other words, in a large work, Wagner's motives presented the aural impression of organic growth rather than of dissolution or fragmentation; but it is the reverse of this process that occurs in the third act of *Tristan.*[9]

Joseph Kerman felt that it was a fine inspiration on Wagner's part to keep the shepherd's tune sounding throughout what Kerman calls Tristan's second cycle of introspection.[10] But the dramatic purpose behind the inspiration was, I think, even more remarkable. Bernard Shaw was closer to the mark when he noted that the shepherd "carries on the drama at one of its most deeply felt passages by playing on his pipe."[11] The shepherd's tune not only carries on the drama but, in a sense, is the drama. Tristan grows in act 3, but he grows through dissolution: Tristan the hero dissolves to become Tristan the human being. The shepherd's tune does not merely help him do this; it forces him. The tune is broken apart so that Tristan may be broken apart; and to make this process obvious, Wagner first presents the tune in its entirety. By unceasing repetition, the tune demands that Tristan remember his past. Wherever his thoughts turn, some fragment of the tune is there to call him to account and to make him remember. With its relentless melodic and harmonic insistence, the tune refuses to give Tristan peace until he has examined every stage in the development of his relationship with Isolde and has come to realize that he is himself responsible for his actions. The shepherd's tune does not cease to sound until Tristan can admit his part in the tragedy he has played. When Tristan at last comes to this knowledge of himself, he is ready to die with Isolde. As a sign of this change, his music at last escapes F minor.

The use of musical motives that have been related to poetic ideas is the most obvious way in which the poetic intent can be seen to operate in the delirium scene of act 3. This equation of music with various incidents in the libretto is, moreover, the one aspect of the poetic intent that is probably most often associated with Wagner and his theories about opera. But an equally important aspect of the poetic intent found in this scene is Wagner's use of music to reflect Tristan's varying physical and emotional states, shown in two extremes at the beginning and end of the scene. No "exhaustion" motive, for example, is necessary to indicate Tristan's feebleness when he first awakens. His condition is conveyed by other musical means: sparse instrumental accompaniment; numerous sustained chords; slow rhythmic motion; low dynamic levels; and short, fragmented vocal phrases separated, even within phrases, by frequent rests. As Tristan becomes more and more excited, the musical setting likewise intensifies so that, by the time the climax of the scene is reached in the measures immediately preceding Isolde's entrance, the dynamic level has reached *forte/fortissimo*; the vocal tessitura has climbed to the top of the tenor's range; the vocal phrases tumble out one after the other in a torrent of words; the instrumental forces have grown to include almost every instrument in the orchestra; and the rhythmic and metrical activity has increased from frenetic to eccentric. In all of this, a poetic intent is at work; but the principal means by which it is conveyed have nothing to do with individual words in the text, previously identified musical motives, or any of Wagner's "new" ideas about opera advanced in *Oper und Drama*. Wagner employed instead what, in the light of his evolutionist theories about opera, can only be regarded as reversions—traditional musical conventions for depicting emotions and states of mind. As a result, even though much of the scene can be considered to follow Wagner's theories closely, part of it, at least, conforms to musical practices as old as opera itself. In the application of both the old and the new, a poetic intent operates to suggest musical responses to ideas arising from the text.

When Tristan recovers consciousness for the last time, he is delirious and clairvoyant. Already he sees clearly what the shepherd has not yet seen: Isolde making her way toward Tristan, sailing across the ocean's vast expanse, on waves of luminous flowers. (Tristan's music in the "Wie sie selig" section here blossoms lyrically and radiantly in E major, foreshadowing the opera's B-major conclusion and contrasting strongly with the act's previous insistence on F minor.) Eventually, the ship sails into range of the shepherd's sight, and his second tune confirms the reality of Tristan's vision. It is not too forced an allusion, I think, to say that the shepherd's second tune is as different from his first as day is from night.

Whereas the first was sad, grave, oppressive, the second is joyful, open, buoyant. The second tune dances (there is no question here of rhythmic ambiguity) and, hardly deigning to touch the tonic, leaps gaily from the dominant to the supertonic, the mediant, and the subdominant degrees of the C-major scale (see example 5.9, measures 17–33). When the time-values of the tune are halved (measure 63), the resulting display of energy seems boundless. The second tune is a diatonic intrusion from the world of daylight and reality, but it is an intrusion that reconciles that world with the lovers and, thus, serves them; and, as an obvious indication of this fact, the tune itself takes on new chromatic elements (see example 5.9, measures 75–87). When Tristan learns that the flag on the mast of the ship is the flag of joy, his final doubt is quenched. Isolde has come bringing healing once again to the wounded man; and the tune, now perpetual motion, climbs step by step from dominant to dominant in an amazing show of musical and dramatic strength. This for Tristan is real joy—Isolde coming one last time, not at night under the cloak of darkness, but "Hell am Tage," in broad daylight. The final barrier has been removed, and nothing remains for the lovers but death and eternity together.

The final outcome of the opera, Tristan and Isolde's union in death, is prefigured in the long second-act duet that forms the dramatic center of the opera. The duet is divided into two halves, the first of which deals with past events in the love affair and the second of which deals with the lovers' present and future. The first half contains the famous (and, for some writers, interminable)[12] discussion of day and night—the two worlds that exert contradictory forces on the lovers; in the second, Tristan and Isolde pledge their love to night and to death. Because of its narrative, explanatory nature, the first half is largely declamatory; the second half, which deals primarily with the expression of feelings and emotions, is more lyrical. In neither half of the duet is there a great deal of physical action, and Wagner himself joked that there seemed to be so much more music than action in the act that it had made some people lose their sense of hearing.[13] This is not to imply, however, that because there is no action in the love duet there is no drama. On the contrary, there is drama but it is drama of a rarefied order. Consequently, the love duet provides an excellent example of how the poetic intent can use the lyrical aspects of music to create drama. For more reasons than one, the sexual image of poetry as the fertilizing seed and music as the womb that receives that seed in order to produce drama is particularly apt to the declaration of love that occurs in act 2 of *Tristan und Isolde.*

The drama that takes place in the second half of the duet (for which the first half is extended exposition) begins with the lovers' invocation to night. Tristan and Isolde beg night to sink down upon them and make

Example 5.9 *Tristan und Isolde*: The shepherd's
second tune (pp. 265–68)

Example 5.9 *Continued*

Example 5.9 *Continued*

Example 5.9 *Continued*

them forget that they are alive, to take them up into its bosom and set them free from the world:

> O sink hernieder,
> Nacht der Liebe,
> gib Vergessen
> dass ich lebe,
> nimm mich auf
> in deinen Schoss,
> löse von
> der Welt mich los!

The first two lines of verse are sung by Tristan alone and then are repeated by Isolde just as Tristan is finishing. Before she finishes her repetition, Tristan begins the next two lines. Again, as he is finishing his lines, Isolde begins to repeat them. This pattern of repeated lines dovetailing into one another is continued throughout the first eight lines of text.

Does the repetition of words in the love duet contradict Wagner's assertion in *Zukunftsmusik* that there was no longer a trace of word repetition in the musical setting of *Tristan*?[14] My own opinion is that it does not. I think the kind of word repetition Wagner was referring to is that in which words are repeated solely to fill out preconceived melodic lines. The repetitions in the love duet from *Tristan* are different: they serve a dramatic rather than a musical purpose that is, I think, essential to the realization of Wagner's poetic intent. In the musical setting of the text, not only do the beginnings and ends of the phrases overlap, but the melodies themselves overlap (see example 5.10, measures 1–16) in the sense that the melodic lines intertwine. Isolde's first phrase wraps itself melodically around Tristan's, just as Tristan's second phrase wraps itself around both Isolde's first and second phrases. The lovers exchange time signatures, rhythmic patterns, and melodic ideas as they exchange words. There is a repeated alternation and exchange of lines that rise and fall, fall and rise. Underneath, the pulsating rhythm in the orchestra unifies the lovers' mutual exchange.

The dramatic concept is continued in the next ten lines of text:

> Verloschen nun
> die letzte Leuchte;
> was wir dachten,
> was uns deuchte;
> all' Gedenken,
> all' Gemahnen,
> heil'ger Dämmerung
> hehres Ahnen
> löscht des Wähnens Graus
> welterlösend aus.

Example 5.10   *Tristan und Isolde*: "O sink'
               hernieder, Nacht der Liebe"
               (pp. 163–65)

Example 5.10 *Continued*

Example 5.10 *Continued*

Tristan and Isolde alternately develop a single, continuous thought in these lines, as if one person were speaking.[15] The similarity between the two lovers' development of this thought is realized musically by alternating melodic phrases that imitate one another as they rise sequentially, by the continuation of the orchestra's unifying rhythm, and by the introduction of a new instrumental motive that sounds throughout the musical setting of these lines (see example 5.10, measures 17–40). Even though the vocal phrases do not at first overlap, the length of alternating phrases becomes shorter and shorter, shrinking from three measures, to two, to one. At that point, the lovers are singing together again—Tristan leading, Isolde following one measure behind—echoing thoughts and notes in sequential imitation that rises by half steps to the duet's first climax.

The next eight lines of verse bring a degree of relative calm:

> Barg im Busen
> uns sich die Sonne,
> leuchten lachend
> Sterne der Wonne.
> Von deinem Zauber
> sanft umsponnen,
> vor deinen Augen
> süss zerronnen.

After the climax of the preceding section, the lovers again attempt to sing separately as individuals (see example 5.11, measures 1–12); Isolde sings the first four lines, Tristan the second four. The verbal and musical separation is the most extended the lovers have yet endured: Tristan waits until the last beat of Isolde's second phrase before he starts to sing. But the lovers appear to have grown too much alike for separation to make a distinction in their identities. Even though what Tristan has to say ("Enfolded by your magic, swooning before your eyes") is decidedly different from what Isolde has just said ("The sun lies hidden in our breast; the stars shine on us"), his melody is, nevertheless, the same as hers. He confirms her move from A-flat to A major and, following her lead in the musical sequence, drives the second half of the phrase from A major up to B-flat.

The effect of distance that the preceding six-measure solos give the lovers serves as a dramatic foil for the succeeding eight lines of text, which speak directly to their physical closeness and during the singing of which Tristan and Isolde are drawn musically closer together again:

> Herz an Herz dir,
> Mund an Mund,
> eines Atems
> ein'ger Bund;

Example 5.11 *Tristan und Isolde*: "Barg im Busen uns sich die Sonne" (pp. 166–69)

Example 5.11   *Continued*

Example 5.11 Continued

Example 5.11   *Continued*

> bricht mein Blick sich
> wonn'-erblindet,
> erbleicht die Welt
> mit ihrem Blenden.

In the setting of these lines (see example 5.11, measures 13–22), two measures at first separate the lovers' alternating vocal entrances, but the distance quickly shrinks to only half a measure. Twenty-nine lines into the duet, the first explicit verbal statement of the poetic image that animates the musical setting appears: the breath of each of us bound together in one breath. Identical vocal lines rise alternately by half steps in more sequential imitation.

The next four lines,

> die uns der Tag
> trügend erhellt,
> zu täuschendem Wahn
> entgegengestellt,

continue the thoughts begun in the preceding lines but offer again brief, dovetailing solo phrases for the lovers that serve as a temporary respite before the duet's second climax. Tristan and Isolde unite again in the lines

> Selbst dann
> bin ich die Welt

with intertwining phrases that come into rhythmic synchronization on "bin" and into melodic synchronization and climax on "Welt" (see example 5.11, measures 23–32).

The lines following the climax contain a second explicit statement of the poetic image that the music throughout seeks to realize: "wonne-hehrstes Weben," sublime, rapturous weaving. The poetic intent that calls forth the musical drama of the duet is, thus, a combination of two concepts—binding and weaving. The idea of weaving, moreover, suggests not just joining two people together but intertwining them through and through. This the music does. Still intertwining, the vocal lines gradually subside in half-step surges that, with lengthening note-values, finally cease to sound. As the vocal lines fall, the lovers themselves sink down side by side and Brangäne, in the tower above, begins to sing her song of watch and warning.

Of course, it is possible to see the love duet in *Tristan* as nothing more than a musical depiction of an act of physical love.[16] The music contributes more than its share of physical suggestiveness in musical gestures that are almost too graphic. Near the end of the scene, for example, the drive towards the final climax is prefaced by a vivid orchestral introduction that includes reiterated *forte-piano* dynamic surges, chromatic sequences that rise increasingly faster to their melodic peaks, and syncopated melodic figures that simultaneously rise and fall by half steps (see example 5.12). The overlapping entrances of the lovers, moreover, only serve to reinforce the orchestral images. Simultaneously, over orchestral rhythms that pound away in tension and release, the lovers approach *fortissimo* a dissonance that strains toward resolution. The approach is repeated more gently (*piano* and with attenuated orchestral force and rhythm) a minor third lower, only to be repeated again *fortissimo* and a half step higher than the first attempt. Such music, particularly in the context of a love duet, lends itself all too easily to a sexual connotation. As a result, one could make a fairly good argument in support of the contention that sexual intercourse is the poetic intent that underlies the musical realization of the duet. But the poetry and the majority of the music in the duet suggest—and the subsequent outcome of the drama confirms—that Wagner's overall poetic intent for the duet encompassed more than the mere portrayal of licentious behavior or "unconsummated passion."[17]

In the middle of the second half of the duet, Wagner plants a musical and poetic seed that bears the opera's ultimate dramatic fruit. This portion of the duet comes as the pendant to a long discussion between Tristan and Isolde about the fate their love would suffer from death. Tristan tries to convince Isolde that his love for her is so strong that even death could not destroy it. Isolde feels that their love links them in life as well as death but demands the same from each of them. If Tristan dies, she says, so must I. The idea makes so great an impression on Tristan that he replies in words that form the central verbal focus of the whole act:

> So stürben wir,
> um ungetrennt,
> ewig einig,
> ohne End',
> ohn' Erwachen,
> ohn' Erbangen,
> namenlos
> in Lieb' umfangen,
> ganz uns selbst gegeben,
> der Liebe nur zu leben!

Up until this point, the poetic intent has been mentioned specifically in two words only (*binding* and *weaving*) in isolated lines of text. Here,

Example 5.12 *Tristan und Isolde*: "O ew'ge Nacht,
süsse Nacht!" (pp. 183–84)

Example 5.12 *Continued*

though, practically every line addresses in one way or another the principal dramatic intention that the music seeks to realize: So might we die undivided, ever one, without end, without waking, without fear, namelessly embraced in love, given completely to each other, to live only in love.

In setting these lines to music (see example 5.13), Wagner again employed, in a musical context, the idea of joining the lovers together. Thus Tristan, as if following out in his mind the implications of Isolde's suggestion, sings all ten lines at first by himself. When he has finished, Isolde repeats the first two lines exactly; Tristan, as an extension of her melody and personality (just as she is an extension of his) follows with a repetition of lines 3 and 4. The musical distance separating the lovers closes as Isolde sings line 5 and Tristan sings line 6. By the eighth line, the lovers are singing together in rhythmic synchronization and in the intertwining melodic lines that have come to characterize their love. In the last two lines, Tristan and Isolde sing together in unison. I suggest that this is verbal and melodic repetition that is allowable, even in a strictly construed *Oper und Drama* sense, because it is repetition that has a dramatic meaning: the making of two individuals into one being.

The appearance of oneness that the lovers' unison suggests is confirmed by the two sections of the duet that flank this central portion. In the first, Tristan sings,

> Lass' mich sterben! . . .
> Nie erwachen! . . .
> Lass' den Tag
> dem Tode weichen!

In the second, Isolde sings the same words to the same melody, a musical image of Tristan. The exchange of identities, which the words of the central portion of the duet hold up as a desirable outcome of the lovers' death, is, thus, already under way (compare example 5.14, measures 15–36, with example 5.15, measures 3–23).

Wagner wrote in *Zukunftsmusik* that the "inner movements of the soul"[18] determined the whole course of the action in *Tristan und Isolde,* which is another way of saying that the principal subject matter of the opera is emotional and therefore musical. Certainly this is true of the second half of the love duet, where the individual words the lovers sing are obviously not responsible for affecting the specific motion of the melodies to which they are set. The duet is an extended lyric passage in the drama that develops not from outside circumstances but from those "inner movements of the soul." At this point in the opera, the emotions

Example 5.13   *Tristan und Isolde*: "So stürben wir,
                um ungetrennt" (pp. 178–80)

Example 5.13 *Continued*

Example 5.13 *Continued*

Example 5.14 *Tristan und Isolde*: "Lass' mich
sterben!" "Neid'sche Wache!"
(pp. 172–73)

Example 5.14 *Continued*

Example 5.15 *Tristan und Isolde*: "Lass' mich
            sterben!" "Muss ich wachen?"
            (pp. 181–82)

Example 5.15 *Continued*

arising from the dramatic situation take precedence over the words that describe or comment on that situation. Because Wagner has led up to and captured a general emotional state, any melody (or parts of it) associated with that state and epitomizing it can be used, just as in a strophic song, to set many different lines of verse—as long as the verses set contribute to or reflect the emotional state called forth. In this regard, Wagner never required the musician to treat words in lyric passages the same way he would treat them in explanatory, narrative, or conversational passages. The melodies in the duet generally accommodate the words, but the emotional level the lovers have attained in the duet is far too exalted (by Wagnerian standards) to demand the kind of text-setting that declamation requires.

Thus, the dramatic seed that Wagner plants in the duet is primarily a musical and emotional one that is tied, not to specific words, but to a general idea that a number of words have been used to describe. The seed lies dormant, its meaning hidden, until near the end of act 3, when it blooms in the monologue Isolde sings over Tristan's dead body. Tristan's death is the test not only of Isolde's love but also of her philosophy. The *Liebestod* proves the truth of both. Musically, the aria is a formal element that recalls the love duet and culminates in the duet's long-awaited cadence in B major.[19] A musician can appreciate this fact without understanding a word of the opera's libretto, but the libretto gives the musical form a dramatic function as well so that the *Liebestod* vindicates as it recapitulates. The *Liebestod,* as a function of the poetic intent, gives the concept of love advanced in act 2 a sense of reality by providing a dramatically appropriate association of ideas, emotions, and music. In this process, individual words play a small part. It is the overall view that both the music and the drama seize on. For the dramatist, the function of the *Liebestod* is not so much a question of form as it is a question of the apt coincidence of form and meaning. The *Liebestod* succeeds as music, possibly, because of its formal associations; but it succeeds as drama, not because it repeats the love duet, but because, by repeating it, it proves the truth of it.

We have seen that the principal poetic images used by Wagner in setting the words of the love duet are those of binding and weaving. It is no accident, I think, that Wagner's explanatory program for the prelude to *Tristan,* written for the Paris concerts in 1860, concludes with a reference to the ivy and the vine that "sprang up in locked embrace over Tristan and Isolde's grave."[20] This, indeed, seems to be the real drama of the opera as Wagner conceived it: two lovers, misunderstanding one another, separated by the world's folly and their own, struggling to overcome barriers, to be joined into one co-eternal, co-conscious, co-extensive being. Their union, moreover, presents a dramatic act such as only music can portray, since the act is incapable of physical portrayal. For this very reason, Wagner's little joke about there being so much music to hear in act 2 of *Tristan* and so little action to see is, in reality, no joke at all: it is no more than a frank acknowledgment that the central dramatic action of the opera takes place in the music because there is no place else for it to occur.

6

"Ideal Naturalism and the Singing Tongue": *Die Meistersinger von Nürnberg*

Just as the presence of end-rhyme in *Tristan und Isolde* forces us to revise Wagner's strictures in *Oper und Drama* about the use of *Stabreim*, so the setting of *Die Meistersinger von Nürnberg* forces us to revise his strictures about the use of myth as subject matter for musical drama. The story of *Die Meistersinger* is not even remotely mythic; it takes place at a definite period of time and deals with an historically recognizable central character, city, and musical practice. Set as it is in the sixteenth century, *Die Meistersinger* is even less far removed in time than *Rienzi,* which is set in the middle of the fourteenth century. From a purely temporal point of view, therefore, *Die Meistersinger* can be regarded as the most historical of all Wagner's operas. And yet, for all its historical associations, *Die Meistersinger* is surprisingly free from the faults of historical opera that Wagner criticized so severely in *Oper und Drama.* In *Oper und Drama* terms, *Die Meistersinger* is both of history and above history.[1]

In *Eine Mittheilung an meine Freunde,* Wagner related how he conceived *Die Meistersinger* as a comic pendant to *Tannhäuser und der Sängerkrieg auf Wartburg,* which he had just finished composing. He wrote that it was the folk element in the *Meistersinger* story that most appealed to him at the time. Wagner considered Hans Sachs to be the "last manifestation of the art-productive spirit of the folk,"[2] and it was in this capacity that he saw Sachs set in contrast and opposition to the "pettyfogging bombast"[3] of the other mastersingers and their pedantic rules. Wagner thus set the story at what might be considered the outside limit of history (the "last manifestation") acceptable to him for operatic treatment. Even so, it is clear from Wagner's account in the *Mittheilung* that what appealed to him in the story had nothing to do with the usual political intrigues that plagued historical opera as he saw it: there was nothing nonmusical in the *Meistersinger* story that had to be explained in order to make the story comprehensible. History, as such, intrudes on the opera primarily in the rules of the mastersingers, which have to do not with politics but with music. One need only look at David's first-act aria and Kothner's reading of the *Leges Tabulaturae* to see how fit these rules are (and this history is) for musical treatment. Song forms and wordpainting come as naturally to David's recital as chanting and melodic flourishes do to Kothner's. Thus, considered even as history, the story of *Die Meistersinger* has all the human simplicity of myth and none of the complicated political ramifications of history.[4] The history contained in *Die Meistersinger* is musical history.

In *Die Meistersinger,* Wagner found a view of art, compatible with his own, that could be propounded in opera. He also found the same things that drew him to myth in the first place: simple, easily understood, human relationships among clearly defined, true-to-life people. Thus, Walther's wooing of Eva and his becoming a *Meistersinger* in order to win her are the principal subjects of Wagner's original poetic plan for the opera; and about both of these subjects Wagner reveals a good deal in the first sixty or so measures of the opera.

When the curtain rises on the first act, the stage setting indicated makes it immediately apparent that the opera is set in historical times rather than in the legendary past. The chorale tune the congregation sings as the overture ends also helps place the action. But the chorale does much more than place the action. It foreshadows the straightforward melodic, rhythmic, and harmonic nature of most of the music yet to come and allows Wagner to proclaim right from the start that the opera's libretto will be in rhymed verse with little or no *Stabreim*:

> Da zu dir der Heiland kam,
> willig deine Taufe nahm,
> weihte sich dem Opfertod,
> gab er uns des Heil's Gebot:
> dass wir durch sein' Tauf' uns weih'n,
> seines Opfers werth zu sein.

The musical setting of these lines (see example 6.1), with its rhythmic regularity and cadences on chords clearly in C major, confirms what the overture has already made abundantly clear: in *Die Meistersinger,* Wagner has abandoned the musically ambiguous world of Tristan and Isolde and returned to a musical style that for him is the equivalent of plain speaking.

In terms of the poetic intent, the first scene of the opera provides a considerable amount of information about the opera's dramatic conflicts. In the formal context of a service in the *Katharinenkirche,* Eva and Walther

Example 6.1 *Die Meistersinger von Nürnberg*: "Da
zu dir der Heiland kam" (pp. 14–17)

Erster Aufzug.
Erste Scene.

Die Bühne stellt das Innere der Katharinenkirche in schrägem Durchschnitt dar; von dem Haupt-
schiff, welches links ab, dem Hintergrunde zu, sich ausdehnend anzunehmen ist, sind nur noch die
letzten Reihen der Kirchenstühlbänke sichtbar: den Vordergrund nimmt der freie Raum vor dem
Chor ein; dieser wird später durch einen schwarzen Vorhang gegen das Schiff zu gänzlich geschlos-
sen.
In der letzten Reihe der Kirchenstühle sitzen Eva und Magdalena; Walther von Stolzing steht, in
einiger Entfernung, zur Seite an eine Säule gelehnt, die Blicke auf Eva heftend, die sich mit stum-
men Gebärdenspiel wiederholt zu ihm umkehrt.

First Act.
First scene.

The stage represents an oblique view of the church of St. Katharine; the last few rows of seats
of the nave, which is on the left stretching towards the back, are visible: in front is the open space
of the choir which is later shut off from the nave by a black curtain.
In the last row of seats Eva and Magdalena sit; Walther von Stolzing stands at some distance at
the side leaning against a column with his eyes fixed on Eva, who frequently turns round towards
him with mute gestures.

Example 6.1 Continued

Example 6.1 *Continued*

Example 6.1 *Continued*

are set off physically from the rest of the congregation. The church building is the visual embodiment of the formalism that surrounds the lovers
(the mastersingers meet here as well as the church's congregation); the
aural embodiment is the chorale tune. Set in visual contrast to the church
and its service are the earnest, impetuous, entreating gestures that Eva
and Walther exchange; set in aural contrast to the organ-accompanied
chorale is the instrumental music, played by a chamber ensemble, that
accompanies those gestures.

The score reveals a conflict between musical styles that is as obvious
as the two lovers' uninhibited behavior in church (see example 6.1, measures 1–13). In the first two interludes, the asymmetrical melodic line of
the lovers' music, with its two-and-a-half and three-and-a-half measure
phrases, is in direct contrast to the four-measure regularity of the chorale.
The lovers' melody, moreover, is syncopated and droops in fits and starts
from the height of desire (as the stage directions indicate) to the depth of
frustration, embarrassment, and near-despair. At the same time, the lovers' music is distinguished from the chorale by increasingly chromatic
tendencies. The melodic motive that begins these first two interludes appears later as an integral melodic component of the *Stollen* of Walther's
prize song. At the moment, however, the motive serves to presage the
expression of Walther's feelings and to introduce an expansion in the
scene's harmonic vocabulary. With its leading-tone diminished-seventh
over a tonic pedal and its chromatic inner voices, the lovers' music presents a somewhat more daring first appearance than the chorale does; but
the pedal tone, continuing from the end of the first chorale phrase into
the lovers' music, nevertheless binds the two musical worlds together.[5]

In the third and fourth interludes, Wagner employs a melodic fragment that will later become part of Walther's first attempt at creating a
Meisterlied (see example 6.1, measures 17–27). Again, a melodic motive
is used to relate the experience of love in the first scene to a subsequent
expression of that love. With the introduction of this slightly chromatic
motive, the rhythmic activity of the lovers' music becomes more consistent, and the melody itself begins to climb. The lovers are apparently
taking courage; and as they become more and more unconcerned for the
situation in which they find themselves, their music gradually begins to
encroach upon the chorale. In fact, the fifth and sixth phrases of the
chorale are not separated by an interlude at all, since the music that would
have constituted the interlude is absorbed into the chorale phrases and
actually continues throughout the whole sixth line of the congregation's
singing (see example 6.1, measures 26–35). The music characterizing Eva
and Walther has, thus, persevered in the face of formalism and convention; the lovers' triumph, beginning as the chorale phrase ends, is cele-

brated by an instrumental statement of what will eventually become the beginning of the prize song's *Abgesang*.[6]

It is at this point of triumph for the lovers that the chorale's verse structure changes, and the impact of that change can be felt dramatically as well as musically. The final four lines of text are

> Edler Täufer!
> Christs Vorläufer!
> Nimm uns gnädig an,
> dort am Fluss Jordan!

The four-measure regularity of the chorale's first six lines has now been replaced by a different sort of regularity (see example 6.2). The first two lines of the text are set to two complementary two-measure phrases, while the final two lines are set to three- and four-measure phrases, respectively. The cadences that mark the ends of the first two lines are on secondary dominants, which resolve into the first chord of the following phrase and emphasize, as none of the chorale's previous cadences have, the chromatic aspects inherent in the opera's diatonicism. What is more, all four of the last lines are sung consecutively, with fragments of the instrumental motives depicting the lovers' effusions played underneath them. Because each of the three phrases before the last ends with the dominant of the chord that begins the succeeding phrase, the music drives continuously and relentlessly toward its final cadence in C major.

The words of the chorale provide no verbal reason for the musical effect achieved in the final portion of the chorale; but I think the poetic intent in the dramatic situation does. If not one of cause and effect, there is at least some sort of relationship between the eleven-measure melodic span that concludes the chorale and the understanding reached between Walther and Eva that coincides with it. This is not to say that the congregation is aware of what is going on behind its back, but it is to say that the folk's music, under the influence of the poetic intent, is susceptible to change and growth and organic development: because the chorale is not all four-measure regularity, the folk's music is able to absorb that of the lovers. When, at the end of the chorale, the full orchestra announces Walther and Eva's love, it is an instrumental body that includes the organ, the instrument that alone accompanied the folk in their singing. Right at the beginning of the opera, consequently, the poetic intent reveals artistic tendencies in the folk's own artwork that correspond to Walther's artistic nature and eventually make it possible for the people of Nuremberg to recognize in Walther a kindred spirit and bestow on him the title of *Meistersinger* as well as the hand of the woman he loves.

Example 6.2   *Die Meistersinger von Nürnberg*:
"Edler Täufer! Christs Vorläufer!"
(pp. 18–19)

Example 6.2 *Continued*

In *Die Meistersinger,* convention and creative impulse, artistic restraint and artistic freedom are juxtaposed. These contradictory forces are what separate Eva and Walther, and the workings of these forces can be seen most succinctly, I think, in the three songs that precipitate the finales of each of the opera's three acts: Walther's trial song, "So rief der Lenz"; Beckmesser's wooing song, "Den Tag seh' ich erscheinen"; and Walther's prize song, "Morgenlich leuchtend."[7] All three songs have to do with fitting creativity to the rules of convention and with judging the success or failure of the fit and, by extension, the appropriateness of the rules. "So rief der Lenz" apparently obeys none of the rules; and, unable to understand it, the mastersingers condemn it. Beckmesser's song contains several flagrant errors, even though Beckmesser, as the guild's Marker, presumably knows all the rules and how to use them. Sachs marks "Den Tag seh' ich erscheinen" fairly but loudly and, as a result, draws the whole neighborhood into the riot that makes it impossible for Beckmesser to sing the song in public again. "Morgenlich leuchtend," as the prize song, must be assumed to satisfy the artist's desire to express himself with freedom, while at the same time meeting enough of the rules to give the song form and render it, therefore, comprehensible. Set in contrast to Beckmesser's parody of it, "Morgenlich leuchtend" easily wins the people over. Walther's sincerity of expression, as something that cannot be codified, allows him to go beyond the rules in his singing and yet be understood.

The trial song is a spur-of-the-moment inspiration, full of youthful ardor and enthusiasm.[8] The words are unabashedly romantic: Spring cried to the forest, "Begin!"; and the sound swelled, echoed, and grew until the whole forest rang like the clanging of bells and, with new life, answered Spring's call. This is the essence of the first part of the first verse. The second part offers in contrast Old Winter, consumed with jealousy, hiding in a thorn hedge and plotting ways to harm Spring's joyful singing. In the second verse, Walther likens his love to Spring's call and draws the obvious physical analogy between the effect of Spring on the plants in the forest and the effect of love on his body. He has hardly finished the first part of the second verse, however, when Beckmesser comes tearing out of the Marker's box, his slate full of chalk marks indicating the errors Walther has committed so far. Beckmesser adroitly turns the other guild members' wonder at the effect Walther's strange new song has produced on them to open condemnation of a thing they do not understand. Only Hans Sachs approves of Walther's efforts; and, as the other masters grow more and more upset and vociferous, Sachs urges Walther to complete his verse. Walther, beginning where he was interrupted, at the second half of the second verse, complies. Soaring over the growing tumult, he catalogs the ravens, crows, magpies, and jackdaws of the forest that, with their hollow screeching and hoarse croaking, voice their envy of Spring: the verbal conceit thus reflects the dramatic situation. In the final lines of the poem, Walther describes the beautiful bird that rises up from the forest and beckons him to fly away, back to the green meadows and hills of his home, where he can sing as he pleases songs in honor of the woman he loves. With a gesture of contempt, and suiting his exit from the church to the words of his poem, Walther quits the singer's chair and leaves the building.

The first six lines of the song—

> So rief der Lenz in den Wald,
> dass laut es ihn durchhallt:
> und wie in fern'ren Wellen
> der Hall von dannen flieht,
> von weither naht ein Schwellen,
> das mächtig näher zieht

—are alternately seven and six syllables in length; but whereas the last two pairs of lines are set to four-measure phrases, the first pair is extended to five measures to accommodate the long held g on the second syllable of "durchhallt," echo throughout (see example 6.3, measures 11–16). (Walther's melodic line on "laut es ihn durchhallt" is imitated in diminution by the first violins.) After this exuberant outburst and unorthodox beginning (especially from the mastersingers' point of view), Walther moderates his ardor somewhat, and the song's phrase structure becomes more regular. The second and third pairs of phrases bring the first mention of waves ("Wellen"), the poetic idea which has animated the song's chromatic, triplet accompaniment from the beginning. In these lines, the "waves" find vocal expression in the dotted-quarter, eighth-note rhythm and in the rising and falling triadic motion of the song's melodic line.

In the next eight lines of text, Walther's excitement gradually increases:

> Es schwillt und schallt,
> es tönt der Wald
> von holder Stimmen Gemenge;
> nun laut und hell,
> schon nah' zur Stell',
> wie wächst der Schwall!
> Wie Glockenhall
> ertost des Jubels Gedränge!

In this part of the song, shorter, more excited four-syllable phrases, separated by eighth rests, lead to longer, complementary eight-syllable phrases

Example 6.3   *Die Meistersinger von Nürnberg*: "So
rief der Lenz in den Wald" (pp. 144–46)

Example 6.3 *Continued*

Example 6.3 *Continued*

that recall the expansiveness of Walther's first phrase (see example 6.3, measures 24–34). The melody of these short phrases takes on the chromaticism and triplet motion of the accompaniment as the poem describes the forest echo swelling and resounding. Like the tide (the analogy is apt, even though there is no mention of the sea until the second verse), the melody advances and recedes in its efforts to attain a tonic *f.* This tidelike impetus is revealed in the formal structure of the song as well. The group of two four-syllable antecedent phrases and one eight-syllable consequent phrase is followed asymmetrically by a group of four four-syllable antecedent phrases and one eight-syllable consequent phrase. Musically, the two extra four-syllable phrases in the second group are used to drive the melody up from *G* to *B-flat, c,* and finally *e.* The second eight-syllable phrase rises briefly to a *g* (the first had risen only to *f*) only to fall precipitately and syncopatedly back to the same *c* that marked the end of the first eight-syllable phrase. Wagner's use of melodic and rhythmic motion in these phrases is a musical realization of the poetic intent that is remarkably suggestive of the water's quick rush to a high point on the shore and its slower return out to sea.

Although the pitch level reached by the end of the fourteenth line of the poem is the same as that reached by the end of the ninth, the song has, nevertheless, developed and advanced melodically. The insertion of the two extra four-syllable phrases in lines 12 and 13 of the poem has provided melodic impetus. The singer has, in effect, now built up sufficient strength not only to reach the high *f* and hold it but to climb from there all the way up to a high *a* (see example 6.3, measures 34–40). This melodic progress is reflected with almost breathless excitement in the two shortest lines of the poem,

> Der Wald,
> wie bald . . . ,

which are answered by two longer consequent lines,

> antwortet er dem Ruf,
> der neu ihm Leben schuf.

The subsequent lines, however, are set to descending melodic lines; and in each of the two the melody returns, as it has previously done in the two preceding eight-syllable lines, to *c.* Although Walther's attempts to climb melodically have returned each time to the scale's dominant, his efforts have given him assurance. In the first section's penultimate line, Walther, recalling the song's "Fanget an!" motto opening, leaps grandly up a perfect fifth to a sustained *a,* which he relinquishes only after he has held it four beats. In the final line of the first section,

> das süsse Lenzes-Lied . . . ,

with a gentle melodic motion (marked *dolce* in the score), he encircles the tonic *f* and cadences on it.

The sound of Beckmesser in the Marker's box, ill-naturedly chalking up errors on his slate, comes as a rude interruption to Walther's ecstatic mood and obviously furnishes him with the inspiration for the song's subsequent reference to cruel Old Winter, cowering in a thorn hedge amid the dry rustling of leaves. The poem and its musical setting at this point take on a symmetry that contrasts noticeably with the musical and poetic phrases in the first section but yet fits well the idea of confinement embodied in the mastersingers' rules, the Marker in his box, and, by extension, Old Winter in the thorn hedge. The predominant sound of the verse, moreover, seems at this point to shift from vowels to consonants:

> In einer Dornenhecken,
> von Neid und Gram verzehrt,
> musst' er sich da verstecken,
> der Winter, Grimm-bewehrt:
> von dürrem Laub umrauscht,
> er lauert da und lauscht.

Up until now in the song, no one has paid much attention to the Marker, since Walther and his song have been the focus of all eyes and ears. But now Beckmesser's disapproval is made glaringly obvious, not by his physical presence, but by the prominence the orchestra gives to a single, regularly reiterated tone and its preceding downward flourish which characterize Beckmesser's busy tallying (see example 6.4, measures 1–15). At the same time, the intervals of Walther's song become more disjunct as the supporting harmony becomes further removed from the home tonality of F major.

The final two lines of this section of the song,

> wie er das frohe Singen
> zu Schaden könnte bringen . . . ,

bring a change of verbal emphasis away from Beckmesser and back to singing, but back to singing that is now tinged with sadness. The reiterated notes and flourishes cease as Beckmesser ceases to be dramatically im-

Example 6.4 *Die Meistersinger von Nürnberg*: "In
einer Dornenhecken, von Neid und
Gram verzehrt" (pp. 147–50)

Example 6.4 *Continued*

Example 6.4 *Continued*

Example 6.4 *Continued*

portant. Walther's melody is marked *cantabile*; his melodic intervals become less angular, and the harmony begins to suggest A minor. The simple setting of these lines brings the score's first premonition of poignancy, poignancy that will eventually be associated not with Walther but with Sachs, Walther's only supporter among the masters. Walther's words remind him of how much he has to lose. He rises from the singer's chair and plunges into the second verse of his song.

Musically, the second verse is almost identical to the first; but its beginning, supported by submediant harmonies rather than tonic, suggests the sadness Walther has briefly experienced (see example 6.4, measures 21–32). The melody rises more quickly than it did in the first verse, as Walther tries to counteract the mood that has come upon him. And, indeed, almost immediately Walther's attempt seems to work. He recalls the dreamlike state from which the call of love awoke him:

> Da fühlt' ich's tief sich regen,
> als weckt' es mich aus dem Traum . . .

The descending orchestral figure in thirds (measures 29–32) that accompanies these words and later symbolizes Sachs's recollection of Walther's song marks the tranquilizing effect of the dream; over this figure, the melody begins to resume its original shape and mood. By the time Walther reaches

> Mein Herz mit bebenden Schlägen
> erfüllte des Busens Raum:
> das Blut, es wallt'
> mit Allgewalt,
> geschwellt von neuem Gefühle;
> aus warmer Nacht,
> mit Übermacht,
> schwillt mir zum Meer
> der Seufzer Heer
> in wildem Wonne-Gewühle.

his song has attained much the same musical shape it had in the first verse, and appropriately so. The image of blood coursing through the lover's veins in answer to the effect of love on his body is the poetic equivalent of the waves of sound that greeted Spring's return and brought new life coursing through the veins of the plants in the forest. The second verse's lines

> Schwillt mir zum Meer
> der Seufzer Heer

recall this equivalent, and the music in both verses reinforces the similarity: the poetic intent in both verses is the same.

Throughout the trial scene, Wagner places traditional musical forms at the service of the poetic intent. Walther appears before the masters so that he can create a *Meisterlied,* be accepted into the guild, win the contest the following day, and carry off Eva as his prize. Preliminary to this program of activities and in response to Kothner's questions of who instructed him and in what school he learned, Walther sings the narrative "Am stillen Herd." Curiously enough, the song's form is a perfect *Bar*: two *Stollen* ("Am stillen Herd in Winterzeit" and "Wann dann die Flur vom Frost befreit"), which Vogelgesang compliments ("Zwei art'ge Stollen fasst' er da ein"), followed by an *Abgesang* ("Was Winternacht, was Waldespracht"). And because of this perfection of form, on one level the song is both poetically and musically ironic, since even before his trial, even as Kothner is asking him if he is ready to show the masters that he can create a worthy poem and melody, Walther is doing just that. On another level, however, "Am stillen Herd" supplies the specific information (both verbal and musical) that proves that Walther is not completely untutored in the singer's art: as he reveals in the song, he has indeed been taught. His instruction has come from his study of an old book of songs written by Walther von der Vogelweide, the thirteenth-century *Minnesinger.* Beckmesser's response to this statement is, of course, characteristic: how could anyone who has been dead so long teach Walther the rules? This question assumes some importance as the scene progresses.

The trial song itself, which follows "Am stillen Herd," is also in *Bar* form; but in it the form is greatly extended, since the *Stollen* have two parts and the normal progress of the song is interrupted by lengthy segments of dialogue. The song's form, excluding interruptions, is therefore represented not by the usual AAB of *Bar* form but by the following schematization:

A—"So rief der Lenz in den Wald" . . . . *Stollen* 1
B—"In einer Dornenhecken"
A—"So rief es mir in der Brust" . . . . *Stollen* 2
B—"Aus finst'rer Dornenhecken"
C—"Auf da steigt, mit gold'nem Flügelpaar" . . . . . . *Abgesang*

Carl Dahlhaus has suggested that Beckmesser interrupts Walther in the trial song after the second statement of A ("So rief es mir in der Brust") because, as a result of the length and bipartite nature of the *Stollen,* Beckmesser mistakes the *Bar* form of the song for a *Bogen* (ABA).[9] If this mistake is in fact what Wagner intended to convey by Beckmesser's interruption, then the mistake is natural enough. Dahlhaus's interpretation, however, is not one that the scene strongly supports. Short of waiting patiently for Walther to finish singing, there is no way that Beckmesser (or anyone else; certainly not a spectator in the theater) can foresee the eventual, overall form Walther's song will take. Dahlhaus implies that one of Beckmesser's faults as the guild's Marker is his impatience; but, actually, even this is not the case. Beckmesser may be impatient, but he has marked down, according to his own count, over fifty errors in Walther's singing when eight are enough to disqualify him. When Beckmesser finally interrupts Walther, it is not because he thinks the song is over but because his slate is full: there is no more room to mark down Walther's mistakes.

In his fury at Walther's presumption in attempting to become a mastersinger without any formal training, Beckmesser reels off some of Walther's more egregious errors. Certainly form is among them ("Who would seriously call that a *Bar*?"); but it is not the first error Beckmesser mentions, nor is it emphasized by him in any way. Indeed, it is all but obscured by the other faults he has noted: false number, false grouping; phrases too long, phrases too short; no beginning, no end; no *Bar* form; a hodge-podge of "Adventure" and "Blue-larkspur" melodies, "High fir-tree" and "Proud youth" tones; no pauses; no coloratura; not a trace of melody; unspeakable words; affixes; vices; misplaced rhymes and inversions; obscure meanings, equivocations, and disagreements; breaths in the wrong places; surprise; a "patch-song" (*Flickgesang*) between the *Stollen*. One could say, therefore, that Beckmesser is not really criticizing Walther's use of form so much as he is Walther's ignorance of all the little rules that had grown up to govern the melodic and verbal adornments of form. This is the reason, perhaps, why a *Minnesinger,* who even from a book could have taught Walther everything he needed to know about *Bar* form, is not an adequate teacher, in Beckmesser's view, of the *Meister-singer* rules. Sachs, however, in his instruction of Walther in the third act of the opera, goes back to the essentials of form, teaching Walther what, in effect, he already knows.[10]

As another possible interpretation of the trial scene that relates a verbal idea to a musical response, one could say that Beckmesser himself is responsible for the unusual length of the *Stollen* in the trial song. He is the reason the ordinary proportions of the *Bar* are spoiled. In each of the *Stollen,* the extension ("In einer Dornenhecken" in the first; "Aus finst'rer Dornenhecken" in the second) comes as a response or allusion to Beckmesser. Were it not for Beckmesser's antagonism, Walther would have little reason to extend the form of his song to include references to forces (which Beckmesser personifies) thwarting his love for Eva. Beckmesser himself, consequently, is the cause of the "Flickgesang" he objects to.

Lorenz tried to show that Wagner's predilection, as a musician, for forms like the *Bar* influenced his writing of poetry so that musical forms, with Wagner, were translated into poetic structures, which were in turn translated back again into music. If one accepts Lorenz's premise, which Wagner himself confirmed in *Oper und Drama* and *Eine Mittheilung an meine Freunde,* then one accepts the fact that musical form in Wagner's operas proceeded from Wagner the musician, not Wagner the poet. In all three of Walther's songs in *Die Meistersinger,* there is not the least question that the overall form is musical rather than poetic. And yet, in the trial scene, we see quite clearly that musical form answers a verbal, poetic need and that the poetic intent, while it does not determine the musical form, does determine the use to which that form is put. In the case of *Die Meistersinger* at least, the very fact that the forms of Walther's songs are musically inspired gives them the little dramatic meaning they possess. A more obvious use by Wagner of a poetic intent to determine musical form occurs in Beckmesser's "theft" of the prize song in act 3. There, since Wagner has given the music he uses associative meanings, the ordering of the musical segments is determined by the logic of the associations, not by the logic of the music.

Left to themselves, the mastersingers would probably have been merely bewildered by Walther's trial song and uncertain of the sort of response to make to it. Their reactions to "Am stillen Herd" suggest that they would have responded similarly to the trial song. But instead of bewilderment or even polite disinterest, malice toward Walther is both felt and expressed; and that this is so is due entirely to the machinations of Beckmesser. Making use of his position of authority as Marker, he plays on the masters' uncertainty, rouses it to resentment, and causes the uproar that finally drives Walther from the church in disgust. It is no more than poetic justice, therefore, and a natural extension of Wagner's poetic intent that Beckmesser's serenade in the second act and Sachs's judging of it should lead to a far greater public uproar than anything Beckmesser's ill nature has been able to produce in act 1.

Master though he may be, Beckmesser's art (if Wagner will allow it to be called that) does not extend to making songs about things he knows nothing of. True love for Eva is beyond his ken, and the mere sense of acquisitiveness he feels in place of love is simply not enough to serve as the basis for a true *Meisterlied.* The thoughts Beckmesser chooses to express in his song show plainly that he does not know the first thing about the business at hand. In the first verse, he praises the day, his courage, the fact that he is thinking not of dying but of wooing, the beautiful girl he wants to wed, and her dear father who has destined her for matrimony. Things do not improve in the second verse. Beckmesser dwells on the conditions of Pogner's offer of Eva, the money the groom will inherit from her wealthy father, and the singing skill the successful suitor will need to display. Beckmesser devotes the third verse almost entirely to himself as he describes his burning, hungering, thirsting desire for the prize. He affirms that he knows all the necessary rules, and he calls on the Muses (a little late, one might say) to inspire him as he uses the rules. He has brought, as he says in conclusion, his skin, his honor, his office, his dignity, and his livelihood (everything but love) to the contest so that his singing might please the judges and persuade Eva to look with favor on him as a husband.

The poem, alas, is hardly the stuff of which love songs are made; but Beckmesser, with an eye to the main chance, is either too vain or too inexperienced to realize how inappropriate his poem really is. That Beckmesser knows nothing about what he has undertaken is made all the more obvious by the tune he chooses for setting his poem (see example 6.5, measures 6–15). The tune itself is not bad. Unremittingly diatonic and strongly rhythmic (except for the languishing coronas Beckmesser observes in the first verse), it is rather jaunty and even catchy. But it is a walking song, not a love song. Its regular rhythm (underscored by the bass line of the orchestral accompaniment to the second verse) and proud coloratura flourishes ill accord with the serious expression of a lover's passion.

Wagner was not content, however, to let Beckmesser write a ridiculous love poem and then set it to entirely the wrong sort of music. The poetic intent, in Beckmesser's case, encompassed an even greater folly: Wagner made the hapless Marker ignorant of even the most rudimentary rules of prosody. Practically every weak accent in the poem is made to fall on strong beats of measures with embarrassing regularity. Something of the magnitude of Beckmesser's ignorance can be seen in an English translation showing the misplaced accents in the first four lines of the poem:

> The dáy see Í now dáwning,
> which ímparts gréat pleasúre;
> it dóth my héart so éxcite,
> promísing sóon raptúre.[11]

Beckmesser's errors in text-setting are compounded by his extended coloratura passages, which regularly give spectacular emphasis to whatever word or syllable happens to fall on them. An excruciating example occurs

Example 6.5 *Die Meistersinger von Nürnberg*:
"Den Tag seh' ich erscheinen"
(pp. 299–301)

Example 6.5 *Continued*

Example 6.5 *Continued*

in the line "Wie gelobt hat er" (see example 6.5, measures 19–21), where even the misplaced accent on "gélobt" pales in comparison to the four-beat, sixteen-note emphasis given to "hát."

Beckmesser is so proud of his coloratura that his zeal to show it off makes him destroy the four-beat regularity of his phrases. The result, in *Oper und Drama* terms, is that effect takes precedence over both content and form.[12] Normally, the phrases in Beckmesser's serenade begin on the upbeat to the third beat of the measure; but because of the coloratura at the end of the *Stollen,* the last two phrases are displaced—in the first instance, to the upbeat to the fourth beat and, in the second, to the upbeat to the second beat (see example 6.6, measures 3 and 4). In the opera, Walther's free manner of phrasing comes from a natural, sincere expression of passion; but Beckmesser's liberties are the result of vanity (or perhaps the inability to control the coloratura forces he unleashes). Walther's sincerity gives his asymmetrical phrases meaning; Beckmesser's vanity makes his phrases ridiculous.

As one of the lyrical elements in the drama, Beckmesser's wooing song provides an example of how individual words can retain much of their own identity and yet come under the sway of an overall lyricism. In the song, Wagner's poetic intention has been to present Beckmesser as an artistic dunce. This we notice almost immediately, not in the words, but in the music's utter inappropriateness to the matter at hand (a situation prepared for, of course, by a number of words). We can appreciate part of the joke on Beckmesser without understanding a word that he sings. If, however, we go beyond the music, we can add to the musical joke the fact that the Marker is careless, heedless even, of verbal accents. On this level, we see that almost any words Wagner might have chosen could have been used to make the prosodic point of the joke. But Wagner did not choose just any words. He picked instead words that are just as inappropriate for a love song as the music itself is. Beyond the musical and prosodic jokes, there is, then, a verbal joke. In the whole song, therefore, Wagner's poetic intent, while maintaining a lyrical aspect in the music, makes use of words in increasingly specific ways to give that lyricism a dramatic meaning.

Wagner offers no explanation of how the Marker can be so artistically inept. Did Beckmesser see other people's errors more clearly than his own? Did the unwonted nature of his subject make him careless in handling it? Did Pogner's offer come upon him too quickly for him to do anything but put together a poem hastily and then adapt it to an old tune that happened to be lying around the house? Obviously, Wagner felt that it would serve little purpose dramatically to explain how one entrusted with guarding the rules could know so little about them; an explanation

Example 6.6 *Die Meistersinger von Nürnberg*: "Für den, der ihn beerben will" (p. 305)

might even have weakened the comedy. What mattered instead was showing that Walther in act 1 had been at the mercy of a man who did not
know what he was talking about and who had yet risen to a position of
power and influence. In the first act, Beckmesser humiliates Walther; in
the second act, Beckmesser causes his own humiliation. In both acts, the
poetic intent is realized dramatically even though we do not know or care
how the Marker came by his office or his power. The verse condensation
Wagner had recommended in *Oper und Drama* stood him in good stead
in *Die Meistersinger*; it made it possible for him to eliminate these explanations of Beckmesser's background as unimportant, undramatic, and
therefore unnecessary. We feel (again in *Oper und Drama* terms) rather
than know that Walther's trial song rightly soars above the argument that
ends act 1 and that Beckmesser's serenade rightly lies at the bottom of
and serves as a fit musical foundation for the riot that ends act 2.

The third act of *Die Meistersinger* offers an opportunity for compro-
mise between artistic freedom and artistic restraint. Walther is disgusted
with the mastersingers and all their rules, but Hans Sachs persuades him
to conform to the rules enough to mold his creativity to a form that the
masters can understand. Sachs's instruction, consequently, consists almost entirely of advice about form. Not for him, at this point, a bewil-
dering recital (like David's in act 1) of the masters' elegant poetic devices.
Sachs simply tells Walther to cast his song in *Bar* form: Make two *Stollen*
and follow them with an *Abgesang*. When Walther asks Sachs why he
should follow his first verse with a second, Sachs merely tells him that
the second verse will reinforce the impression of the first and prove to
everyone his desire to marry the woman of his choice. That, of course,
is all the explanation Walther needs, and he complies immediately. When
it comes to the *Abgesang,* however, a little more explaining is required;
but Sachs again puts the rule in terms Walther can understand. If the first
two verses are a true pair, Sachs says, it will show in the child that springs
from the pair. The *Abgesang* is the child, which should be similar to the
parent verses but not exactly the same. It should be rich in its own tones
and rhymes and distinguish itself from and for its parents.

Sachs's instructions are extremely simple compared to David's; but
then Sachs, by discussing form, is emphasizing the very foundation of the
art, whereas David had emphasized the devices with which the foundation
could be ornamented. Sachs singles out from all the rules the most important and then explains that rule in the simplest way possible by showing the reason behind it. More importantly for Walther, though, Sachs
reveals the human nature that lies behind the reason that created the rule:
make two *Stollen* that complement each other, so that from their union
an *Abgesang* can emerge that is like them but different, as a child is like

but different from its parents. It should nevertheless be remembered that Sachs instructs Walther because it is demanded by the dramatic situation. The lesson itself is an illusion. Sachs's lines, which would reveal their embarrassing naiveté clearly in a play, fulfill the dramatic needs of the opera without having to meet the further demands of logic. The illusion the lines create is sufficient, since the real goal of the scene is musical, not verbal: the object is not the instruction but the song. Nothing shows this more clearly than the prize song itself, which, when it comes, is perfect. There is nothing for Sachs to do when he hears it but listen and admire.[13]

Walther's trial song in act 1 has been created extemporaneously, but the song he sings for Sachs in act 3 is inspired by a dream. With encouragement from Sachs, he sings his first stanza, describing an enticing garden in which stood the tree of life and a beautiful woman who embraced him and urged him to eat the fruit of the tree. In the second stanza, Walther describes night in the garden with the woman of his dream; but he finds it impossible to create a third verse that will, as Sachs suggests, interpret the dream. "Where might I find that?" Walther asks. Two scenes later, when Walther sees Eva dressed as a bride, all in white, the answer and the third verse spring to his lips. In this verse, the woman of the dream twines a garland of flowers around her husband's head and pours the joys of paradise into his heart. The end of the opera proves Walther's dream to have been amazingly prescient as his dream-world becomes reality.

The phrase structure and rhyming patterns of the first *Stollen* of the first *Bar* of Walther's song—

> Morgenlich leuchtend in rosigem Schein,
> von Blüt' und Duft
> geschwellt die Luft,
> voll aller Wonnen
> nie ersonnen,
> ein Garten lud mich ein,
> Gast ihm zu sein—

are reflected in the second *Stollen* of the first verse and each of the *Stollen* of the two remaining verses. It would be difficult, however, to find a more asymmetrical *Stollen* than the one Walther has created. The first line contains ten syllables, set to three and a half measures of music. The next two lines, which are rhymed, contain four syllables each and are set to two measures of music that begin and end on half measures. The second pair of rhymed lines has five and four syllables, respectively, set to two and a half measures of music; while the last rhymed pair, with six and four syllables, is set to three measures of music (see example 6.7, measures 6–16). The entire song is eleven measures long. It has no interior rests and is encompassed by only one phrase mark that runs from the first note to the last, thus recalling the concluding melodic span of the folk's chorale in the opening scene of the opera.

Even though Walther has created the appearance of an unbroken span of melody, there are, nevertheless, melodic phrases within the span to which the lines of text correspond. The first line of the melody, like the first line of the poem, is unique and has no corresponding companion line. It contains, however, the important motive of a descending fourth and the song's characteristic appoggiaturas. The remaining lines of the melody are divided into three phrases that correspond to the three remaining pairs of rhymed lines. The melody of the first pair,

von Blüt' und Duft
geschwellt die Luft

mirrors the rhyme with which each line ends. Thus, the text is set to two phrases whose melodic rhythm and contour are exactly the same: three eighth notes, ascending stepwise, followed by a drop of a perfect fifth to a dotted quarter note. The three-eighth-note upbeat is used rhythmically to link the phrase of the first rhymed pair to the phrase that follows, but the rhymes in the succeeding lines ("voll aller Wonnen / nie ersonnen") are de-emphasized melodically by dissimilar settings. Lines 4 through 7, however, are united by a rhythmic figure (two eighth notes followed by a quarter and two eighth notes) and by a melodic figure (a descending fourth followed by an ascending third) into a five-and-a-half-measure span that balances the first half of the song and recalls melodically the opening phrase's descent to the dominant.

At the climax of the second *Stollen,* as Walther describes the wonderful tree standing in the center of the garden, his poetic inspiration leads him to a cadence on the dominant and a sustained, concluding high *g,* approached stepwise (see example 6.7, measures 30–35). Sachs points out that ending a *Stollen* in another key (even a closely related one) offends the masters and transgresses on their rules. He sees, however, the poetic and musical justification for the transgression ("im Lenz wohl müss' es so sein"), approves it, and declares that he will learn from it. This is all Walther needs to hear. With Sachs's approval, the question of modulation ceases to be important. Since it is necessary to the song, we assume that the other masters, like Sachs, will recognize the need for it and likewise approve it. In this regard, Sachs is the *deus ex machina*; neither Walther nor the drama need any further assistance. Walther, con-

Example 6.7 *Die Meistersinger von Nürnberg*:
"Morgenlich leuchtend in rosigem
Schein" (pp. 389–90)

Example 6.7 *Continued*

sequently, having arrived at a new key and a sustained high *g,* can begin his *Abgesang* from a position of strength.

The *Abgesang* that Walther creates is almost twice as long as the individual *Stollen,* but it is far more regular than they:

> Sei euch vertraut
> welch' hehres Wunder mir gescheh'n:
> an meiner Seite stand ein Weib
> so hold und schön ich nie geseh'n;
> gleich einer Braut
> umfasste sie sanft meinen Leib;
> mit Augen winkend,
> die Hand wies blinkend,
> was ich verlangend begehrt,
> die Frucht so hold und wert
> vom Lebensbaum.

The first four lines of this one-sentence effusion are set to an eight-measure phrase that is divided into two unequal parts (see example 6.8, measures 9–16). The opening motive of the first half, a descending fifth followed by an ascending third, is a variation of the first four notes of the *Stollen.* The opening motive of the second half ("an meiner Seite"), three eighth notes ascending a third to drop a fifth to a dotted quarter note, and the appoggiaturas at its conclusion are derived from the *Stollen* as well. The appoggiaturas appear in the very first phrase of the *Stollen*; the motive itself, in the phrase immediately following. Thus, at the beginning of his *Abgesang,* Walther has done a creditable job of following Sachs's advice to make the *Abgesang* similar to the *Stollen* but not exactly the same ("Den Stollen ähnlich, doch nicht gleicht").[14]

The last seven lines of the *Abgesang* (beginning with "gleich einer Braut") are divided into three phrases of five, four, and six measures (see example 6.8, measures 17–31). An important melodic motive of these measures is one that appears earlier in the *Abgesang* (measure 11) but does not appear in the *Stollen*: a tonic-triad ascent from *c* to *g* followed by a chromatic descent to *f.* The last half of the motive, the chromatic descent, appears under the rhyming lines

> Mit Augen winkend,
> die Hand wies blinkend . . .

The level of excitement is subsequently raised as the entire motive is repeated twice more, twice as fast in eighth notes, under the final rhyming lines,

> Was ich verlangend begehrt,
> die Frucht so hold und wert . . .

Example 6.8 *Die Meistersinger von Nürnberg*: "Sei
euch vertraut welch' hehres Wunder
mir gescheh'n" (pp. 392–93)

Example 6.8 *Continued*

that lead triumphantly to the climax of the whole *Bar*: the ascent to a sustained high *a* at the mention of the tree of life that stands at the center of the garden.

During the remainder of the act, Walther sings two more verses that are almost exactly similar to the first. Since the song is strophic, it does not attempt to express specific verbal conceits; but it does portray, in a general way, an overall mood of serenity that gradually grows in excitement. The *Stollen* express the lover's continuing wonder; the *Abgesang*, his mounting passion. Like the love duet in *Tristan und Isolde,* the prize song is lyrical rather than declamatory; and the music to which it is set, therefore, responds to a general emotional climate rather than to individual words.[15] Sachs thinks the song meets the rules of the guild well enough to win the prize. And yet, the only rule the song seems to conform to is that of *Bar* form. The song is not "regular" in any sense of the word, but it is balanced. What is more important perhaps in terms of the drama is that, throughout the song, there is the appearance of sincerity and truth that only honest emotions can create. These are the qualities that make the song a *Meisterlied* in Sachs's opinion and that, in the final analysis, render the question of the degree to which Walther follows the rules moot.

The *Meisterlied* that Sachs approves is not, however, exactly the one Walther sings at the contest. For one thing, Walther sings only one *Bar* of his song at the contest. But more significantly, he makes substantial additions to the original version of the *Bar* that alter its shape dramatically and, in effect, destroy what little tie the song has to the mastersingers' rules. At the contest, Walther creates such a mesmerizing impression on the masters and the people with the first nine measures of his song that Kothner, who has been holding the copy of the poem, lets the paper fall unnoticed to the ground. Only Walther is quick enough to see what has happened. With his audience in his hand and no one to notice whether or not he is following his text, he replaces the four-note phrase ("Gast ihm zu sein") that closes the first *Stollen* with a seven-line, thirteen-measure appendage.

The words Walther adds to the first *Stollen* at the contest are these:

> Dort unter einem Wunderbaum,
> von Früchten reich behangen,
> zu schau'n im sel'gen Liebestraum,
> was höchstem Lustverlangen
> Erfüllung kühn verhiess,
> das schönste Weib:
> Eva im Paradies!

The first four lines, rhyming alternately, are set to alternately corresponding phrases, the second and fourth of which are derived from Walther's original *Abgesang* (see example 6.9, measures 4–17). The fifth line is a melodic condensation of the first and third phrases; the sixth is a parenthesis that suggests the dominant ending of the second *Stollen* in the original song; and the seventh line, set most effectively of all as far as individual words and their meanings go, highlights the main point of the whole excursion: Eva as the woman in Walther's paradise. An extended version of the song's original orchestral interlude gives the spectators opportunity and time to make flattering comments on Walther's artistic ability.

The second *Stollen* of the modified song follows the same structure and rhyme scheme as the first verse, but the entire second verse (all thirteen lines of it) is completely different from anything Walther has created so far. The melody is virtually the same as the first expanded *Stollen,* but the interruption in the song's original structure does not continue in C major the second time around (see example 6.9, measures 25–46). Instead, it is transformed over tremolo strings and a diminuendo to a radiant B major that gradually leads to the original G-major ending of the second *Stollen.* At the end of this second addition, Eva is once again praised, this time as the Muse of Parnassus. The proclamation accompanies the dominant preparation for the G-major cadence and Walther's stepwise ascent to the new tonic. An expanded eight-measure interlude over a G pedal-tone gives the chorus a second opportunity to express approbation.

The new *Abgesang,* when it comes at last, follows the original version of the song closely. The poem again has different words from those in the original, but the mood it expresses is the same. The first twenty measures of music, consequently, are exactly the same as the original *Abgesang.* Wagner simply extends the original cadence on C from two measures to twelve. He increases the sense of excitement in this extension by adding the chorus beneath Walther's singing (their music is absorbed into his song just as the lovers' music was originally absorbed into the folk's chorale) and by repeating in the orchestra the principal cadential motive, derived from the song itself, nine times in eleven measures, with almost as many dynamic surges from *piano* to *forte* (see example 6.10).

The conclusion of Walther's singing is not the end of his success, however. After he has finished, another eighteen measures of choral singing and orchestral accompaniment, built on the same motivic material as the preceding twelve, underscore everyone's decision to award the garland of myrtle and laurel to Walther. The same dynamic surges mark Eva's eagerness to bestow the prize on her lover. To the melody of the

Example 6.9 *Die Meistersinger von Nürnberg*:
"Dort unter einem Wunderbaum"
(pp. 539–43)

(An dieser Stelle lässt Kothner das Blatt, in welchem er mit den andern Meistern eifrig nachzulesen begonnen, vor Ergriffenheit unwillkürlich fallen, er und die Uebrigen hören nur noch theilnamvoll zu.)
(*Kothner, who with the other Masters had begun to follow the written words of the song, deeply moved, here lets the paper fall. He and the rest listen with interest.*)

Example 6.9   *Continued*

Example 6.9 *Continued*

Example 6.9   *Continued*

Example 6.9 *Continued*

Example 6.10   *Die Meistersinger von Nürnberg*:
"Am lichten Tag der Sonnen"
(pp. 547–49)

Example 6.10 *Continued*

Example 6.10 *Continued*

opening phrases of the song's *Abgesang*, Eva tells Walther that no one knows how to woo like him (see example 6.11). At the end of Eva's phrase, a trill, executed on the unaccented second syllable of "werben" (emphasized not only by the trill but by extended note-values and a rallentando as well), appears as a sly allusion to Beckmesser's folly. This joke, directed against one unrequited lover, makes the subsequent orchestral reference (the opening motive from Sachs's "Wahn" monologue) to the other all the more poignant and bittersweet: Sachs has vindicated youth in art and in love, but at a price.

As in much of the love duet in *Tristan und Isolde*, Wagner's poetic intent in *Die Meistersinger* does not necessarily function on a word-to-word basis. That is to say, the lyric nature of the whole piece and its lyric subject matter (songs and love) obviate the sort of dramatic declamation that more serious, less constantly lyrical subjects require. I do not wish to imply, however, that specific words are unimportant in *Die Meistersinger* or that Wagner little regarded them. He was justifiably proud of his ability to set even the *Knittelvers* of the sixteenth-century folk poets, and he offered the seemingly inexhaustible rhythms of the vocal lines in *Die Meistersinger* as proof that music could indeed be used "to fix beyond all doubt an infinitely varied life of discourse."[16] Nevertheless, the word treatment in *Die Meistersinger* suits the subject matter; and, in the majority of cases, the subject matter is unfailingly lyrical. Even in the non-lyrical dialogue sections, the opera's lyricism, if not expressed in the vocal lines, appears in the orchestral melodies that support and surround the dialogue and set the boundaries within which the melodic line can move. A constant interchange of melodic motives between vocal and instrumental bodies maintains the overall lyric flow practically continuously. When Wagner does interrupt this flow, as in the *secco* recitative setting of Sachs's instruction of Walther, the very sparseness of the musical setting emphasizes all the more strongly the persistence of the lyricism that the recitative sets off.

Wagner wrote that he wanted to show in *Die Meistersinger* that it was possible to achieve "a singing tongue wherein an ideal naturalism should take the place of the unnatural affectation of our actors ruined by un-German rhetoric."[17] In this regard, certainly the words of *Die Meistersinger* are individually and collectively important; but, as opera and as drama, they are generally lyrical rather than declamatory. Sachs's final address to the folk is an example of this. Although the speech is primarily hortatory (Honor the masters who have nourished and preserved German art), it is also dramatically important since, by convincing Walther to accept a place among the mastersingers, it precipitates the opera's happy ending. The main consideration in setting the speech, however, is musical

Example 6.11 *Die Meistersinger von Nürnberg*:
"Keiner wie du so hold zu werben
weiss!" (pp. 553–54)

Example 6.11 *Continued*

rather than verbal: Sachs's lines are incorporated into a reprise of various sections of the opera's overture. Thus, the melody Sachs sings may appear to meet the demands of effective text-setting, but it does so only secondarily. The first requirement the vocal line meets is that of conforming to the preestablished lyrical framework the orchestra supplies. Within that framework, there is some latitude in the matter of text-setting; but Sachs's melodic line must necessarily either double that of the orchestra or appear as a contrapuntal melody dependent on and subordinate to the orchestral melody.

When Wagner wants to make a particular verbal point, he abandons the lyrical framework in favor of a setting that gives much more prominence to the words. This happens in the "Habt acht!" section of the final speech, where Sachs warns the folk to beware lest they degenerate and, no longer upholding what is German and true, succumb to foreign rule and foreign vanities. In this section, Wagner interrupts the reprise of the overture, shifts the tonality from C major to C minor, writes tremolos and sustained chords for reduced orchestral forces, slows down the rhythmic and harmonic motion of the orchestra, lowers the dynamic level of the accompaniment, and allows Sachs to declaim his lines clearly in rhythms and notes that emphasize his words to the virtual exclusion of the music (see example 6.12). That Wagner should have chosen this manner of setting the speech is not perhaps surprising; what is surprising is that he should have chosen to set it at all. No foreign enemies have threatened the honor or art of Germany. The threat, if a buffoon can threaten, has come entirely from within, from one of the mastersingers' own number. The words may support Wagner's own prejudice against "foreign" influences (against, especially, foreign musical influences), but they have nothing whatsoever to do with *Die Meistersinger von Nürnberg*. The warning against foreigners, therefore, is dramatically meaningless. The setting of this speech meets the needs of the warning, but the warning does not meet the needs of the drama. The result is a failure of judgment on Wagner's part that marks a failure of the poetic intent as well. It is something of a paradox, consequently, that the setting of these words should be so closely related to those parts of *Oper und Drama* that recommend text-incited melodic movement when the words themselves are so obviously an alien element in the musical-dramatic world the mastersingers inhabit.

Example 6.12   *Die Meistersinger von Nürnberg*:
"Habt acht! Uns dräuen üble
Streich' " (pp. 562–63)

Example 6.12 *Continued*

"Music Divorced from the Reasoned Word": *Parsifal*

Early on, Wagner had envisioned a perfect dramatic artwork made up of three principal components: words, music, and gestures. All three are mentioned in both *Das Kunstwerk der Zukunft* and *Oper und Drama* as equal sister arts; and yet, Wagner's treatment of them in *Oper und Drama* often makes the equality of the arts seem doubtful. Poetry, in particular, occasionally receives so much attention that it appears to be the most important component of the three, while the comparatively few references to gesture make it seem to be less important than either words or music. This appearance of disparity is due in part, I think, to Wagner's desire to explain and justify *Stabreim* and root-syllables as new elements in opera librettos; gestures needed no such description or justification. Wagner felt, moreover, that it was difficult to write about gestures and that no verbal description of a movement could take the place of the movement itself.[1] More importantly, though, as far as the role of gesture in the artwork of the future is concerned, Wagner in 1850 was primarily interested in reforming opera's musical structures; and it was his view of words, not of gestures, that provided the theoretical justification for the musical alterations he eventually carried out. When the reform had been accomplished and Wagner's "endless melody"[2] was a matter of history rather than hypothesis, the reforming emphasis on words ceased to be as meaningful or appropriate as it had originally been. It was replaced in Wagner's later writings by what appears to be a compensating emphasis on gestures.

In many ways, *Parsifal* reaffirms and vindicates the role of gesture in opera as originally conceived by Wagner, since gesture is given a dramatic prominence in *Parsifal* not found in Wagner's other works. Some writers see this as indicating a fundamental change in Wagner's opera theory, but I suggest that it is not. The prominence given to gesture in *Parsifal* seems to me to be a natural outcome of the opera's subject matter.

That is to say, the poetic intent operates differently in a story that deals with a medieval monastic community than it does in stories about warring gods and mortals, a pair of star-crossed lovers, or a guild of mastersingers. The religious life, as treated in opera, practically demands a dramatic use of ceremony and the concomitant motions of ritual: there is no more stately dance. I believe that Wagner used this "dance" (and I use the word in its *Oper und Drama* meaning that encompasses all motion) for dramatic reasons because his conception of the opera demanded it, not because (as has been suggested or implied) he was at last learning how to write music that was independent of words and would soon be able to use this skill to write a symphony.[3]

In *Oper und Drama,* one of the three functions Wagner assigned the orchestra was that of "recreating" motion. He wrote that a musical gesture should occur in the orchestra at the same time a physical gesture occurred on stage and should convey to the ear the same impression the physical gesture conveyed to the eye.[4] The orchestra, therefore, was to vindicate gesture in the same way it vindicated verse. Later, in *Beethoven,* Wagner wrote that music could create such a vivid sense of motion that it could create the impression of physical action even when gesture itself was absent.[5] Wagner used the "gesturing" capability of music to good effect in *Parsifal*; and there are, consequently, numerous places in the score where a musical gesture in the orchestra answers a physical gesture on stage: the harp *glissando* as Klingsor hurls the sacred spear at Parsifal; the slow, grave, halting descent of the motive that signals the arrival and departure of Amfortas's litter; the vigorous, dotted brass entries that herald Parsifal's approach in act 3; the sinuous ascending and descending chromatic lines associated with Kundry's spell; and the headlong descent of the motive that accompanies her first stage entry.

None of the motives mentioned above, however, are necessarily dependent on an association with specific lines of verse. On Kundry's approach at the beginning of act 1, for example, the squires and knights reveal that she is riding a horse and that both she and the animal are reeling from exhaustion. But this is almost gratuitous information as far as the music is concerned (see example 7.1, measures 6–18). The dotted-eighth-and-sixteenth-note figure in the orchestra is an obvious musical symbol for riding; but the motion of this figure is not constant. The contradictory melodic motions of the treble and bass lines seem to inhibit the progress of the figure. Its galloping rhythm is slackened by eighth notes that, on the last beats of measures 6 and 7, are set against the rhythm of a descending triplet figure, which together serve as the musical equivalent of stumbling or faltering. In the next measure and a half, the eighth-note rhythm stumbles over the triplet figure three more times. The melodic and

Example 7.1   *Parsifal*: "Die Mähre taumelt"
             (pp. 13–14)

Example 7.1 *Continued*

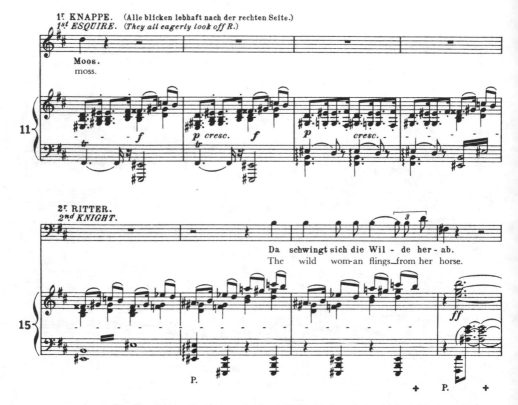

1ᵣ KNAPPE. (Alle blicken lebhaft nach der rechten Seite.)
1ˢᵗ ESQUIRE. *(They all eagerly look off R.)*

Moos.
moss.

2ᵣ RITTER.
2ⁿᵈ KNIGHT.

Da schwingt sich die Wil - de her - ab.
The wild wom-an flings from her horse.

(Kundry stürzt hastig, fast taumelnd herein. Wilde Kleidung, hoch geschürzt; Gürtel von Schlangen-
häuten lang herabhängend; schwarzes in losen Zöpfen flatterndes Haar; tief braun-röthliche Gesichts-
farbe; stechende schwarze Augen. zuweilen wild aufblitzend, öfters wie todesstarr und unbeweglich.)
*(Kundry rushes hastily in, almost staggering. She wears a wild garb, and a snakeskin girdle with
long hanging ends: her black hair is loose, her complexion deep red-brown, her eyes dark and pier-
cing, sometimes flashing wildly, more often fixed and staring.)*

KUNDRY. (sie eilt auf Gurnemanz zu und dringt ihm ein kleines Krystallgefäss auf.)
(hastening up to Gurnemanz, and forcing into his hand a small crystal vial.)

Hier!
Here!

harmonic ideas traverse the same ground over and over in an almost literally dogged attempt to advance. Progress comes only after repeated musical efforts. When Kundry finally staggers on stage and throws herself onto the ground, it is the music more than the words of the squires and knights that makes her physical condition believable. The musical realization of her condition, however, is derived from the dramatic situation, which is itself dependent on words for its specific expression.

Because we are conditioned by a concept associated with a musical idiom, motions such as Kundry's ride and collapse can be realized in music with little or no aid from words. Words may, however, clarify or make specific the musical evocation of a gesture where no corresponding physical movement immediately occurs. We have already seen an example of such a musical realization of gesture in the love duet from *Tristan und Isolde*. The scene with the flower maidens in Klingsor's magic garden provides another. Parsifal has fought his way through a cordon of the Grail's finest knights who have been bewitched by Klingsor's magic. The youth arrives in the garden only to be beset by the paramours of the men he has bested. The flower maidens storm on stage to an accompanimental figure that is propelled forward by a driving rhythmic energy but is held back harmonically by a dominant pedal point (see example 7.2). The harmonic progress of the figure is restrained because the women, in their confusion, do not let the music, or the dramatic situation, advance. Each fighting to be heard, their vocal entrances practically tumbling over one another, the flower maidens act at cross purposes. The orchestra portrays their dizzy swirls of activity in reiterated string-triplet figures that rise in pitch as the women become more and more excited and make increasingly greater efforts to be heard above each other. Their vocal lines of lament, moreover, emerging out of the musical turmoil the women have created, have no real strength or character: they are descending chromatic sighs that droop musically like the wilting flowers the women are. The words the flower maidens sing may tell us why the women are upset—

> Mein Geliebter verwundet!—
> Wo find' ich den meinen?—
> Ich erwachte alleine!—

but it is Wagner's poetic intent, operating in the music, that conveys to us their confusion and tells us, as a result, what the women are really like.

Later, when the flower maidens finally calm down enough to be heard distinctly, it becomes apparent that what they have to say is not really very important; indeed, it is not important at all. The flower maidens are,

Example 7.2 *Parsifal*: "Hier! Hier war das Tosen!"
      (pp. 127–31)

Example 7.2 *Continued*

Example 7.2 *Continued*

Example 7.2 *Continued*

Example 7.2   *Continued*

in fact, practically mindless, and what little mind they have is occupied entirely with being pretty and being loved. Words, as the flower maidens use them, consequently, have extremely limited scope and meaning. The women's anger is no more real than their love, and their words reflect this. Not fifty measures after they have begun reviling Parsifal, they are attempting to seduce him. Forgetting wounded lovers, each tries to prove that she looks prettier or smells sweeter than the others. When Parsifal declares that he will gladly be their new playmate, they rush off stage to adorn themselves as flowers. When they return, it is with the fixed intention of "blooming" for him.

On returning, the women dance around Parsifal to graceful, seductive, waltzlike music. In full harmony, they entice the fool:

> Komm'! Komm'! Holder Knabe!
> Komm'! Komm'! Lass' mich dir blühen!
> Komm'! Dir zur Wonn' und Labe
> gilt mein minniges Mühen!
> Komm'! Holder Knabe!

The message could not be simpler or more direct. In the first ten measures alone, the women encourage Parsifal to come no fewer than six times (see example 7.3). There is no subtlety here. The vocal lines, with their periodic rests and recurring motion of gentle rise and fall, present the aural equivalent of flowers swaying seductively in the breeze. Here in the lines the women sing is the verbal image that characterizes the flower maidens and points up their only reason for existing: "Lass' mich dir blühen!" This is the flower maidens' primary physical function; it is also the poetic intent that animates their musical response. From the massed choruses, solo voices rise and unfold musically like petals of a flower: the maidens bloom in sound, if not in actual, physical fact. Overlapping words, together with overlapping vocal phrases, over slow-moving tonic and dominant pedals add a cloying, almost overpoweringly narcotic effect to the blooming.

In an attempt to portray these musical and verbal images, the women entwine Parsifal with their arms and bodies. Singly, in pairs, and in groups, they weave their spell in melodic lines that rise only to fall chromatically in graceful, coquettish three-note flourishes (see example 7.4).[6] Like birds or bees or flower petals themselves, the women's vocal lines create the impression of fluttering descent that permeates the music. Aside from the musical portrayal of *blühen*, though, the words have little to do with the poetic image the music evokes. Whether the women are singing "Let me cool your brow," or "Let me stroke your cheeks," or "Let me kiss your

Example 7.3 *Parsifal*: "Komm'! Komm'! Holder
Knabe!" (p. 147)

Example 7.4 *Parsifal*: "Lass' mich dir erblühen"
         (p. 149)

lips" is of relatively little importance to the drama. What is important is the musical gesture and its implications, communicated to the audience even though the words the flower maidens sing may be confused, unintelligible, or unimportant.[7] The flower maidens, if not actually plants, at least have natures like plants: they are beautiful but mindless. Completely unaware of what they are doing and without the least flicker of emotion, they surround Parsifal, lull his suspicions, and almost lead him to his doom. The flower maidens' gestures and the poetic intent realized in their music suggest this more clearly, I think, than mere words ever could.

Related to music in *Parsifal* that suggests motion is music that suggests change or transformation. This type of music also develops from an association of ideas derived from the text. In act 1, for example, Gurnemanz and Parsifal walk from the forest to Montsalvat; during the entire scene neither man speaks. Music alone accompanies their journey and, at the same time, represents it. Music marks the progress of the two men and forebodes events yet to come in the drama: the stately dotted rhythm of the theme that begins the journey gradually becomes more and more influenced by the music associated with Amfortas's agony. Amfortas's theme mounts in intensity as Gurnemanz and Parsifal approach the sanctuary that Amfortas's presence defiles. The theme is quelled at last only by the trombones' *fortissimo* insistence on one of the Grail's sacred themes. Pealing bells announce the journey's end and the arrival of Gurnemanz and Parsifal in Montsalvat's pillared festival hall. In the whole transformation scene, walking is the only physical motion that is suggested (and that only by the dotted rhythms that occur at the scene's beginning, middle, and end); and yet, by the juxtaposition of different musical ideas within a dramatic context, a sense of movement and change is conveyed. As much by the music as by the scenic transformation, Gurnemanz and Parsifal are brought closer and closer to Amfortas.

In all Wagner's mature operas, there are scenes in which the dramatic action is dominated by orchestral music and movement (Tristan and Isolde's drinking of the love potion and Beckmesser's theft of the prize song represent two extremes in this regard). But none of Wagner's other operas can compare, I think, with *Parsifal* in the number or dramatic significance of these scenes. Ritual, of course, is primarily responsible for this emphasis on movement to the exclusion of words. In act 2 of *Parsifal,* for example, there is almost no movement on stage that does not accompany dialogue. The exceptions are Klingsor's conjuring of Kundry (a sort of ritual in itself), the vanishing of Klingsor's castle, Kundry's kiss that gives Parsifal knowledge, and the withering of Klingsor's magic garden—altogether about fifty measures out of hundreds. What movement there is in act 2 is generally of secondary dramatic importance, but acts 1 and 3 are another matter altogether. In these acts, ritual is a primary concern; and attention focuses on the ritual motions of prayer, eucharist, baptism, and anointing as important events in the course of the drama.

In the ritual scenes of the opera, the relationship between music and gesture is often tenuous: more often than not, music reflects the emotions called up by the ritual act rather than the motions used to carry out that act. When Gurnemanz and his squires pause to pray at the beginning of act 1, for example, there are no audible words or visible motions—merely silent prayer and solemn music. In the celebration of the love feast that comprises the last third of the act, moreover, although gesture plays an important part in much of the ritual, this circumstance is not always reflected in the music. There is, in fact, a musical disassociation from gesture as Wagner draws nearer to the heart of the mystery surrounding the descent of the light from heaven. At this point in the drama, not only gestures but words as well shrink in significance; and the resulting music, divorced to a large extent from both of its conditioning agents, becomes almost entirely and unfailingly lyric. The reason for this lyricism is provided by Wagner himself in *Religion und Kunst*, where he advanced his belief that religious dogma was not suitable for musical expression but that the "rapturous worship"[8] that dogma inspired was. Even though religious poetry had to be faithful to dogma, Wagner felt that the lyrical aspects of its expression could be poured into music without regard for the constraints of abstract terms. It is for this reason that, as far as the drama is concerned, the knights' words during the central portion of the feast signify little, and their actions scarcely more. The real dramatic value of the ritual lies in the emotional stores it untaps and in the background of sanctity it gives to Amfortas's sin and suffering.

As the knights march into the hall and begin the preliminaries of the rite, their primary emotional attitude is one of confidence. Their first lines of text,

> Zum letzten Liebesmahle
> gerüstet Tag für Tag

are set to a melody that leaps at the outset an octave from tonic to tonic (see example 7.5, measures 3–7). The melody descends at midpoint to the mediant level only to march from there firmly and squarely straight back to the upper tonic. Underneath the melody lies the sturdy, martial rhythm of Gurnemanz and Parsifal's journey to Montsalvat and a C-major harmonic underpinning, associated appropriately enough with the knights' spotless purity. Later, after the elements have been consecrated and the knights prepare to partake of the transformed substance, their strength

Example 7.5 *Parsifal*: "Zum letzten Liebesmahle gerüstet Tag für Tag" (p. 69)

and confidence increase; and the music reflects this change in their emotional demeanor (see example 7.6, measures 1–33). Like the blood now coursing vigorously through the knights' veins, the orchestral rhythm pulses steadily in reiterated triplets, the knights' melodic line rises in jaunty syncopations, and the bass line descends diatonically in half notes with firm harmonic purpose. Even without understanding the religious implications of the knights' actions, the listener can perceive the effects of the rite on the knights' physical and emotional states.

As the spiritual feast begins to affect their physical bodies, the knights (as befits Christ's warriors) become stronger, more powerful, and better able to fight on Christ's behalf. The poetic intent guiding the musical response is summed up in the words the knights sing: "Take the bread; turn it confidently into bodily strength and power. Turn the wine into the fiery blood of life." Following this specific verbal reference to the change the knights are undergoing, the music becomes even more assertive (see example 7.6, measures 34–46): reiterated triplets in the orchestra give way to a dotted march rhythm; the bass line strides diatonically down and up with increased speed and energy in figures again reminiscent of Gurnemanz and Parsifal's journey during the transformation scene; and the vocal line, broadening, outlines the ascending E-flat major tonic triad. In a sense, the entire transformation scene (so striking in its visual impact), recalled at this point in the ritual, serves merely to "forebode" and heighten the effect of the emotional transformation experienced by the knights. As they sing

> Wandelt es kühn
> in Leibes Kraft und Stärke . . .

their strength seems boundless. From the first syllable of "wandelt" to the first syllable of "Leibes," the melodic ascent is a diatonic E-flat major scale. A syncopated plunge to the mediant degree of the scale on the second syllable of "Leibes" only acts as a springboard that drives the melody from there to a cadence on the dominant, with the knights sustaining an *f* for four beats on the first syllable of "Stärke." Mention of the wine and blood of life in the second verse (see example 7.6, measures 52–66) only serves to increase the rhythmic animation of the bass line and to create the impression of hearts racing with "feurigem Blute."

The Grail rite is not, however, all dotted, diatonic, syncopated confidence; not all of its music is so obviously physically allusive as that of the preceding example. The consecration of the elements, introduced by a statement of the "Dresden Amen" (which is associated by Wagner with the Grail), is preceded by fragments of the motive that begins the opera's

Example 7.6 *Parsifal*: "Wein und Brot des letzten Mahles" (pp. 92–96)

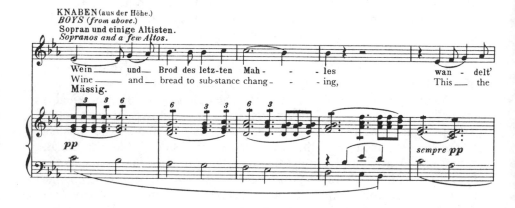

KNABEN (aus der Höhe.)
BOYS (from above.)
Sopran und einige Altisten.
Sopranos and a few Altos.

Wein_____ und___ Brod des letz-ten Mah - - - les wan - delt'
Wine_____ and___ bread to sub-stance chang - - - ing, This ___ the

Mässig.

pp *sempre* **pp**

(Die vier Knaben, nachdem sie den Schrein verschlossen, nehmen nun die zwei
Weinkrüge, sowie die zwei Brodkörbe, welche Amfortas zuvor durch das
Schwenken des Grals-Kelches über sie gesegnet hatte, von dem Altartische,
*(The four Esquires, having enclosed the shrine, now take from the altar-
table the two flagons and baskets which have been blessed by Amfortas with*

einst der Herr des Gra - - les, durch des Mit - leid's___ Lie - - bes -
Grail's dear Lord's ar - rang - - ing, Through the power_ of_____ Love di -

6

vertheilen das Brod an die Ritter und füllen die vor ihnen stehenden Becher mit Wein. Die Ritter lassen sich zum Mahle nieder, so
auch Gurnemanz, welcher einen Platz neben sich leer hält und Parsifal durch ein Zeichen zur Theilnehmung am Mahle ein-
lädt: Parsifal bleibt aber, starr und stumm, wie gänzlich entrückt, zur Seite stehen.)
*the Grail-chalice. They distribute the bread to the Knights and fill their cups with wine. The Knights seat themselves, and Gurnemanz, who
has kept a place empty beside him, signs to Parsifal to come and take part in the meal; but the latter remains standing apart, silent
and motionless, as though wholly entranced.)*

macht, in das Blut, das er ver-goss, in den Leib, den dar_ er -
vine, In - to bread that is His flesh, In - to blood of that_ true

11

pp

Example 7.6 *Continued*

Example 7.6 *Continued*

Example 7.6 *Continued*

Example 7.6 *Continued*

prelude, played now by unison violoncellos over hushed timpani rolls. The effect is solemn indeed; as the heart of the mystery approaches, the music forebodes it (see example 7.7, measures 1–24). As the elements are blessed, the orchestral tremolos continue while unison voices intone the words of the ritual—

> Nehmet hin meinen Leib,
> nehmet hin mein Blut,
> um uns'rer Liebe Willen!

to a full statement of the asymmetrical melody, fragments of which the cellos have just played. The prelude itself, together with the other statements of this melody that have already occurred in the act, has given the melody an emotional significance that far transcends the simple and (from a dramatic point of view) meaningless words of the ritual.[9] The staging suggestions for the scene, moreover, intensify that significance and add to it an even greater element of mystery. As in the prelude, the melody is followed by orchestral tremolos and arpeggios and is then repeated by a solo trumpet, stabbing like a ray of light through the clouds of string and wind configurations. The stage lights dim to complete darkness. The whole passage is repeated at the mediant level; and with the second entrance of the trumpet comes a dazzling ray of light in reality, illuminating the Grail and transforming the elements. Behind the ritual in this scene, there is what Wagner would have called dogma, to be sure; but it is the emotion that lies behind the dogma, not the dogma itself, that forms the basis of the drama. The scene is dramatic because of the feeling of mystery it arouses, not because it expounds or demands belief in transubstantiation of the elements. The poetic intent encompasses this doctrine of the church but concentrates on the mystery associated with the doctrine. In the presentation of this mystery, moreover, neither words nor gestures contribute as much as the music and stage setting do.

In this atmosphere of confidence and mystery, Amfortas's presence is a completely alien and disturbing element. It is, moreover, a profane element that serves dramatically to undermine the confidence and mock the mystery. Amfortas reveals all too obviously and embarrassingly man's intrinsically sinful nature: he is an ever-present reminder of the knights that Klingsor has debased. And yet, Amfortas is much like Christ. It is not by accident but by dramatic design that his entrance into the hall at the beginning of the scene is made to correspond to the knights' reference in their ritual to Christ's suffering on the cross:

> Den sündigen Welten,
> mit tausend Schmerzen,

Example 7.7 *Parsifal*: "Nehmet hin meinen Leib,
nehmet hin mein Blut" (pp. 87–90)

(Die Knaben nehmen die Decke vom goldenen Schreine, entnehmen ihm eine antike Krystallschale, von welcher sie ebenfals
eine Verhüllung hinwegnehmen, und setzen diese vor Amfortas hin.)
(*The Esquires remove the cover from the golden shrine and take from it an antique crystal cup, which they
likewise uncover and place before Amfortas.*)

Example 7.7 *Continued*

Example 7.7   *Continued*

Example 7.7 *Continued*

(Hier dringt ein blendender Lichtstrahl von oben auf die Krystallschale herab;
diese erglüht sodann immer stärker in leuchtender Purpurfarbe, Alles sanft bestrahlend.)
*(A dazzling ray of light falls from above upon the crystal cup, which now
glows, ever-deeper, a shining wine-purple colour, shedding a soft light on all around.)*

(Amfortas, mit verklärter Miene, erhebt den „Gral" hoch und schwenkt ihn sanft nach allen Seiten, worauf er dann Brod und
(Amfortas with a transfigured expression raises the Grail, and waves it slowly to every side, thus consecrating the

TITUREL.

Oh! Hei - - li-geWonne, wie
Oh! Rap - ture from heav-en, how

Wein segnet. Alles ist auf Knieen.)
bread and wine. All are kneeling.)

> wie einst sein Blut geflossen—
> dem Erlösungshelden
> sei nun mit freudigem Herzen
> mein Blut vergossen.

The melody to which these words are set begins, as the knights' first vocal entrance in the scene begins, with a leap of an octave; but here that leap is colored immediately by a chromatic descent which suggests suffering, Christ's by direct reference and Amfortas's by inference (see example 7.8). While the convoluted vocal lines descend chromatically, the underlying E-flat-minor harmony modulates up to E minor. The opposing melodic and harmonic motions are mirrored in conflicting duplet-triplet rhythmic motions as well. The irony and misery of Amfortas's position are painfully evident in the musical setting. The musical motions, centering on Amfortas's efforts to ascend the throne, and the words of the ritual only underscore the obvious: "With a glad heart, I now shed my blood for you." Amfortas's heart is anything but glad; it is no wonder that this is the music that occurs to him later when he sees in his mind's eye Christ suffering on the cross, bleeding from the spear wound in his side.

Amfortas's long monologue in the middle of the rite is the drama that the ritual isolates. Three times, in unaccompanied vocal utterances, Titurel asks Amfortas to serve his office; three times Titurel's requests go unanswered—in silence made more emphatic by muffled timpani beats (see example 7.9, measures 5–16). After Titurel's third request ("Muss ich sterben, vom Retter ungeleitet?"), Amfortas can contain his agony no longer. Underscored by an uprushing string scale that ends in dotted notes that mount by leaps even higher and by chromatically descending chords that surround the motive of Christ on the cross, Amfortas cries out in torment:

> Wehe! Wehe mir der Qual!
> Mein Vater, oh! noch einmal
> verrichte du das Amt!
> Lebe, leb'—und lass' mich sterben!

Beginning in the upper part of the baritone's vocal range, the melody dwells on "Wehe," which, after a pause, is repeated at a lower pitch, jumps up to emphasize the object of the woe ("mir"), and then plunges straight down an octave and a second to dwell on the reason for that woe ("der Qual"). (See example 7.9, measures 18–20.) From this depth of misery, Amfortas pauses only long enough to catch his breath. His melody then jumps up an octave as he beseeches Titurel to fulfill the duties of the office in his son's place. Lengthened note-values, pitch, and metric po-

Example 7.8   *Parsifal*: "Den sündigen Welten, mit
              tausend Schmerzen" (p. 72)

Example 7.9 *Parsifal*: "Mein Sohn Amfortas, bist du am Amt?" (pp. 76–78)

Example 7.9 *Continued*

Example 7.9 *Continued*

sitions highlight the principal words in Amfortas's plea—"Vater," "einmal," and "Amt"—and the resurgence of orchestral activity and the syncopated vocal and orchestral melody on "oh! noch einmal" contribute to the urgency and despair of that plea (see example 7.9, measures 21–23). The energy spent in the first three lines takes away from what is available for the last, but still the contrast between height and depth serves to communicate the poetic intent in the music (measures 23 and 24): life for Titurel (*c-flat* falling to *B-flat* and *A-flat*) and death for Amfortas (*E-flat* falling to *A-flat₁*). Syncopations again animate the urgency behind Amfortas's request; at the same time, however, sparse chordal accompaniment and frequent rests indicate his exhaustion.

Although Wagner in his operas made use of the distinction between lyric and declamatory singing in more or less traditional ways to create dramatic effects, he also, in order to give the appearance of unity and continuity, combined lyricism and declamation in constantly varying proportions.[10] We see such a combination of the two in the few measures we have just been discussing in a proportion that leans more toward declamation than lyricism. Such declamatory lines (or lines that are primarily declamatory in nature) are what Wagner had in mind when he wrote in *Oper und Drama* that the word-verse should determine the melody. The lyric is by its very nature (and by its very definition) musical rather than verbal: its primary element is not the word but the emotion, not the verse but the melody to which the verse is set. The declaimed line is different: in it, individual words are far more important than they are in the lyric; they stand out with greater distinctness because they must be understood.

The declamatory nature of the opening of Amfortas's lament is made even more apparent by the measures that follow. Titurel tells Amfortas again what he already knows very well: Titurel is too weak to come out of his tomb; Amfortas must continue the attempt to expiate his sin by bearing the responsibilities of his position. "No!" cries Amfortas desperately in response; and that one word erupts in a single note that is given both agony and motion by an underlying suspended diminished-seventh harmony and a descending string figure (recalling Kundry's entrance in act 1) that limns the chord melodically in staccato sixteenth notes (see example 7.9, measures 40–42). Throughout the next six lines, Amfortas bewails the contradictory effects of the holy relic and its attendant ceremony on his conscience:

> Nein! Lasst ihn unenthüllt!—Oh!—
> Dass Keiner, Keiner diese Qual ermisst,
> die mir der Anblick weckt, der euch entzückt!

Was ist die Wunde, ihrer Schmerzen Wut,
gegen die Not, die Höllenpein,
zu diesem Amt—verdammt zu sein!

The words here, in true *Oper und Drama* declamatory fashion, appear to determine the melodic motion but not necessarily, of course, the specific pitches of the melody. Again, as in the beginning of the monologue, words of import are set in relief by pitch, duration, metric position, and harmony. The excess of emotion that afflicts Amfortas as he tries to keep the Grail veiled finds vivid expression in the vocal line. Frequent rests set off the individual words and suggest the gasping breaths of the pain-racked man. Some of the phrases, occurring after Amfortas has seemingly choked down air, burst out in melodies that are propelled upward to the principal word by ascending triplet figures. The orchestra is full of throbbing tremolos, and it repeats tellingly the descending melodic figure of Kundry's first-act entrance music and the ascending string scale from the beginning of the lament to mirror Amfortas's agitation. For the most important lines of text (lines 4 through 6 above), however, Wagner reserves sparse, single-chord accompaniment and even complete orchestral silence. As a result, the question that plagues Amfortas—What is the pain of the wound compared to the curse of being a sinner in this office?—receives striking dramatic emphasis (see example 7.9, measures 50–55).

Not all of the declamatory lines in the monologue are set so prominently, however. Many receive extenuated emphasis because they are associated with important orchestral motives and are subjected, consequently, in their melodic motion to the motion of the motive. This does not necessarily imply a lessening in the value assigned the text of the opera but simply indicates, for the most part, that the text is under the influence of another aspect of the poetic intent: there is, in other words, a shift in the dramatic center of attention. During the monologue, for example, Amfortas sees the covering fall from the chalice and a light stream down from heaven to kindle the vessel's contents. This is prevision. It is also dramatic preparation for a physical act which has not yet happened but is about to. The preparation involves associating Amfortas's descriptive words with the orchestral motive first heard, unaccompanied, at the beginning of the prelude. In the monologue, both the melody and the words are equally important; and even though the vocal line must be subjected melodically to the motion of the orchestral motive, the vocal line achieves an emphasis of its own by the sparseness of the orchestral accompaniment and by the correctly accented, intricate speech-rhythms that appear in the chantlike setting of Amfortas's words (see example 7.10, measures 8–17). Later, when the elements are consecrated, when the

Example 7.10 *Parsifal*: "Die Stunde naht: ein
Lichtstrahl senkt sich auf das heilige
Werk" (pp. 81–82)

Example 7.10 *Continued*

vision Amfortas has described becomes a reality, there will be no need for words: music will accompany the action itself rather than the words that have described that action. At that point in the opera, the dramatic emphasis will shift away from words completely to the emotions evoked by the ritual.

In Amfortas's monologue, though, this shift of emphasis has not yet occurred. His vision reaches a verbal climax at the words "des heiligsten Blutes Quell" that coincides with the melodic climax of the orchestral motive accompanying the vision: Amfortas feels Christ's purifying blood rushing into his own sinful heart (see example 7.10, measures 15–17). But his awareness of Christ's cleansing power only serves ultimately to remind Amfortas more forcibly of his sin and its consequences for him. The remembrance causes the motive of the Grail feast to vanish. In its place comes the sinuous, undulating motive associated with Klingsor, a horrible desecration of the temple (see example 7.10, measures 22–26). The motive gives sudden dramatic meaning to all the knights' straightforward, rhythmic diatonicism. Amfortas's words, still declaimed, dwell on the world of sinful passion; and, as a sign of where his thoughts are, his vocal line is subjected to the spell of Klingsor's evil magic. It is the vision of Christ suffering on the cross and the Grail motive accompanying that vision that call Amfortas back. Throughout this brief section of the monologue, the battle for the possession of Amfortas's soul is fought, literally, in the succession of poetic ideas that find musical expression in the orchestra.

The agony afflicting Amfortas is very great, torn as he is between good and evil, sin and salvation. That agony is, moreover, a proper subject for lyric operatic treatment, and in the monologue it finds recurring lyric expression. But even though this lyricism generally de-emphasizes the importance of individual words, there are passages in the monologue where the verse contains so few words that one of them can easily be isolated and associated with the prevailing emotion being expressed. The line "Oh, Strafe! Strafe ohne Gleichen" is an example. Only one idea is conveyed here: punishment. The idea is emphasized by the repetition of "Strafe." In the monologue, the line is set lyrically, being absorbed into the motive of Christ suffering on the cross (see example 7.11, measures 10–14). A leap of an octave from "Oh" to the first syllable of "Strafe" emphasizes at the outset the principal idea of the line. At the same time, the leap also initiates the descending-second interval in the vocal line that is part of the motive's overall harmonic underpinning. By being isolated from other words, the single word is not only emphasized but associated with the lyricism of the motive. Wagner does not, however, insist that "Strafe" is equivalent to the motive. In fact, the repetition of the word shows the beginning of a melodic departure from the motive; and in the

Example 7.11 *Parsifal*: "Oh, Strafe! Strafe ohne
Gleichen" (p. 79)

next line the motive itself takes on an entirely new word and association: "gekränkten," wronged.

We have already seen that this particular lyric element in the monologue is originally associated in the Grail ritual with the sufferings of Christ on the cross and with his dying for man's salvation. Even there, the motive does not serve as a melody determined by the words, although we may say that it is a melody determined by the emotion behind the words. This is what makes the motive lyric and what makes it adaptable in a way that the dramatic, declamatory melodic lines that open the monologue could never be. When Amfortas stills the clamor of his sinful blood by recalling the Grail theme, the conflict produces the agony that drives him immediately to think of the spear:

> der dort dem Erlöser die Wunde stach,
> aus der mit blut'gen Tränen
> der Göttliche weint' ob der Menschheit Schmach,
> in Mitleids heiligem Sehnen.

These words are absorbed into lyricism as both the first and third lines are sung to the same melody representing the wounded Christ suffering on the cross (see example 7.12). Only the note values in the motive are changed to accommodate the different prosodic values of the new words. To point to this melody (or one like it), which in this scene alone is associated with so many different words, and to say that it proves that Wagner had disavowed his earlier theory of words determining melody shows a complete misunderstanding of both Wagnerian melody and theory. The melody exists as a lyric element in the drama, its shape determined not by specific, individual words but by general emotional attitudes. The effect of such a melody on individual words is to take them up into lyricism and to color them emotionally. The presence of lyricism in such a scene, therefore, indicates not the ascendancy of music over words but a shift in the dramatic emphasis of the poetic intent from conversation, narrative, or monologue to a more all-encompassing emotional outpouring.

Perhaps the best example in *Parsifal* (certainly the most obvious) of a dramatic emphasis on lyricism occurs in the third act during the *Karfreitagszauber* music. Kundry has washed and anointed Parsifal's feet; Gurnemanz has anointed Parsifal's head in preparation for his coronation. Parsifal's first act of office is to offer Kundry salvation in baptism. Turning to her, he gazes at the wood and meadow and sees them glowing in the morning light. Out of the music recalling Christ's suffering, the melody of the *Karfreitagszauber* rises in the solo oboe amid a shimmering halo of strings (see example 7.13, measures 25–62). For over a hundred mea-

Example 7.12 *Parsifal*: "Der dort dem Erlöser die Wunde stach" (p. 83)

Example 7.13 *Parsifal*: "Die Taufe nimm und
glaub' an den Erlöser!" (pp. 245–50)

Example 7.13 *Continued*

Wald und Wiese, welche jetzt im Vormittagslichte leuchten).
forest, which are glowing in the morning light).

PARSIFAL.

Wie dünkt mich doch die Au — e heut' so schön!
How beau - ti - ful the mead - ows seem to - day!

Wohl traf ich Wun - - - - - der-blu - men
Well I re - call the won - drous

Example 7.13 *Continued*

Example 7.13 *Continued*

Example 7.13 *Continued*

Example 7.13 *Continued*

sures, until the end of the scene, the Good Friday music exerts its spell; and everything else in the drama yields to its magic. We see the influence of the melody and its magic in Parsifal's very next line ("Wie dünkt mich doch die Aue heut' so schön!"), which hardly moves melodically for the singer's wonder. When the vocal line does move, it stays within the contours imposed upon it by the orchestral motive. The lyric mood of the magic spell takes precedence over everything Parsifal has to say; his melody, consequently, must accord with the mood to which his words are mere reaction. When the words do take precedence over the lyric mood, when the focus of attention shifts to them from the mood, then the Good Friday music ceases—as it does when Gurnemanz offers the brief explanation that gives the music its name: "Das ist Karfreitagszauber, Herr!" (measures 62–66). Sung over sustained chords played by tremolo strings and in the complete absence of orchestral melody, Gurnemanz's words are given all the prominence of a signpost in the drama. The mention of Good Friday reminds Parsifal of how much man has to weep for on this particular day (the knowledge he has acquired since act 1 has been substantial). His reaction to Gurnemanz's words brings, therefore, a contrasting mood, characterized by the Grail motive, which Parsifal incorporates into the vocal line of his subsequent outburst. Parsifal's new mood, however, is not strong enough to prevail over the Good Friday spell. Even as he is singing the word "weinen," the Good Friday magic has already begun again, its melody growing radiantly into D major out of Parsifal's E minor (measures 73–78).

Gurnemanz's subsequent words of explanation are similar to Parsifal's previous words of wonder in that both speeches exist entirely within the framework of the spell (see example 7.13, measures 73–101). Like Parsifal, Gurnemanz cannot resist for long the beneficent influence of the Good Friday music. At the words

> Nun freu't sich alle Kreatur
> auf des Erlösers holder Spur,
> will ihr Gebet ihm weihen

Gurnemanz's melody unites with the Good Friday theme. Like Parsifal again, Gurnemanz recalls Christ's suffering on the cross; and when he does, the Good Friday music ceases. Gurnemanz, however, mentions the cross only to say that the man who has been redeemed need no longer look to Christ suffering; instead, this man

> . . . fühlt sich frei von Sündenlast und Grauen,
> durch Gottes Liebesopfer rein und heil.

At these words, the Good Friday music reasserts itself, growing out of the motive of the spear and enveloping Gurnemanz's vocal line in the musical equivalent of Christ's gesture of love (measures 112–20). From this point to the end of Gurnemanz's speech, there are no more interruptions in the Good Friday music. It only increases in dynamic strength and power as Gurnemanz sings of all nature absolved from sin and giving thanks for the absolution. Throughout the scene, Kundry has been weeping passionately, a visible symbol of the meaning of Good Friday. At the end of the scene, as if to point and crown its meaning, Parsifal turns to Kundry to bless her tears:

> Auch deine Träne ward zum Segenstaue:
> du weinest!—sieh'! es lacht die Aue!

Under the influence of the Good Friday spell, Kundry's sins are forgiven and washed away. By the music as much as by her tears, she is made whole and clean. As the spell dissolves into the music that begins the transformation scene, Parsifal seals Kundry's salvation with a kiss. It is a gesture of great importance, made doubly dramatic by the sinful implications attached to Kundry's kiss in act 2.

The dramatic center of *Parsifal* is the great confrontation between Parsifal and Kundry that occurs in act 2. It is this scene that gives Parsifal's kiss in act 3 its meaning.[11] Everything else in the opera either leads up to or away from this crucial event and helps set it in relief. Even the stage settings isolate this scene from the rest of the opera, the precincts of the Grail with their solemnity and ordered ritual contrasting strikingly with the lush riot of Klingsor's garden and the kaleidoscopic colors of his enchanted flower maidens. We could go even further and say that not only is the scene between Parsifal and Kundry isolated, not only is it the dramatic center of the opera, but it is, in effect, the entire drama of the opera. In this scene, Parsifal begins to acquire knowledge; and from it, we can understand every important thing Wagner has to say about the young fool. Amfortas, Titurel, Gurnemanz, the knights, Klingsor, and the flower maidens—everything else in the opera is of secondary importance compared to the enlightenment Parsifal experiences under Kundry's expert, though reluctant, instruction. And although there are lyric moments in the scene, there is no true lyric repose. Everything that happens here contributes to the ongoing drama; the whole scene, consequently, is almost unceasingly, unfailingly dramatic. More than anything else Wagner ever wrote, I think, the scene between Parsifal and Kundry fulfills simultaneously all the conditions outlined in *Oper und Drama* for the complete artwork. In *Oper und Drama* terms, the scene is a well-nigh perfect example of an equal union of words and music that produces an exalted level of gripping drama immediately perceptible to the feeling. Excepting a consistent use of *Stabreim,* there is nothing in the Wagnerian theoretical canon that it lacks.

In act 2, Kundry brings enlightenment to the pure fool, although her only purpose is seduction. Both the intention and the result are plainly and simply stated in two words at her first stunning, dramatic entrance: "Parsifal! Weile!" Possibly Kundry's vocal line here is a subconscious expression on her part, but not on Wagner's: the descending fifth and ascending minor third to which she sings Parsifal's name recall the prophecy vouchsafed Amfortas. The intervals form the conclusion to the first line of the prophecy: "der reine Tor." Later, when Kundry explains the derivation of Parsifal's name,

> Dich nannt' ich, tör'ger Reiner,
> "Falparsi,"
> Dich reinen Toren: "Parsifal" . . .

she encapsulates the whole first line of the prophecy in her melody (see example 7.14, measures 3–9). The setting of "Falparsi," with its descending diminished fifth and ascending minor sixth recalls the prophecy's first words—"Durch Mitleid wissend"—while that of "Parsifal" recalls its conclusion ("der reine Tor"). In all this, the orchestra supplies sparse harmonic support for Kundry's vocal phrases, which, in striking contrast to the elaborate music of the flower maidens, combine words and melody to produce an immediate effect on the already bewildered boy. Kundry calls his name, and almost instantly he remembers what up until then he had forgotten—that Parsifal is the name his mother had once called him in a dream. In one word and three notes, Kundry has unlocked the wells of memory for Parsifal. The musical process whereby this feat is accomplished is similar to that of the shepherd's tune in act 3 of *Tristan,* but in *Parsifal* the process is infinitely more economical. There is no doubt that the music will bring about the psychological awakening of Parsifal. The poetic intent makes this clear. As the flower maidens disappear laughing, the *Mitleid* motive sounds in the orchestra to preface Parsifal's question: "Dies Alles—hab' ich nun geträumt?" During the course of the scene, the distinction between dream and reality becomes increasingly important to Parsifal and increasingly obvious.

The opening of the scene relies primarily on an almost recitativelike setting of the text. Orchestral activity is reduced to little more than sustained chords that support the vocal line and to fragments of motives that add an extra dimension to the text. The words are prominently set with

Example 7.14 *Parsifal*: "Dich nannt' ich, tör'ger
Reiner, 'Falparsi' " (p. 173)

great care for their prosody, but they are, nevertheless, dispatched quickly. In a few measures, Kundry explains the derivation of Parsifal's name. She tells him where he was born, who his father was, and that his father named him as he died. She insists that the desire to know these things drew Parsifal to her; and as she insists, her vocal line assumes the descending diminished fifth and ascending minor sixth of the knowledge-through-compassion motive. The implication of Kundry's use of this motive is, of course, that Parsifal's compassion will make him emotionally susceptible to her seduction. Actually, however, the effect of Parsifal's compassion will be just the reverse. This compassion (for Herzeleide, Amfortas, and even Kundry herself), which Kundry has already begun to arouse, will eventually give Parsifal the knowledge and strength he needs to resist Kundry's blandishments. The stage is set in the opening of this scene, but the drama has only been poised for advance. The beginning of the scene is, thus, both important and unimportant: it contains essential background information, but it is preliminary to the drama itself. Nothing makes this more obvious than the relative inactivity of the orchestra during this part of the scene and the conversational setting of the text.

With Kundry's Herzeleide narrative, the drama begins to move forward. The setting of the narrative, however, has all the appearance of a lyric interlude; the narrative itself has even been called an aria or cavatina in 6/8 time.[12] But this appearance could not be more deceptive: lyric though it is, the narrative is intensely dramatic. We assume that Kundry's intention at this point is to work on Parsifal's emotions: she wants to get him into her arms by reminding him of his mother and by returning him, as a result of the remembrance, to a state of childish dependence on her as a maternal surrogate. This Kundry does plainly enough in the rhyming iambics of her poem with their visions of Herzeleide caring for her child, guarding him from harm and from knowledge of the world, anxiously awaiting his return whenever he roamed too far or too late, and finally dying of sorrow when at last Parsifal wandered away never to return.[13] Kundry skillfully and relentlessly piles the burden of guilt and responsibility more and more heavily on Parsifal's shoulders; but we may well doubt that Kundry's words alone (especially in rhyming iambics) could ever have much effect on Parsifal's mind, never (at least up to this point in the opera) very retentive or accessible. Kundry's (and Wagner's) real psychological acumen is shown by the setting her words are given. In 6/8 time certainly, but just as certainly not an aria or a cavatina, Kundry's narrative is a lullaby. It is a stroke that is masterly in its simplicity and is both lyric and dramatic at the same time.

The words of Kundry's narrative have the appearance of a lullaby, at least at the outset:

> Ich sah das Kind an seiner Mutter Brust,
> sein erstes Lallen lacht mir noch im Ohr . . .

so too the music (see example 7.15, measures 7–22), which begins with a sustained G-pedal point and hypnotic chromatic inner-voice movement in the orchestra and with a gentle, lilting melodic line (doubled by the first violins), rising and falling in slow undulation, in the vocal part. The appearance of a lullaby is, however, subterfuge; and Kundry, having begun to lull Parsifal's awareness more insidiously than the flower maidens ever could, begins to intertwine joy and sorrow in her singing. Her words start to take up subjects that have no place in a lullaby:

> das Leid im Herzen,
> wie lachte da auch Herzeleide,
> als ihren Schmerzen
> zujauchzte ihrer Augen Weide!

The combination of joy and sorrow in the words is made even more disorienting by the shifting harmonies under the words—G major (measure 14), F-sharp minor (measure 16), B major (measure 17), F-sharp minor (measure 19), G major (measure 20).

The second verse increases the tension of the conflicting emotions being aroused in Parsifal. Again, the verse begins with comforting, reassuring words—

> Gebettet sanft auf weichen Moosen,
> den hold geschläfert sie mit Kosen

that serve to connect Herzeleide's love and care for her child with a subsequent statement of her love, sorrow, and longing for the child's dead father. Again, as in the first verse, the initial stable harmonies begin to shift—this time even further, to B-flat major (measure 32), E-flat major (measure 33), G major (measure 35), F-sharp minor (measure 37), G major (measure 38)—and the vocal line begins to twist and turn in disjunct motion. When the second verse finally returns to G major at its end, however, it does not return with a comforting thought, as the first verse does ("Augen Weide"), but with a distressing one ("Mutterthränen"). This is reflected in the music (measure 41) by an avoidance of the cadence Wagner has been preparing for three measures: the return to G major occurs as a dominant-seventh in C; and the cadence, therefore, is neither

Example 7.15   *Parsifal*: "Ich sah das Kind an seiner
                Mutter Brust" (pp. 175–76)

Example 7.15 *Continued*

comforting nor satisfying. From this point, the subsequent mention of Herzeleide's tears leads directly and disconcertingly to her love for Gamuret and from there to a change in meter and tonal level for an intensification of the attack.

With the disturbing reference to Gamuret and Herzeleide's love in the immediate background, Kundry shifts back to Herzeleide as mother rather than lover. She reminds Parsifal of Herzeleide's protective, maternal instincts and her desire to keep him safe from knowledge of weapons and the world. The shift is another psychological feint that offers a plausible reason for introducing the increased rhythmic activity that accompanies the shift to 9/8 (see example 7.16). There is, moreover, a relentless insistence about the recurring dotted-eighth-note motive in the bass line, a motive vaguely but recognizably reminiscent of both halves of the prophecy motive and associated now in this scene with Parsifal's acquisition of knowledge through Kundry. The underlying rhythmic ostinato of this motive continues, in fact, when the reiterated eighth notes above it have ceased and Kundry is no longer singing about weapons and battles. As she sings

> Hörst du nicht noch ihrer Klage Ruf,
> wann spät und fern du geweilt?

her vocal line, sung over the continuing bass ostinato, becomes increasingly chromatic and sinuous.

Herzeleide's subsequent joy at Parsifal's return from wandering is depicted in an ascending chromatic vocal line surrounded on either side by lines that continue to encircle each other and intertwine. Kundry scarcely pauses for breath as she climbs to the climax of her song; the energy of her attack creates an emotional turmoil that leaves Parsifal completely unprepared for the lullaby's dénouement. The rhythmic activity nearly ceases; the whirl of eighth notes subsides to sustained chords; the meter shifts from 9/8 to 3/4 in the vocal part as Kundry sings "Ward dir es wohl gar beim Küssen bang"; and once again, at the crucial moment, the cadence on G is aborted—this time to E-flat major. In comparison to what has gone before as the lullaby has become an emotional vortex, these rhythmic, harmonic, melodic, and dynamic shifts give Kundry's words a startling clarity that makes the leap from b to f-$sharp^1$ and e^1 on "beim Küssen" seem superfluous. But, of course, the dramatic emphasis on "Küssen" is not superfluous; even though this is the first mention of the word in this scene, it is the goal that has been foremost in Kundry's mind from the beginning. She, consequently, allows time for her point to strike home and then, continuing to alternate between 9/8

Example 7.16 *Parsifal*: "Den Waffen fern, der
Männer Kampf und Wüten"
(pp. 177–79)

Example 7.16 *Continued*

Example 7.16   *Continued*

and 3/4 and with a gradual slowing of tempo, offers the conclusion of her narrative. From "kisses" to "death" is the work of a mere twenty measures, during which time Parsifal is beset by motivic figures (the ascending chromatic triplets and the reiterated simultaneous seconds) that seem to insist on a response from him. In her final devastating lines,

> ihr brach das Leid das Herz,
> und—Herzeleide—starb . . .

Kundry returns, as if nothing had happened, to the 6/8 rhythm of the lullaby's beginning, the rhythm with which she began her seduction.

Kundry's verbal and musical psychology works. She brings Parsifal to his knees in remorse, and her convoluted lyricism gives way to his anguished declamation:

> Wehe! Wehe! Was tat ich? Wo war ich?
> Mutter! Süsse, holde Mutter!
> Dein Sohn, dein Sohn musste dich morden!
> O Tor! Blöder, taumelnder Tor.
> Wo irrtest du hin, ihrer vergessend,
> deiner, deiner vergessend?
> Traute, teuerste Mutter!

Parsifal's response is little more verbally than interjection and ejaculation. His speech fragments are translated into melodic fragments of three or four notes only, separated by rests that create the musical parallel of sobbing (see example 7.17). In contrast to the words of Kundry's lullaby, Parsifal's words are given a varied rhythmic setting that strives toward the patterns of speech rather than of song. The importance of his words as dramatic agents is given further emphasis by the isolation in which the melodic fragments are set. Practically every word is separated from the others, and the impact of this separation is only increased by lengthened note-values and extremes of vocal range for the setting of words of principal import: "Wehe," "Mutter," "Süsse," "holde," "Sohn," "morden," "Tor." The orchestra, moreover, in no way competes with the singer here; but the orchestral activity does increase as Parsifal's emotional state becomes more troubled. His agitation is mirrored, for example, in the orchestral tremolos that pulse with recurring *forte-piano* surges. The vocal phrases are surrounded and cushioned by tremolo chords; or they are emphasized even more obviously by complete orchestral silence; or they are preceded by orchestral motives out of which the vocal phrases rise like capstones or echoes. Like many of the declamatory scenes in Wagner's later operas, this scene in which Parsifal reacts to Kundry's

Example 7.17 *Parsifal*: "Wehe! Wehe! Was tat ich?
Wo war ich?" (pp. 180–81)

Example 7.17   *Continued*

manipulation seems to fulfill ideally the conditions first outlined in *Oper und Drama*; the words do seem in fact to determine the melodic movement, which in turn seems to determine the supporting orchestral activity.

Kundry's response to the outburst she provokes is confident and sure (see example 7.18). The orchestra sounds the three descending half steps that announced the beginning of the original lullaby; but, at this point in the drama, Kundry has no need to repeat her beguiling preliminaries. The memory of the lullaby, which the three descending half steps evoke, is enough.[14] Kundry goes immediately from this brief introduction to the 9/8 rhythm that had earlier insinuated itself into the lullaby; the pulsing, reiterated eighth notes sound insistently and assist Kundry to persuade Parsifal that confession will free him of guilt and shame. Kundry, however, has not the power to tell Parsifal the truth about her intentions. Only the descending figure that recalls her first-act entrance and that seems almost to slither down alternately in the first violins and clarinet at first suggests the falsehood that lies behind her words.

Ultimately, of course, Wagner betrays Kundry's true allegiance and the source of power that animates her existence, as the writhing, ascending chromatic line that recalls Kundry's sorcery and relationship to Klingsor is heard in the orchestra (see example 7.18, measure 13). Like an evil spirit, the motive enters her vocal line at the most dramatically appropriate words: "Die Liebe lerne kennen" (measures 14 and 15). With a completely unbalancing effect, she shifts from the sorcery motive to the kindred twining phrases of the lullaby for the lines that follow, the psychologically all-important lines that link Herzeleide and Gamuret's child with their lovemaking:

> die Gamuret umschloss
> als Herzeleid's Entbrennen
> ihn sengend überfloss!

The triumph Kundry already feels is hers is signaled by a climactic *f-sharp*[1] ("überfloss"), which the violins, again recalling Kundry's first appearance on stage in the opera, punctuate like a cry. The clarinet rises from the *G* to which the violins have plunged, and the motive it plays is the motive of Kundry's sorcery (measures 21 and 22). Her final words, rising and falling hypnotically in the motive of her magic, complete the spell. Kundry has awakened Parsifal's compassion and given him enough knowledge to draw him to her. In a strikingly dramatic use of gesture, Parsifal sinks into Kundry's arms and receives from her the long, long kiss (at least five measures, *sehr langsam*) that makes his knowledge complete. In the space of ten measures, Parsifal has become Amfortas.

Example 7.18 *Parsifal*: "Bekenntnis wird Schuld in
Reue enden" (pp. 182–84)

Example 7.18 *Continued*

Example 7.18   *Continued*

Wagner wrote in *Religion und Kunst* that music could end any conflict between reason and feeling by showing that the power of feeling was greater and its truth more apparent than that of reason. It was this quality of music as an organ of feeling that, according to Wagner, made it possible for music used in religious contexts to bypass dogma and "to quite divorce herself from the reasoned word."[15] In many ways, *Parsifal* supplies Wagner's own evidence which proves that his view of music's power was correct. Certainly, in the Grail rites, music makes no attempt to explicate or argue on behalf of the doctrine of transubstantiation. Instead, music presents the miracle as a fait accompli: something that is mysterious but that nevertheless works; therefore, it is true. The appeal is emotional rather than intellectual. The same can be said for Amfortas's reaction to the Grail and Kundry's reaction to Parsifal. What the music here builds on is not the explanations of these situations but the emotions that the situations call into play. In both cases, there is the same attraction and revulsion, the same agony and desire. Words help prepare both situations, and in that preparation reasoning and logic are important; but once the situations have been prepared and emotional outpouring is imminent, then words become less important and emotion more so. In this sense, the relation between religion and musical drama, at least as Wagner conceived them, is remarkably similar.

8

Conclusions

From the beginning of this study, we have distinguished between a fundamental idea advanced in *Oper und Drama* and various peripheral ideas related to that fundamental idea but distinct from it. In this regard, it can be shown that many of these peripheral ideas underwent modification and change during the second half of Wagner's compositional career and that various parts of the *Ring des Nibelungen, Tristan und Isolde, Die Meistersinger von Nürnberg,* and *Parsifal* obviously do not follow to the letter Wagner's recommendations for musical drama outlined in *Oper und Drama.* This fact supports Wagner's own statement that the artwork of the future must be ever newly born, "springing directly from, and belonging only to the present . . . mirroring the face of life itself in all its countless traits."[1] We have viewed the ideas advanced in *Oper und Drama,* consequently, not as part of an unchanging, unalterable artistic creed but as points along a starting line from which subsequent creative departures might reasonably be expected to be made. Wagner's later theoretical writings confirm the validity of this approach by showing a change of emphasis among the components that make up the perfect drama in music. In these later writings, music and gesture seem to receive more emphasis than formerly; poetry, less. Most recent critical opinion seems to regard this change of emphasis as a reversal of Wagner's earlier view of the *Gesamtkunstwerk,* a more or less complete change of artistic faith which Gutman's characteristically outspoken view ("After years of dialectic rambling and reams of paper, [Wagner] had ended by defining grand opera. *Sicut erat in principio.*"[2]) more or less sums up.

In contrast to what appears to be a majority opinion, we have recognized the change of emphasis in Wagner's later theoretical writings but have tried to show that the fundamental idea of *Oper und Drama,* as the foundation upon which Wagner's opera theories and compositions were built, did not change. The idea that the poetic intent incites the musical response and calls it forth as drama remained constant in everything Wagner wrote, both theoretical and practical, after *Oper und Drama.* This idea is repeatedly stated in *Oper und Drama*, although the emphasis Wagner placed on words there often overshadows the role that the idea gives to music in realizing the artwork. In Wagner's later writings, the emphasis on words gradually subsides; and music more and more assumes its rightful and, I think, intended place in the creative act.

Many years after writing *Oper und Drama*, Wagner apparently confessed his awareness of the confusion his emphasis on words in it had caused. Cosima Wagner wrote in her diary on 11 February 1872:

> Of *Opera and Drama*, which he is correcting, he says: I know what Nietzsche didn't like in it—it is the same thing which Kossak took up and which set Schopenhauer against me: what I said about words. At the time I didn't dare to say that it was music which produced drama, although inside myself I knew it.[3]

One is tempted to say that this knowledge was hindsight, but I suggest it is more likely that Wagner actually meant what he said. Clearly, the composer of *Der fliegende Holländer, Tannhäuser, Lohengrin,* and *Die Walküre* knew that music created drama—it was not something he suddenly discovered while he was writing the second act of *Tristan*; and he said as much in *Oper und Drama* by assigning music the feminine, bearing role in the creative process. Nevertheless, Wagner also knew that the dramatic moment which music created arrived as a result of or in response to a verbal stimulus. It was this stimulus that he called the *dichterische Absicht,* the poetic intent.

Related to the fundamental concept of the poetic intent and supplementing it is a substantial emphasis in *Oper und Drama* on the importance of words in opera. To understand this emphasis, one must remember the sort of operas Wagner's reforms were intended to combat and vanquish. These were epitomized in Wagner's own mind by the works of Giacomo Meyerbeer, operas that Wagner vigorously denounced for what he considered to be absurd librettos and musical effects without dramatic causes. Wagner felt that in the operas of Meyerbeer the creative process was reversed, that the poem existed solely for the purpose of explaining the music. In place of operas like *Robert le Diable, Les Huguenots,* and *Le Prophète,* Wagner proposed to offer operas in which the relationship between music and poetry would be natural and proper: music would help give meaning to the words and would come into being, therefore, as a natural outgrowth of the libretto. As opposed to operas like Meyerbeer's, Wagner proposed to create works that would attune the audience in an opera house to "a reverent reception of the highest and sincerest things the human mind [could] grasp."[4] With this as the point of view from which he regarded opera, it is only natural that Wagner should have emphasized in *Oper und Drama* the importance of the poem in creating the worthwhile artwork. For him, only a worthwhile poem could bring forth worthwhile music.

As far as musical effects were concerned, Wagner did not denounce or forbid them. After all, the musician achieved drama by the use of musical effects; but the effects had to be called for by the libretto. What Wagner did denounce was the musical effect that existed of and for itself or as the justification for the libretto. He demanded that musical effects grow out of the libretto and not the libretto out of musical effects. Many years after *Oper und Drama* first appeared, in *Über die Anwendung der Musik auf das Drama,* Wagner pointed to examples of what might be considered "harmonic" effects in his own operas: the openings of the first three *Ring* operas. He made it clear, however, that the stories of the operas, not the whims of the musician, determined or suggested these effects. Although music made the effects possible, Wagner felt that poetry called this music—and instrumental music at that—into being.

In further consideration of the emphasis on words in *Oper und Drama,* one should also remember that this emphasis includes another important aspect of Wagner's reform of opera: his intention to alter completely what he considered to be opera's outmoded musical structure. Time and again in *Oper und Drama,* Wagner reiterated his desire to break down the barriers that divided opera's lyric and declamatory moments into arias and recitatives. His aim was to unite both elements into a more or less seamless musical texture, an ongoing musical development that, because it did not start and stop, would make it possible for the emotional level of an opera to remain in a constantly uplifted state. This meant that Wagner, having settled on a worthwhile story suitable for musical treatment, had to choose carefully the words that told that story. Like the story, the words had to be appropriate to and capable of musical realization. The poet, as Wagner said in *Oper und Drama,* had to concentrate words and actions to a point most accessible to the feeling. In other words, the poet had to remove everything nonmusical from the libretto. The musician then had to expand the point of concentration musically until it fulfilled its emotional potential.

In this admittedly vague process, words played an important role, part of which Wagner saw as new to operatic composition. Obviously, portions of text which required a lyrical musical treatment presented no problems that the composer had not met before; in them, the composer was concerned primarily, as he had ever been, with portraying in music one general mood conveyed in several lines of text. Because lyric moments presented no new problems, Wagner had little to say about them in *Oper und Drama*—a fact that gives what he said about setting declamatory passages a deceptive appearance of all-importance.

Because Wagner wanted opera to develop as a continuous musical form, he was particularly anxious to show how declamatory passages, which had formerly been relegated to recitative, might be set in order to achieve a musical ambience, that endless melody, out of and into which lyrical passages could grow with every appearance of organic unity. In practical terms, this meant that in most of the declamatory passages (and in some of the lyrical passages) lyricism and declamation had to be combined in ever-varying proportions that changed almost from measure to measure. This continuous combination and recombination of lyricism and declamation was an aspect of the Wagnerian musical drama that was completely new and that, like *Stabreim,* had to be discussed and explained at some length in *Oper und Drama*. Words, which would always be of secondary importance in lyric moments, would be determinative in the declamatory, narrative, conversational, nonlyric passages of the opera; in these passages, words would play a major role in shaping the melodic response.[5] The words in these passages, consequently, had to be important enough to receive the musical attention Wagner was determined to give them. They had not only to incite the musical response but also, to a large extent, to determine its course. Wagner said in 1873 that he felt

> conscious of having, if not achieved, at least deliberately striven for this one advantage, the raising of the dramatic dialogue itself to the main subject of the musical treatment; whereas in opera proper the moments of lyrical delay, and mostly violent arrest of the action, had hitherto been deemed the only ones of possible service to the musical composition.[6]

In this attempt, words provided the reason behind the structural alterations that Wagner carried out in his efforts to make declamation lyric.

As important as Wagner considered words to be in the reform of opera, they were not everything in the drama that he envisioned. He wrote about the limitations of poetry in *Das Kunstwerk der Zukunft*:

> Thus the poetic art can absolutely not create the genuine artwork—and this is only such a one as is brought to direct physical manifestation—without those arts to which the physical show belongs directly. Thought, that mere phantom of reality, is formless by itself; and only when it retraces the road on which it rose to birth, can it attain artistic perceptibility. In the poetic art, the purpose of all art comes first to consciousness: but the other arts contain within themselves the unconscious necessity that forms this purpose. The art of poetry is the creative process by which the artwork steps into life: but out of nothing only the god of the Israelites can make something. The poet must have the something; and that something is the whole artistic man, who proclaims

in the arts of dance and tone the physical longing become a longing of the soul, which through its force first generates the poetic purpose.[7]

In this essay, Wagner stated his belief that each art evolved along a line of force which eventually brought the art to the limits of its expressive ability, at which point another art's expressive powers began. That poetry was limited primarily to thought and the intellect was one postulate of Wagner's reasoning; that music was a vehicle of the feeling was another. Wagner believed that the word could only indicate an emotion but that music could realize that emotion. "Through an intimate conjunction of both arts," he wrote in an open letter to Hector Berlioz, "the thing impossible to express by either of them singly may be expressed with most persuasive clearness."[8] As declamation became more lyrical and lyricism more declamatory in Wagner's operas, both the thought, embodied in the declamation, and the emotion, embodied in the lyricism, would achieve new dramatic meaning and significance.

In considering Wagner's reform of opera, I think it is a mistake to attribute more importance to his emphasis on words than that emphasis merits. It is also a mistake to confuse the roles of words in lyric and declamatory passages and to treat the two as if they were the same. In this regard, it is particularly a mistake to think of what Wagner had to say about words in terms of dominance and subservience, concepts that appear so frequently in the history of opera whenever words and music are discussed. It is wrong to assume that Wagner, because he assigned poetry the masculine role, intended for poetry to dominate music; or that he meant for music, because he assigned it the feminine role, to be subservient to poetry. Such concepts are far too limited and limiting and do no justice to the varied interplay of words and music in the creation of any musical drama, least of all Wagner's. Neither the emphasis Wagner gave poetry in *Oper und Drama* nor the gender he assigned it there can be taken to mean that he considered words to be more important than music in the creation of drama.

As far as discussion of this emphasis goes, I suggest that a more accurate way of viewing it might be in terms of balance or equilibrium rather than dominance and subservience. Accordingly, Wagner in 1850 was trying to correct the balance of a musical-dramatic genre in which he felt that one of the components, music, had gotten badly out of hand; he was trying to restore the components to a state of equilibrium. To counteract the unnatural influence of music in opera, he had to exert considerable force and give greater emphasis to the importance of words than words would eventually receive. This emphasis was necessary as a corrective and counterbalance. The situation was not unlike a tug-of-war in which one side (music, in this case) is winning. Balance and equilibrium cannot be restored until the losing side is given enough extra help to counteract the momentum of the winning side. Once this happens and equilibrium has been achieved, no additional effort is required to maintain it. In terms of Wagner's writings on opera, once he had achieved what he considered to be a proper balance between words and music, further emphasis would have been not only unnecessary but destructive of the equilibrium he had achieved.

We see the same sort of balancing emphasis on words in the reform efforts of Gluck. In the famous first notice of his intentions that appeared in 1769 in the dedication to the published score of *Alceste,* Gluck could not sufficiently praise Calzabigi for writing librettos which made it possible for the composer "to restrict music to its true office of serving poetry by means of expression."[9] Eight years later, however, when the reform was history, Gluck's opinion about the respective roles of words and music in opera appears to have undergone a modification. In a satirical reply of 1777 to criticisms of his music made by Jean François de la Harpe, Gluck wrote that

> the voices, the instruments, all the sounds, and even the silences, ought to have only one aim, namely that of expression, and that the union of music and words ought to be so intimate that the poem would seem to be no less closely patterned after the music than the music after the poetry.[10]

This change in emphasis in the roles assigned to music and poetry is slight but significant. Gone are the earlier concepts of dominance and subservience; in their place is a view of the union of poetry and music that is more like the sexual one that Wagner conceived and wrote about seventy years later.

The image of a union of poetry and music, seen in sexual terms, is, as far as I know, unique in opera literature before Wagner; but it is nonetheless apt, for all that. Even in the years when Wagner was elaborating his *Ring* theories, he produced no set formula for creating the perfect dramatic artwork. As obvious as it may seem, the point cannot be too often made: Regardless of the impression one derives from reading *Oper und Drama,* the relationship between words and music (and gestures) was not constant in Wagner's opera theories or in his operas; it varied continually. It is for this reason that the sexual image of the union of poetry and music, with its implications of give-and-take, is so well suited to describing the relationship between words and music in opera. Beyond this image, the relationship was never really fixed; I think Wagner never intended it to be. Indeed, the changing proportions of words, music, and gestures in response to the dramatic situation were the essence of Wagner's view of opera, which he described as early as 1849 in *Das Kunstwerk der Zukunft*:

> Thus, supplementing one another in their changeful dance, the united sister arts will show themselves and make good their claim; now all together, now in pairs, and again in solitary splendor, according to the momentary need of the only rule- and purpose-giver, the dramatic action. Now plastic mimicry will listen to the passionate plaint of thought; now resolute thought will pour itself into the expressive mold of gesture; now tone must vent alone the stream of feeling, the shudder of alarm; and now, in mutual embrace, all three will raise the will of drama to immediate and potent deed. For one thing there is that all the three united arts must will in order to be free: and that one thing is the drama. The reaching of the drama's aim must be their common goal.[11]

In the constant give and take of drama, the proportions of all three arts—poetry, music, and gesture—varied, in Wagner's view, in accordance with the demands of the poetic intent, the seed that instigated the dramatic response.[12]

At the same time that Wagner admitted that the relationships among words, music, and gestures should vary in response to the poetic intent, he also realized that opera was a musical genre, which music—especially in the type of opera he envisioned—pervaded, whether or not music was, at any given moment, the focus of dramatic attention. Again in *Das Kunstwerk der Zukunft,* he wrote:

> Not one rich faculty of the separate arts will remain unused in the united artwork of the future; in it will each attain its first complete appraisement. Thus, especially will the manifold developments of tone, so peculiar to our instrumental music, unfold their utmost wealth within this artwork; nay, tone will incite the mimetic art of dance to entirely new discoveries, and no less swell the breath of poetry to unimagined fill. For music, in her solitude, has fashioned herself an organ which is capable of the highest reaches of expression. This organ is the orchestra. . . . The orchestra is, so to speak, the loam of endless, universal feeling, from which the individual feeling of the separate actor draws power to shoot aloft to fullest height of growth: it, in a sense, dissolves the hard, immobile ground of the actual scene into a fluent, elastic, impressionable ether, whose unmeasured bottom is the great sea of feeling itself.[13]

A subsequent note in *Das Kunstwerk der Zukunft* addressed to the poet reiterates the point:

> If, however, the poet's doubt lie deeper, and consist in this, that he cannot conceive how song should be entitled to usurp entirely the place of spoken dialogue, then he must take for rejoinder that in two several regards he has not as yet a clear idea of the character of the artwork of the future. Firstly, he does not reflect that music has to occupy a very different position in this artwork to what she takes in modern opera: that only where her power is the fittest, has she to open out her full expanse; while,

on the contrary, wherever another power, for instance that of dramatic speech, is the most necessary, she has to subordinate herself to that; still, that music possesses the peculiar faculty of, without entirely keeping silence, so imperceptibly linking herself to the thought-full element of speech that she lets the latter seem to walk abroad alone, the while she supports it.[14]

Thus, no matter how one interprets Wagner's emphasis on words in *Oper und Drama,* whether one regards that emphasis as primary or secondary, as unchanging or variable, one must reconcile one's interpretation with the fact that Wagner knew very well—as both his theoretical writings and his operatic compositions attest—music's power and place in the artwork of the future. Wagner chose opera over the play because he believed that music's power of emotional expression was greater than that of words. He knew, as he told Cosima many years later, that music is the means whereby drama is actually created in opera.[15]

Having said this much about the relation of Wagner's emphasis on words in *Oper und Drama* to his fundamental concept of the poetic intent acting as the fertilizing seed, we approach more closely a definition of the *dichterische Absicht.* In the musical analyses of this study, I have tried to show that a poetic idea often instigates the musical response and provides the verbal reason for releasing the power of that response. This poetic idea is not, however, merely the poetry in a libretto, although it is related to that poetry. The poetic intent is, as the word *Absicht* indicates, a purpose, aim, or intention (it may also be a plan or design) that is usually more general than specific.

The concept of the poetic intent embraces, nevertheless, specific words. It can determine, for example, what portions of text are to receive the heightened dramatic emphasis of musical declamation, such as we find in Tristan's awakening and subsequent delirium and in Parsifal's realization of Amfortas's sin. Thus, a poetic design may cause dramatic attention to be focused on several specific words in successive lines of text. It may also dictate that music be used to inform the meaning of single words or phrases scattered throughout several more or less otherwise unemphasized lines of text. This function of the poetic intent includes the association of particular musical motives or fragments of motives with specific words—as in the linking of "Westwärts" in the sailor's song from *Tristan* with the interval that begins the prelude, or as in Kundry's calling Parsifal's name in the same intervals that are used to prophesy the coming of the pure fool—and also includes the more general musical emphases of specific words, such as the wordpainting in David's first-act aria, Eva's trill on the second syllable of "werben" at the conclusion of the prize song, or the cessation of musical motion that gives prominence to Gurnemanz's line "Das ist Karfreitagszauber, Herr!" in the middle of the Good Friday music.

Related to the emphasis of specific words is the use of music to realize verbal images, to call forth musical equivalents of specific words or ideas as single musical images, which often serve as constructive devices that influence larger portions of the musical structure than that encompassed by single words. We have seen this function of the poetic intent in *Tristan* in the extended musical realizations of the images of binding and weaving and in the concept of identity-exchange that affect significantly the overall structure of the love duet. We have also seen it in the melodic and structural realizations of waves and tides in "So rief der Lenz," in the blooming, intertwining vocal lines of the flower maidens' seductive dance, and in the straightforward, vigorous rhythms that indicate the rejuvenation of the knights' blood by the power of the Grail.

In a function kindred to the musical realization of verbal images, the poetic intent may suggest musical equivalents of gestures. We see this function particularly in *Parsifal* in the motives associated with riding, stumbling, carrying, walking, and throwing; with light streaming down from heaven and blood spurting up from a sick man's wounded side. At the same time, we see it in *Die Meistersinger,* where perpetual musical motion answers to the perpetual physical motion of the riot in act 2, and in *Tristan,* where the musical realizations of gestures in the love duet are more heard than seen. In realizing both single words and gestures in music, the action of the poetic intent is the same: the image, whether visual or verbal (or verbal suggesting visual), is associated with the music so that both the image and the music supplement one another in terms of meaning and emotion.

The poetic intent may cause music to be used to realize a general mood that becomes appropriate to the drama as a result of some specified or unspecified verbal stimulus. This appears to be a primary function of the poetic intent, and the examples we can offer of its operation are, consequently, numerous. An obvious one is the hunting music that begins act 2 of *Tristan,* where the music is so clear in its verbal connotations that no words are necessary to draw the parallel between the music and what the music represents. What words do is make the nature of the hunt increasingly specific; they sharpen the dramatic context. Another example of this function occurs in the love duet from the same opera, with its succession of moods, not always verbally specified, that pass from the heavy languor of the invocation to night to the delirious excitement of the final interrupted climax. In *Die Meistersinger,* all three of Walther's songs are responses to a generally undefined mood of growing excitement. Beckmesser's *Werbelied* also depicts a general, unspecified mood, although in this case the mood is the wrong one. Similarly, all three of the finales in *Die Meistersinger* realize moods rather than specific words.[16] In *Parsifal*—in the Grail rites, the dance of the flower maidens, the Good Friday music—again the poetic intent indicates a mood, which the music then goes on to realize as part of the developing drama. Through the operation of the poetic intent, moreover, the mood becomes not only appropriate but dramatic as well. In other words, the poetic intent makes it possible for any mood to be given dramatic significance by being associated with words, actions, or other moods that have already been defined in the drama. It is this juxtaposition of a musical mood with its dramatic meaning that makes Amfortas's entrance into the sanctuary and into the ritual so shocking, Tristan's awakening and self-discovery so meaningful, Beckmesser's serenade in the street before Pogner's house so ludicrous.

By relating music to certain words or ideas, Wagner, through the poetic intent, supplied his operas with various structural devices. We have already seen examples of some of these in the musical realizations of verbal images, but there are others. The poetic intent can cause constructive uses to be made of tonality, as in *Tristan* and *Parsifal,* where diatonicism and "nontonality" take on dramatic meanings by being associated with different aspects of the opera librettos. Even within the overall diatonicism of *Die Meistersinger,* tonality functions in response to the dramatic situation. "You did not end in the same key," Sachs says to Walther at the end of the second *Stollen* of the prize song, "and that offends the masters."[17] In dramatic contrast, Beckmesser's song is just as harmonically bland as Walther's is daring. In *Tristan,* in addition to the dramatic significance attached to chromaticism and diatonicism, tonality gives further, and more subtle, dramatic meaning to larger aspects of the musical structure. Thus, the shifting harmonies in Kurwenal's *Moroldlied* reflect his ambivalent feelings about Isolde and Tristan on an almost subconscious level; the harmonic insistence on F minor in act 3 reinforces the melodic insistence of the shepherd's tune that calls Tristan to account; the E major of Tristan's "Wie sie selig, hehr und milde" serves as the tonal bridge between the A minor of the drinking of the love potion (and of the prelude) and the B major of Isolde's transfiguration that reconciles what Tristan has so long struggled against—both love and death;[18] the tonal move from A-flat major to B major links and confirms the relationship between the love duet and the *Liebestod* at the same time that it points up the relationship of both these lyric moments to Tristan's delirium and the harmonic insistence on F minor that characterizes that delirium.

In addition to suggesting the reasons behind various tonal sequences and relationships, the poetic intent can actually determine the musical structure of a scene by ordering the succession of musical ideas that make up the scene. This aspect of the poetic intent's function includes the use of motives but is not limited to it. For example, in the scene that begins the second act of *Tristan und Isolde,* we could say that the music of the hunting horns comprises one motive, but the music that reflects Isolde's longing and impatience is made up of several different musical ideas that the poetic intent does not necessarily guide. The structure that this intent does guide, however, is the larger overall structure in which the hunting music and Isolde's music are juxtaposed, in relation to the text of the scene, to increasingly greater dramatic effect. On a smaller scale, we see a poetic plan governing the succession of musical ideas in the third-act prelude of *Tristan*; these ideas only receive explicit verbal meaning as the act progresses. And again, on a much larger scale, another poetic plan governs the succession of musical ideas in the love duet and relates those ideas (and the duet as a whole) to the *Liebestod.* In *Parsifal,* Wagner accomplishes the poetic intent of the first-act transformation scene—showing, in music, the approach of Gurnemanz and Parsifal to the castle of the Grail—by allowing the music associated with the two men's walking to be twice interrupted by the music associated with Amfortas's lament, until both themes are overpowered by the ostinato of pealing bells that sound from the castle itself. A similar alternation of musical ideas (this time following the general leading of the text) that culminates in the eventual dominance of a particular musical idea also occurs in the Good Friday music in the last act of the opera.

The poetic intent contributes to the realization of musical moods and motives; it can also actually guide the melodic response. Of course, the poetic intent does not indicate the specific notes of a melody; but it can suggest, I believe, a general melodic shape or progression. Thus, I have tried to show that the way the shepherd's first tune in *Tristan* centers almost obsessively on the tonic of F minor is a melodic response to a poetic idea, just as meaningful dramatically as is the second tune's avoidance of the tonic; the rhythmic motion in both tunes is a direct response to the poetic idea as well. So is the monotonous, halting, "dying fall" of Tristan's utterances on first returning to consciousness in act 3. We see poetic ideas influencing the melodic motion in *Die Meistersinger*: in the ascent to the dominant at the end of the second *Stollen* of the prize song; in the awkward melodic intervals of "So rief der Lenz" alluding to Old Winter in the thornhedge; in the seemingly uncontrollable coloratura of Beckmesser's wooing song.

Poetic ideas can also determine any given melody's phrase-structure. This is particularly apparent in the songs from *Die Meistersinger*—in the tidelike ebb and flow of the phrases in "So rief der Lenz," in the intentional regularity of Beckmesser's serenade and his unintentional destruction of that regularity, and in the illusion of a single melodic phrase in the verse of the prize song. In the love duet from *Tristan,* an idea's influence over the phrase-structure actually makes possible the melodic realization of the images of binding and weaving. But poetic ideas influence the phrase-structure in more traditional *Oper und Drama* ways as well by causing a given phrase to be lengthened or shortened as a response to the degree of excitement or calm, frenzy or exhaustion being portrayed in any given scene at any given moment. One poetic idea suggests the overlapping phrases of the flower maidens' choral song, just as another suggests the brief, abrupt ejaculations of Parsifal's response to Kundry's emotional manipulations. Even the fragmentation of the long phrase that begins the prelude to *Parsifal* when that phrase later precedes the rites of the *Liebesmahl* and the subsequent reunion of those fragments as part of the ritual is, I believe, a melodic response to an unstated stimulus of a poetic idea acting in the phrase-structure of the music to help create drama.

On its most general level, the poetic intent determines the choice of subject matter suitable for dramatic treatment in music. Wagner believed that music had the ability to ennoble whatever art it came into contact with.[19] For this ennobling not to appear ridiculous, therefore, he felt that the other art had to be worthy of its association with music. As far as the art of poetry was concerned, this concept naturally imposed limits on the type of stories that music could treat with any real dramatic effect. Wagner early realized these limitations and embodied them in his preference for myth as suitable subject matter for opera. What appealed to Wagner about myth was its remoteness in time but its nearness in humanness. It told of human beings in human situations that were removed enough from the present to make their treatment in music seem natural rather than forced or absurd. Myth, moreover, while it was about men, was at the same time greater than men: myth was universal. It was simple in deeds but complex in human relationships; perhaps most important of all from Wagner's point of view, myth was inspirational.

Wagner's poetic intent, thus prescribing the simple, human, and remote as suitable subject matter for opera, then went on to require that the story be simplified even more by having the words that told the story condensed to their utmost emotional potential. Whatever tended toward thought rather than feeling was to be eliminated. In this regard, *Parsifal,* with the shortest libretto of all Wagner's mature operas, would seem to be the opera that comes closest to fulfilling the requirements for an opera libretto that Wagner set forth in *Oper und Drama.*[20] At the same time, even though its story has elements of religion in it, the story is above ordinary religion as Wagner saw it in that it takes from religion only what is suitable for musical treatment: the lyric aspects of "rapturous worship."[21] In the same way, *Die Meistersinger* is above ordinary history, since its history is not circumstantial or factual but is, rather, "musical." It is thus that the poetic intent determines the plot and the words that relate the plot by determining the nearness of the relationship of the plot and the words to music.

In seeking for a definition of the *dichterische Absicht*, we have examined several different ways in which a poetic intent seems to operate to stimulate a musical response. From what we have seen of this operation, we could say that the poetic intent not only inspires the musical events in the drama but also informs the course of the drama by giving those musical events meaning. In other words, the musical events do not happen in a merely musical context, as they would in a symphony; the logic is not solely musical. In opera, the musical events happen in a dramatic context as well. It is for this reason that we have considered the music that helps make up the *Liebestod* as much more than a truncated recapitulation of the music that helps make up the love duet. The musical structure has more than a musical meaning, and that it does is a direct result of the action of Wagner's poetic intent using music in a dramatic context. This, I believe, is the sense in which Wagner said in *Oper und Drama* that the poetic structure should determine the musical structure. The means whereby this was to be accomplished was the equation of musical motives with poetic ideas. The structural use of motives, however, was only an initial step in Wagner's musical development. He seems to have discovered gradually that the appearance, recurrence, and modification of motives in varying dramatic situations were infinitely powerful dramatic tools that could serve far more than structural purposes. In *Über die Anwendung der Musik auf das Drama,* he singled out the variety of motives in the *Ring* and their mutations "in closest sympathy with the rising passions of the plot"[22] which, more than Wotan's words (and one might also say, more than the formal structures which underlay the words), gave a picture of the god's fear, depression, and suffering.

When Wagner first began work on the *Ring,* he appears to have relied principally on motives that had been given a specific meaning by the text; later appearances of these motives recalled that meaning and its original dramatic context. These were the motives that Wagner called "reminiscences" in *Oper und Drama* and that he used, at first, somewhat less than subtly (as in the appearance of the sword motive in act 1 of *Die Walküre*). But as he evolved as a creative artist, not only did he make increasing use of motives that corresponded to gestures and conveyed the idea of motion embodied in those gestures, but he also made increasing use of motives that foreboded events yet to come in the drama, motives that had not yet been given specific verbal characterization or meaning.

I believe that Wagner must have realized only gradually the immense dramatic advantage that motives of foreboding had over motives of reminiscence. For one thing, they were infinitely more subtle, since they had, as yet in the drama, no precise meaning or, at most, only a vague meaning. For another, because they were unknown quantities, they were mysterious and corresponded more to the uncertainties of life as it really is. Certainly the dramatic relationships and motivations in *Tristan* and *Parsifal,* not to mention the *Ring,* are complex enough. There are, in these operas, more questions and fewer answers; more possibilities of meaning and fewer definite acknowledgments of what that meaning actually is. Wagner's increasing use of the foreboding function of the poetic intent in his later operas seems to reflect a more acute perception of how to present life dramatically. Motives of foreboding make the musical answers or suggestions seem less pat. Far from showing that Wagner was becoming an absolute musician (as Stein has suggested), I would say that the increasing use of motives of foreboding in preference to motives of reminiscence shows his growing skill and depth as a psychological dramatist.

Every good drama has elements of mystery in it; one wants to know how the dramatic conflict is going to be resolved. The foreboding function of music is the musical equivalent of a mystery that is propounded but not yet solved. We have only to consider the preludes of both *Tristan* and *Parsifal* to see the truth of this assertion. Neither prelude has any dramatic meaning to start with other than the moods and emotional responses the music on its own calls into play. As both operas develop, however, their preludes acquire more and more dramatic significance. This is particularly true of the *Tristan* prelude, the true meaning of which is only revealed at the end of the opera when Tristan dies. Because of the dramatic meaning it acquires during the course of the opera, the prelude, far more appropriately than the monologue that ends the opera, could be called the *Liebestod,* since that, in fact, is what it comes to stand for. In a similar way, the motives that make up the principal sections of the *Parsifal* prelude gain general and specific dramatic meanings by their later association with various parts of the drama so that the acquisition of meaning and the further imparting of meaning are both, in themselves, dramatic events. Even in *Die Meistersinger,* the fragments of the prize song that are scattered throughout the first and second acts at verbally apposite moments can be seen as both constructive devices and musical hints or clues to the solution of the mystery of how Walther will finally win Eva's hand. When he reveals his dream in the last act in the prize song, the clues not only make sense and achieve their true meaning, but they also make the song itself, though new, seem old, familiar, and somehow dramatically and musically right.

The poetic intent determines the course of the verbal drama and, consequently, that of the musical drama as well. Its use of words is born of a knowledge of what ideas, situations, and feelings are capable of musical treatment and expansion. As Wagner wrote in *Eine Mittheilung an meine Freunde,* it was his musical predisposition that first made him an opera poet by showing him that poetry intended for opera had to be conditioned by music's expressive abilities.[23] In its larger structural aspects, the poetic intent determines the alternation of lyric and dramatic moments in opera, the combination of both, or the predominance of one over the other. The poetic intent determines the words or actions suitable for both moments and then offers them to the musician to be realized in music as drama. Thus, it is the poetic intent that, in the final analysis, made it possible for Wagner to achieve his structural goal of a musical-dramatic form without noticeable structural divisions. It was the musician who had the tools to blur or merge the actual lyric and dramatic moments into one another, but it was the poetic intent that gave the musician the rationale, the logic, and occasionally even the inspiration that made possible the use of these tools. It was Wagner's concept of a poetic purpose that allowed him to take lyricism and declamation and put them both in a context that was dramatic. Because of the poetic intent, even the intensely lyric moments of the love duet from *Tristan,* the *Liebestod,* Kundry's lullaby, the Good Friday music, even the chorale that begins *Die Meistersinger* are dramatic.

The poetic intent is, thus, the verbal reason behind the musical results; it provides ideas for the musical form and its realization and then gives that form and realization dramatic meaning. In *Oper und Drama* language, the poetic intent is the cause behind the effect. An excellent example of its operation (and one of the few that is mentioned specifically by Wagner) is the musical depiction of the depths of the Rhine that begins the whole *Ring* cycle. Wagner said that it was the poem of *Das Rheingold* that suggested to him the musical response: over one hundred measures of the same E-flat-major triad. One may believe this statement or not; but no one, I think, would seriously maintain that the creative process was the other way around, that the musical idea suggested to Wagner the creation of the poem.[24]

I should point out again that much of what I have said in the musical analyses of this study is conjecture, my own opinion of how Wagner's operas show evidence of the operation of his poetic intent. A more complete examination of Wagner's extant personal writings, as well as of his musical sketches and drafts for the operas, might well remove the subject from much of its dependence on speculation and supply confirmation or refutation of the ideas suggested here. As valid as I believe the concept of the poetic intent is in Wagner's operas, I do not wish to imply by what I have said that it can in every case explain how Wagner went about composing his operas or that it can account for everything verbal, musical, or dramatic that we find in the operas. No such concept can ever explain the genius or intuition or just plain hard work that goes into the creation of any piece of great music or any great opera. Wagner himself said in *Über das Opern-Dichten und Komponiren im Besonderen* that he would never presume to teach men how to make music but only to guide them in the knowledge of how music that had already been made should be rightly understood.[25] This in itself is a tall order; but it is a goal that, in Wagner's own case, the concept of the poetic intent can help achieve. The concept does not explain creativity, but it helps us see how creativity begins and how it ends. It offers us a reasonable, logical, consistent point of view from which to consider the inspiration for and the results of Wagner's labors; it allows us to judge the fruit, as it were, from the seed.

In 1879, less than four years before his death, Wagner reiterated the fundamental theoretical statement from *Oper und Drama* in the article *Über das Opern-Dichten und Komponiren im Besonderen*: In creating the perfect dramatic artwork, the poet's role is the masculine principle; the musician's, the feminine. As an illustration of this statement, he related the following anecdote:

> A German prince with a turn for composing operas once asked friend Liszt to procure my aid in the instrumenting of a new opera by his Highness; in particular he wanted the good effect of the trombones in *Tannhäuser* applied to his work, in which regard my friend felt bound to divulge the secret that something always occurred to me before I set it for the trombones.[26]

Wagner completed the jest and added its moral by confessing that he could never compose at all unless something first "occurred" to him. He ended by advising composers who wanted to write operas in the dramatic, Wagnerian manner "to never think of adopting a text before they see in it a plot, and characters to carry out this plot, that inspire the musician with a lively interest on some account or other."[27] It is as good a definition as any, I think, of Wagner's manner of composing and of the poetic intent.

Notes

Chapter 1

1. Wagner's own account of this period of his life, seen from the vantage point of later
    years, is recorded in his autobiography: Richard Wagner, *My Life*, 2nd ed. (New
    York: Tudor Publishing Co., 1936), pp. 429–516. The standard biographical account
    of the period can be found in Ernest Newman, *The Life of Richard Wagner*, 4 vols.
    (New York: Alfred A. Knopf, 1933–46), 1:481–509; 2:1–122. A more recent account
    appears in Curt von Westernhagen, *Wagner: A Biography*, trans. Mary Whittall,
    2 vols. (Cambridge: Cambridge University Press, 1978), 1:113–51.

2. Some of Wagner's essays appear as parts of other works, and the titles of these essays
    should properly be enclosed in quotation marks. But since in this study the essays
    themselves are considered to be more important than the works from which they may
    have come, I have put the titles of all Wagner's essays longer than an arbitrarily
    selected length of twenty pages in italics.

    The titles given in German appear in Wagner, *Gesammelte Schriften und Dichtun-
    gen*, 10 vols. (Leipzig: E. W. Fritzsch, 1871–83). At this time Wagner also wrote
    newspaper articles ("On E. Devrient's *History of German Acting*," "Theater Re-
    form," "Man and Established Society," and "The Revolution") that do not appear
    in the *Gesammelte Schriften* but that are included in Wagner, *Richard Wagner's Prose
    Works*, trans. William Ashton Ellis, 8 vols. (London: Routledge & Kegan Paul, 1892–99;
    repr. New York: Broude Brothers, 1966). All of the citations of Wagner's prose works
    refer to these two editions.

    The translations of Wagner's prose works that appear in this study are William
    Ashton Ellis's, modified by me only in matters of spelling, punctuation, and capital-
    ization. The faults in Ellis's writing style—noted, for example, by Ernest Newman
    and Houston Stewart Chamberlain (see Newman, *Life of Richard Wagner*, 2:564–65
    note)—seem to me to be of relatively small consequence compared to the undeniable
    merits of Ellis's translations: literalness, accuracy, consistency, completeness, and
    accessibility.

    An exception to Wagner's essay and article writing during this period is the part-
    sketch, part-libretto *Wieland der Schmiedt*, the story of which is referred to at the
    end of *Das Kunstwerk der Zukunft* as a sort of illustrative moral.

3. Wagner, *Music of the Future*, 3:295 (*Zukunftsmusik*, 7:124—"dass ich mich damals,
    als ich jene Arbeiten verfasste, in einem durchaus abnormen Zustande befand"). This
    form of dual reference to both *Richard Wagner's Prose Works* and the *Gesammelte*

Schriften und Dichtungen is used throughout the study. Not all notes, however, contain the original German of the quotations. I have included the German only where I have felt it might be of interest or help as a comparison.

4. Wagner, *Opera and Drama*, 2:235 (*Oper und Drama*, 4:126–27—"Der Verstand ist daher von der Nothwendigkeit gedrängt, sich einem Elemente zu vermählen, welches seine dichterische Absicht als befruchtenden Samen in sich aufzunehmen, und diesen Samen durch sein eigenes, ihm nothwendiges Wesen so zu nähren und zu gestalten vermöge, dass es ihn als verwirklichenden und erlösenden Gefühlsausdruck gebäre"). The image is evoked more plainly in a subsequent sentence: "This procreative seed is the poetic aim, which brings to the glorious loving woman, Music, the stuff for bearing" (ibid., 2:236 [4:128—"Dieser zeugende Samen ist die dichterische Absicht, die dem herrlich liebenden Weibe Musik den Stoff zur Gebärung zuführt"]).

5. The references in sexual terms to the union of poetry and music in opera are too frequent and specific in *Oper und Drama* and Wagner's other writings to admit of any doubt as to his metaphorical intentions. Sex was a subject that Wagner was not shy about discussing openly. It occurs in the operas as well as the theoretical writings and occurs necessarily, consequently, in this study.

6. Jack M. Stein, *Richard Wagner and the Synthesis of the Arts* (Detroit: Wayne State University Press, 1960; repr. Westport, Connecticut: Greenwood Press, 1973), p. 6.

7. Ibid., p. 7.

8. Ibid., p. 213.

9. Ibid., p. 211.

10. Ibid., p. 213.

11. See Carl Dahlhaus, *Richard Wagner's Music Dramas*, trans. Mary Whittall (Cambridge: Cambridge University Press, 1979), pp. 54–55, where the same distinction between words and drama is also made, but without specific reference to Stein's study.

12. Cosima Wagner, *Cosima Wagner's Diaries*, ed. Martin Gregor-Dellin and Dietrich Mack, trans. Geoffrey Skelton, 2 vols. (New York: Harcourt Brace Jovanovich, 1978-80), 1:544. In view of the succeeding events in the relationship between Wagner and Friedrich Nietzsche (see note 13 below), the sentence that precedes this quotation from Cosima's diary seems to be an almost prophetic psychological coincidence: "R. writes to Prof. Nietzsche, . . . and among other things he encloses a little clipping from a newspaper, in which some tasteless extracts from opera texts are quoted and criticized, with the remark, 'This goes even further than R. Wagner'!"

13. Newman, *Life of Richard Wagner*, 4:490. The relationship between Wagner and Nietzsche was a complicated one that questions about the state of Nietzsche's mental health do nothing to simplify. For two different views, see ibid., 4:320–49, 491–539, 543–46, 587–97; and Robert W. Gutman, *Richard Wagner: The Man, His Mind, and His Music* (New York: Harcourt Brace Jovanovich, 1968), pp. 352–61.

14. Friedrich Nietzsche, *On the Genealogy of Morals*, trans. Walter Kaufmann and R. J. Hollingdale (New York: Random House, Vintage Books, 1969), pp. 102–3. It would be interesting to know how Nietzsche reconciled this observation with his original admiration for *Tristan und Isolde* and subsequent championing of Bizet and *Carmen*.

15. For Noufflard's discussion of *Tristan und Isolde*, see Georges Noufflard, *Richard Wagner d'après lui-même* 2 vols. (Paris: Librairie Fischbacher, 1885), 2:301–16.

16. Houston Stewart Chamberlain, "Notes chronologiques sur *L'Anneau de Nibelung*," *Revue Wagnérienne* 3 (February 1888): 276.

17. Guido Adler, *Richard Wagner: Vorlesungen gehalten an der Universität zu Wien*, 2d ed. (Munich: Drei Masken Verlag, 1923), p. 178.

18. Ibid., p. 179. Writing on Wagner in 1963, Hans Gal repeated the gist of Adler's view of Wagner's theory and practice: "These theories were of vital necessity to Wagner because they strengthened him in the unshakeable belief in his mission, that belief which moves mountains. But the great danger is that a doctrine which is absurd in its very nature must also lead to absurd results unless the instinct of the artist is stronger than all theory. The towering greatness of Wagner's mature works is only thanks to the circumstance that, when it came to the point, he was quite prepared to forget about his doctrines" (Hans Gal, *Richard Wagner*, trans. Hans-Hubert Schön-zeler [New York: Stein and Day, 1976], pp. 161–62).

19. Paul Bekker, *Richard Wagner: His Life in His Work*, trans M. M. Bozman (London: J. M. Dent and Sons, 1931), p. 510. Bekker interpreted Wagner's work in the light of Expressionism and considered the fundamental idea of all Wagner's art to be embodied in a concept that Wagner first stated explicitly in the essay *Beethoven*: musical action made visible.

20. Paul Bekker, *The Changing Opera*, trans. Arthur Mendel (New York: W. W. Norton, 1935), p. 177.

21. Gutman, *Richard Wagner*, p. 319. Gutman's reference is to "the heart of Wagnerian thought . . . revealed in four tracts written [in exile in Switzerland] soon after his flight from Germany" (ibid., p. 138): *Die Kunst und die Revolution, Das Kunstwerk der Zukunft, Das Judenthum in der Musik*, and *Oper und Drama*.

22. Ibid., p. 321. One cannot help but wonder, though, why Wagner, if he had really wanted to hide his new ideas about opera, should have felt compelled to write about them at all.

23. Ibid.

24. Robert Bailey, "The Genesis of *Tristan und Isolde* and a Study of Wagner's Sketches and Drafts for the First Act," Ph.D. dissertation, Princeton University, 1969, p. 6.

25. Dahlhaus, *Richard Wagner's Music Dramas*, p. 5.

26. Richard David, "Wagner the Dramatist," in *The Wagner Companion*, ed. Peter Burbidge and Richard Sutton (New York: Cambridge University Press, 1979), p. 117.

27. George Bernard Shaw, "The Tone Poet," in *Shaw on Music*, comp. Eric Bentley (Garden City, New York: Doubleday, Anchor Books, 1956), p. 113.

28. Ibid., p. 114.

29. Ibid., p. 115.

30. Ibid.

31. Ibid.

32. Ibid., p. 116.

33. See Alfred Lorenz, *Das Geheimnis der Form bei Richard Wagner*, 4 vols. (Berlin: Max Hesses Verlag, 1924–33). Lorenz found three forms to be the most prevalent in

Wagner's operas: strophic, *Bar,* and ternary (or *Bogen*) forms. These formal structures were found to be more obviously operative in the more musical, more lyrical
sections of the operas than in the more argumentative or declamatory sections. Lorenz, however, sought for the forms everywhere. For a summary of his work, see
Gerald Abraham, *A Hundred Years of Music,* 3rd ed. (Chicago: Aldine Publishing
Co., 1964), pp. 121–29.

Recently, scholars have tried to find less categorical explanations of Wagner's formal structures than those that appear in Lorenz's work; see, for example, Dahlhaus,
"Wagners dramatisch-musikalisches Formbegriff," in *Colloquium Verdi-Wagner (Rom
1969)* ed. Friedrich Lippman (Cologne and Vienna: Böhlau Verlag, 1972), pp. 290–303;
and Rudolf Stephan, "Gibt es ein Geheimnis der Form bei Richard Wagner?" in *Das
Drama Richard Wagners als musikalisches Kunstwerk,* ed. Carl Dahlhaus (Regensburg: Gustav Bosse Verlag, 1970), pp. 9–16.

34.   Bryan Magee, *Aspects of Wagner* (New York: Stein and Day, 1969), p. 13.

35.   Ibid., p. 14.

36.   See Irmtraud Flechsig, "Beziehungen zwischen textlicher und musikalischer Struktur
in Richard Wagners Tristan und Isolde," in *Das Drama Richard Wagners als musikalisches Kunstwerk,* pp. 239–56.

Flechsig's study stemmed from August Halm, "Über Richard Wagners Musikdrama," in his *Von Grenzen und Ländern der Musik* (Munich: G. Müller Verlag, 1916),
pp. 32–47. Halm tried to show by reference to a portion of *Das Rheingold* that Wagner
created musical equivalents to the verbal syntax. For a discussion of Halm's work,
see Westernhagen, *Wagner: A Biography,* 1:185–86.

37.   Bailey, "Genesis of *Tristan und Isolde,*" p. 10.

38.   Ibid., p. 60.

39.   See Bailey, "The Method of Composition," in *The Wagner Companion,* p. 293.

40.   Deryck Cooke, *I Saw the World End: A Study of Wagner's "Ring"* (New York: Oxford
University Press, 1979), p. 73.
      Another study by Cooke deals, like those by Flechsig and by Halm (see note 36
above), with the subject of musical syntax in Wagner's operas: see Cooke, "Wagner's
Musical Language," in *The Wagner Companion,* pp. 225–68.

41.   Cooke, *I Saw the World End,* p. 65.

42.   In this regard, Carl Dahlhaus maintains that "Wagner himself was not primarily
concerned with whether the music was subordinate to the text in musical drama or
vice versa." Dahlhaus goes on to say that "if readers bring to a theoretical text a
question that it was not originally asking, it is hardly the fault of the text if the answer
they find there seems confused or contradictory" (Dahlhaus, *Richard Wagner's Music
Dramas,* p. 55).

Chapter 2

1.   This chapter does not trace the musical influences affecting Wagner as a composer.
     For discussions of these, see John Warrack, "The Musical Background," in *The
     Wagner Companion,* pp. 85–112; Edward J. Dent, *The Rise of Romantic Opera*
     ed. Winton Dean (Cambridge: Cambridge University Press, 1976); Robert Tallant

Laudon, "Sources of the Wagnerian Synthesis: A Study of the Franco-German Tradition in Nineteenth-Century Opera," Ph.D. dissertation, University of Illinois, Urbana, 1969. All three writers emphasize the importance of contributions from the French musical tradition to the German art form that Wagner developed.

2. For discussions of the influence of German romantic literature on Wagner, see Donald J. Grout, *A Short History of Opera*, 2d ed. (New York: Columbia University Press, 1965), pp. 376–79; see also Ronald Gray, "The German Intellectual Background," in *The Wagner Companion*, pp. 34–38.

3. Ernest Newman, *The Wagner Operas* (New York: Alfred A. Knopf, 1949), p. 188. In this book, Newman traces the literary backgrounds of most of Wagner's opera librettos.

4. For the discussion from which these chief ideas of the German romantic writers are drawn, see Michael Black, "The Literary Background: Poetry, Poetic Drama and Music Drama," in *The Wagner Companion*, pp. 60–84.

5. Wagner, "On E. Devrient's *History of German Acting*," 8:218. The third of five volumes of Devrient's *Geschichte* appeared near the end of 1848. Wagner's review was sent, together with a cover letter dated 8 January 1849, to the Augsburg *Allgemeine Zeitung*. The review was not accepted for publication but was preserved all the same by a member of the newspaper staff. The review does not appear in the *Gesammelte Schriften*, even though it was eventually published in Wagner's lifetime. For details of the publication history, see Carl Friedrich Glasenapp, *Life of Richard Wagner*, trans. William Ashton Ellis, 6 vols. (London: Kegan Paul, Trench, Trübner & Co., 1900–1908), 2:303 note.

6. Wagner, "On E. Devrient's *History of German Acting*," 8:218.

7. Ibid., 8:219.

8. Wagner, "Art and Climate," 1:262 ("Kunst und Klima," 3:265).

9. See ibid., 1:263 (3:265–66).

10. Wagner, *Music of the Future*, 3:306 (*Zukunftsmusik*, 7:136). In this essay, written in 1860, Wagner retraced the important stages to date in the development of his theory of opera. The phrase quoted here comes from his view of the purpose he was trying to accomplish in *Die Kunst und die Revolution*.

11. Wagner, *Art and Revolution*, 1:34 (*Die Kunst und die Revolution*, 3:15).

12. This assertion receives support from the fact that Wagner's personal library in Dresden contained no political works (see Curt von Westernhagen, *Richard Wagners Dresdener Bibliothek: 1842–1849* [Wiesbaden: F. A. Brockhaus, 1966]). Westernhagen considers the absence of such writings in Wagner's library to indicate that, in spite of his political activities, "politics as such hardly impinged at all on his inner life" (idem, *Wagner: A Biography*, 1:133).

13. Wagner, *The Artwork of the Future*, 1:182 (*Das Kunstwerk der Zukunft*, 3:176).

14. See Grout, *Short History of Opera*, pp. 376–77, for examples.

15. August Wilhelm Schlegel, *Über dramatische Kunst und Literatur* (Heidelberg, 1817), 3:8, translated as *A Course of Lectures on Dramatic Art and Literature* by John Black, rev. A. J. W. Morrison (London, 1846), quoted in Black, "The Literary Background," p. 84.

16. See Michael Tanner, "The Total Work of Art," in *The Wagner Companion*, pp. 150–51.

17. See Wagner, *The Artwork of the Future*, 1:191 (*Das Kunstwerk der Zukunft*, 3:187); see also idem, *Music of the Future*, 3:308–9 (*Zukunftsmusik*, 7:138–39).

18. Wagner, *Opera and Drama*, 2:17 (*Oper und Drama*, 3:282—"dass ein Mittel des Ausdruckes [die Musik] zum Zwecke, der Zweck des Ausdruckes [das Drama] aber zum Mittel gemacht war"). The quotation comes from the introduction to *Oper und Drama*; it is set in bold type and is the first statement of the error that appears in the book.

19. See Wagner, letter to Theodor Uhlig, [20 November 1851], *Sämtliche Briefe*, ed. Gertrud Strobel and Werner Wolf, 4 vols. to date (Leipzig: VEB Deutscher Verlag für Musik, 1967–), 4:197.

20. Wagner, *Opera and Drama*, 2:25 (*Oper und Drama*, 3:292—"mit der spröden Unvermischungsfähigkeit alles Unnatürlichen").

21. In *Über naive und sentimentalische Dichtung* (1795–1796), Schiller had discussed classicism and romanticism in poetry—the conflict between the old and the new, the reflective and the spontaneous, the sentimental and the naive. In *Oper und Drama*, Wagner applied Schiller's poetic distinctions to opera.

22. Wagner, *Opera and Drama*, 2:26 (*Oper und Drama*, 3:293).

23. Ibid., 2:27 (3:294).

24. Ibid., 2:28–9 (3:295).

25. Ibid., 2:32 (3:300).

26. See ibid., 2:35 (3:303). It is important to remember when discussing Wagner's view of opera that throughout *Oper und Drama*, as in the reference here, he made it clear repeatedly that he knew music's ability to stir the emotions with little or no help from poetry.

27. Ibid., 2:36 (3:305). Wagner's idealized view of Mozart's relation to his librettists is not supported by documentary evidence. Mozart's letters to his father reveal that he was extremely demanding of his poets. For example, in one of the letters written during the composition of *Die Entführung aus dem Serail*, Mozart wrote: "Everyone abuses Stephanie. . . . But after all he is arranging the libretto for me—and, what is more, as I want it—exactly—and, by Heaven, I do not ask anything more of him" (Wolfgang Amadeus Mozart, letter to Leopold Mozart, 26 September 1781, *The Letters of Mozart and His Family*, trans. and ed. Emily Anderson, 2d ed., prepared by A. Hyatt King and Monica Carolan, 2 vols. [New York: St. Martin's Press, 1966], 2:770).
    As far as composers placing demands on poets goes, Wagner was particularly critical of Weber's treatment of Helmina von Chezy and Meyerbeer's treatment of Eugène Scribe (see Wagner, *Opera and Drama*, 2:83–87; 2:93–94 [*Oper und Drama*, 3:357–62; 3:368–69]). In Wagner's own case, however, he found it impossible to work with any librettist other than himself.

28. Wagner, *Opera and Drama*, 2:48 (*Oper und Drama*, 3:318—"als absolut ohrgefällige Tonweise").

29. Ibid., 2:64 (3:336—"matten und inhaltslosen Schema").

30. Ibid., 2:77 (3:350).

31. Ibid., 2:94 (3:369—"ein ungeheuer buntscheckiges, historisch-romantisches, teu-flisch-religiöses, bigott-wollüstiges, frivol-hei[l]liges, geheimnissvoll-freches, senti-mental-gaunerisches dramatisches Allerlei"). Wagner encapsulated in the quotation his description of the librettos of *Robert le Diable, Les Huguenots,* and *Le Prophète.*

32. Ibid., 2:103 (3:380—"gänzlichen Unvermögens").

33. Ibid., 2:111 (3:389—"wenn er vom Gedanken des Dichters befruchtet wird").

34. Wagner, letter to Theodor Uhlig, 20 January 1851, *Sämtliche Briefe,* 3:498.

35. Wagner, *Opera and Drama,* 2:134 (*Oper und Drama,* 4:22—"seiner zwitterhaften, unnatürlichen Gestalt"). The discussion of the works of Goethe and Schiller, referred to here in passing, forms a large part of part 2, chapter 1.

36. Ibid., 2:155 (4:42).

37. Wagner called the effect of this compression of dramatic material the poetic "won-der." His discussion of this wonder and its difference from religious wonders (or miracles) appears in part 2, chapter 5. Wagner's view was that the events of real life, when shorn of their religious and political trappings and concentrated into a brief span of time, seemed miraculous. It was this concentration of life that allowed the drama to remain natural and yet to become supernatural.

38. Wagner, *Opera and Drama,* 2:191 (*Oper und Drama,* 4:81).

39. Ibid., 2:235 (4:127).

40. Wagner, letter to Theodor Uhlig, 20 January 1851, *Sämtliche Briefe,* 3:498.

Chapter 3

1. Wagner, letter to Theodor Uhlig, [12 December 1850], *Sämtliche Briefe,* 3:477.

2. Wagner, *Music of the Future,* 3:295 (*Zukunftsmusik,* 7:124—"das Labyrinth theore-tischer Spekulation").

3. See Wagner, *Richard Wagner's Prose Works,* trans. William Ashton Ellis, 2:xvi.

4. Bryan Magee has written of Wagner's prose style in the following terms: "I must say, though, that anyone who wants to avoid reading his prose has my sympathy. He writes like an autodidact, with flowery expressions, a vocabulary intended to impress, unnecessary abstractions and elaborate sentence structures. . . . One forms the con-viction that the prose was improvised, poured out without forethought or discipline— that when Wagner embarked on each individual sentence he had no idea how it was going to end. Many passages are intolerably boring. Some do not mean anything at all. It always calls for sustained effort from the reader to pick out meaning in the cloud of words. Often one has to go on reading for several pages before beginning to descry, like solid figures in a mist, what he is saying" (Magee, *Aspects of Wagner,* pp. 14–15).

5. Wagner, letter to Theodor Uhlig, [15 February 1851], *Sämtliche Briefe,* 3:511.

6. General dates for the composition of Wagner's operas appear in the chronological table in Herbert Barth, Dietrich Mack, and Egon Voss, comp. and ed., *Wagner: A*

Documentary Study, trans. P. R. J. Ford and Mary Whittall (New York: Oxford University Press, 1975), p. 252. More specific dates of composition can be found in the list of works that appears at the end of *The New Grove Dictionary of Music and Musicians,* 1980 ed., s.v. "Wagner, Richard," by Curt von Westernhagen, Carl Dahlhaus, and Robert Bailey. Robert Bailey prepared the chronological table in the list of works as well as the bibliography for the article.

7. The summary in this chapter necessarily repeats much that has appeared before in other summaries of *Oper und Drama,* although it differs in a number of points. For comparisons, see Gerald Abraham, *A Hundred Years of Music,* pp. 98–109; Edward Arthur Lippman, "The Esthetic Theories of Richard Wagner," *The Musical Quarterly* 44 (1958): 209–20; Magee, *Aspects of Wagner,* pp. 13–35; and Jack M. Stein, *Richard Wagner and the Synthesis of the Arts,* pp. 67–79.

8. Wagner, *The Diary of Richard Wagner: 1865–1882,* presented and annotated by Joachim Bergfield, trans. George Bird (London: Cambridge University Press, 1980), p. 130.

9. The definite article before words like "feeling" and "understanding" reflects Ellis's translation of a typically German construction that, although occasionally awkward in English, seems appropriate, since Wagner's concept of these intangibles was at once universal (as in "the feeling of all people") and specific (as if "feeling" were a definite thing that always exhibited the characteristics ascribed to it by Wagner). More idiomatic English usage would omit the article or possibly replace it with a word like "our" or "one's."

10. Wagner, *Opera and Drama,* 2:241 (*Oper und Drama,* 4:134).

11. Ibid., 2:247 (4:139—"bereicherte und gewürzte Nahrung").

12. Ibid., 2:249 (4:142—"der sinnlichen Fassung").

13. Ibid., 2:251 (4:144—"dass sie eine Wiederkehr bestimmter melodischer Momente in einem bestimmten Rhythmos enthält; kehren solche Momente entweder gar nicht wieder, oder machen sie sich dadurch unkenntlich, dass sie auf Takttheilen, die sich rhythmisch nicht entsprechen, wiederkehren, so fehlt der Melodie eben das bindende Band, welches sie erst zur Melodie macht").

14. Ibid., 2:252 (4:145—"zur überzeugenden Fülle der Melodie").

15. Ibid.

16. Ibid., 2:256 (4:151).

17. Ibid., 2:257 (4:151–52).

18. Ibid., 2:262 (4:157).

19. Ibid. ("Die Anordnung der stärkeren und schwächeren Accente ist daher maassgebend für die Taktart und den rhythmischen Bau der Periode").

20. Ibid., 2:264 (4:159).

21. Ibid., 2:267 (4:163—"unendlich flüssiges Element").

22. Ibid., 2:269 (4:165—"in einem einheitlichen Ausdrucke").

23. *Stabreim,* or alliterative verse, pairs related speech-roots into one collective image that Wagner felt could be rapidly absorbed by the emotion. According to him, *Stab-*

reim drew its resemblances from initial vowel sounds (*Erb'* and *eigen, immer* and *ewig*), initial consonants (*Ross* and *Reiter, froh* and *frei*), or from final determinative consonants (*Hand* and *Mund, Recht* and *Pflicht*). Wagner discusses *Stabreim* and his concept of the natural development of language in *Oper und Drama*, part 2, chapter 6. For a brief discussion of *Stabreim* and Wagner's use of it, see Deryck Cooke, *I Saw the World End: A Study of Wagner's "Ring,"* pp. 74–76.

24. Wagner, *Opera and Drama,* 2:269 (*Oper und Drama,* 4:165—"Eine gemischte Empfindung dem bereits bestimmten Gefühle schnell verständlich zu machen").

25. Ibid., 2:274 (4:171).

26. Ibid., 2:275 (4:172).

27. Ibid., 2:281 (4:178—"des unendlich bedingten dichterischen Gedankens").

28. Ibid., 2:288–89 (4:187—"er sah vor sich Nichts wie eine unendliche Wogenmasse von Möglichkeiten, in sich selbst aber ward er sich keines, diese Möglichkeiten bestimmenden Zweckes bewusst"). The quotation summarizes Wagner's views on the dissolution of form.

29. Ibid., 2:290 (4:189—"der aus der dichterischen Absicht auf dem Wortverse emporwachsenden Melodie").

30. Ibid., 2:291 (4:189).

31. Ibid., 2:292 (4:191—"würde unwillkürlich zu dem bestimmenden Leitton werden").

32. Ibid., 2:294 (4:193).

33. It is from part 3, chapter 3, that Alfred Lorenz drew many of the statements he used as the basis for his study of form in Wagner's operas.

34. See Wagner, *Opera and Drama,* 2:296 (*Oper und Drama,* 4:195–96).

35. Ibid., 2:297 (4:196).

36. Ibid., 2:298 (4:197—"aus der nackten Harmonie").

37. Ibid., 2:299 (4:198—"miterklingende Harmonie").

38. Ibid., 2:300 (4:199).

39. Ibid., 2:305 (4:204–5—"Die Umgebung nämlich muss sich unserem Gefühle so darstellen, dass wir jedem Gliede derselben unter anderen, als den nun einmal gerade so bestimmten Umständen, die Fähigkeit zu Motiven und Handlungen beimessen können, die unsere Theilnahme ebenso fesseln würden, als die gegenwärtig unserer Beachtung zunächst zugewandten").

40. Ibid., 2:305 (4:205—"aus den vor unseren Augen zusammengedrängten Motiven").

41. Ibid., 2:306 (4:205—"wohlunterschiedene Gliederung selbständiger Individualitäten").

42. Ibid., 2:306 (4:206—"als blosse harmonische Unterstützung der Melodie").

43. Ibid., 2:307 (4:207—"verwandtschaftlichen Neigungen").

44. Ibid., 2:310 (4:210—"aus dem inneren Bereiche der musikalischen Harmonie wohlbedingten und gerechtfertigten zur Wahrnehmung").

45. Ibid., 2:313 (4:214).

46. Ibid., 2:317 (4:218).

47. Ibid., 2:320 (4:221).

48. Ibid., 2:324 (4:226—"Mittheilung selbst des Gedankens").

49. Ibid., 2:329 (4:231).

50. Ibid., 2:330 (4:231—"unwillkürliche Wissen des in der Empfindung verwirklichten Gedankens").

51. Ibid., 2:330 (4:232).

52. Ibid., 2:333 (4:235).

53. Ibid.

54. Ibid., 2:335 (4:238—"der bewegungsvolle Mutterschooss der Musik").

55. Ibid., 2:336 (4:239—"das volle Aufgehen des Sprachgedankens in die musikalische Empfindung").

56. Ibid., 2:339 (4:241).

57. Ibid., 2:339 (4:242).

58. Ibid., 2:341 (4:243—"in dieser bestimmten Lebenslage befindlichen, von dieser Umgebung beeinflussten, von diesem Willen beseelten, und in diesem Vorhaben begriffenen").

59. Ibid., 2:341–42 (4:244—"sich aus der bereits tönenden Wortsprache zu der wirklichen Tonsprache erheben kann, als deren Blüthe die Melodie erscheint, wie sie von dem bestimmten, versicherten Gefühle als Kundgebung des rein menschlichen Empfindungsinhaltes der bestimmten und versicherten Individualität und Situation gefordert wird").

60. Ibid., 2:342 (4:245).

61. See ibid., 2:343 (4:245–46). The underlying implication is that the breakdown of form that had occurred in instrumental music in the first half of the nineteenth century should be extended to include a breakdown of form in opera as well.

62. Ibid., 2:343 (4:246).

63. Ibid., 2:344 (4:247—"der eine umfassendste Absicht des dichterischen Verstandes am entsprechendsten dem Gefühle mitzutheilen vermag").

64. Ibid., 2:345 (4:248—"mit einem fast schon durchsichtigen Tonschleier").

65. Ibid., 2:346 (4:248—"gesenkter oder vorbereitender Situationen").

66. Ibid., 2:347 (4:250—"dass in ihrer wohlbedingten wechselseitigen Wiederholung ihm ganz von selbst auch die höchste einheitliche musikalische Form entsteht").

67. Ibid., 2:348 (4:252—"der vollendeten einheitlichen Form").

68. Ibid., 2:350 (4:254—"Zeit und Raum durch die Wirklichkeit des Drama's vernichtet"). The idea expressed here later appears in the libretto of *Parsifal*. As the transformation scene in act 1 begins, Gurnemanz says to Parsifal: "Du sieh'st, mein Sohn, zum Raum / wird hier die Zeit."

69. Ibid., 2:351 (4:255–56).

70. Ibid., 2:351 (4:255—"ein willkürlich erdachtes System").

71. Ibid.,2:374 (4:281—"der eigenwilligste, grausamste und schmutzigste Kunstbrotgeber").

72. Ibid., 2:375 (4:282—"den Schutt").

73. Ibid., 2:354 (4:258–59—"Erklären wir dem Musiker daher, dass jedes, auch das geringste Moment seines Ausdruckes, in welchem die dichterische Absicht nicht enthalten, und welches von ihr zu ihrer Verwirklichung nicht als nothwendig bedingt ist, überflüssig, störend, schlecht ist; dass jede seiner Kundgebungen eine eindruckslose ist, wenn sie unverständlich bleibt, und dass sie verständlich nur dadurch wird, wenn sie die dichterische Absicht in sich schliesst; dass er, als Verwirklicher der dichterischen Absicht, aber ein unendlich Höherer ist, als er in seinem willkürlichen Schaffen ohne diese Absicht war,—denn als eine bedingte, befriedigende Kundgebung ist die seinige selbst höher als die der bedingenden, bedürftigen Absicht an sich, die wiederum dennoch die höchste, menschliche ist; dass er endlich, als von dieser Absicht in seiner Kundgebung bedingt, zu einer bei Weitem reicheren Kundgebung seines Vermögens veranlasst wird, als er es in seiner einsamen Stellung war, wo er— um möglichster Verständlichkeit wegen—sich selbst beschränken, nämlich zu einer Thätigkeit anhalten musste, die nicht seine eigenthümliche als Musiker war, während er gerade jetzt zur unbeschränktesten Entfaltung seines Vermögens nothwendig aufgefordert ist, weil er ganz nur Musiker sein darf und soll.

    "Dem Dichter erklären wir aber, dass seine Absicht, wenn sie im Ausdrucke des von ihm bedingten Musikers—so weit sie eine an das Gehör kundzugebende ist— nicht vollständig verwirklicht werden könnte, auch keine höchste dichterische Absicht überhaupt ist; dass überall da, wo seine Absicht noch kenntlich ist, er auch noch nicht vollständig gedichtet hat; dass er daher seine Absicht als eine höchste dichterische nur darnach bemessen kann, dass sie im musikalischen Ausdrucke vollkommen zu verwirklichen ist").

74. Ronald Gray, "The German Intellectual Background," p. 36. Gray mentions, in this regard, Hegel's "polarities" in which the spirit of the universe manifests itself, Schiller's *naiv* and *sentimentalisch* poets, Goethe's poet Tasso and man-of-affairs Antonio, Marx's thesis and antithesis, Heine's Hellene and Nazarene, and Nietzsche's Apollonian and Dionysian aspects of tragedy.

75. Wagner, *Opera and Drama*, 2:81 (*Oper und Drama*, 3:356).

76. Ibid., 2:82 (3:356).

77. Ibid.

78. Ibid., 2:351 (4:255—"Möglichkeiten des Ausdruckes bezeichnet").

Chapter 4

1. See Wagner, *Richard Wagner's Prose Works,* trans. William Ashton Ellis, 2:viii–x.

2. Wagner, letter to Theodor Uhlig, [15 February 1851], *Sämtliche Briefe,* 3:511.

3. Ibid., 3:512.

4. Wagner, *Music of the Future*, 3:295 (*Zukunftsmusik,* 7:124). Wagner seems never to have gotten over altogether this feeling of repugnance for *Oper und Drama*. It figures

in the amusing entry in Cosima's diary for 16 October 1878: "A bad night! R. frequently out of bed. . . . In the morning we wonder whether it was a tough partridge he ate in the evening which so upset him, or the reading of *Opera and Drama,* or a very evil-smelling ointment he put on his sore thumb" (Cosima Wagner, *Cosima Wagner's Diaries,* 2:172).

5. Wagner, *Music of the Future,* 3:321 (*Zukunftsmusik,* 7:152–53—"Nichts kann aber der künstlerischen Natur fremder und peinigender sein als ein solches, seinem gewöhnlichen durchaus entgegengesetztes, Denkverfahren. Er giebt sich ihm daher nicht mit der nöthigen kühlen Ruhe hin, die dem Theoretiker von Fach zu eigen ist; ihn drängt vielmehr eine leidenschaftliche Ungeduld, die ihm verwehrt, die nöthige Zeit auf sorgfältige Behandlung des Styles zu verwenden; die stets das ganze Bild seines Gegenstandes in sich schliessende Anschauung möchte er in jedem Satze vollständig geben; Zweifel daran, ob ihm diess gelinge, treibt ihn zur fortgesetzten Wiederholung des Versuches, was ihn endlich mit Heftigkeit und einer Gereiztheit erfüllt, die dem Theoretiker durchaus fremd sein soll. Auch aller dieser Übel und Fehler wird er inne, und durch das Gefühl von ihnen von Neuem beunruhigt, endigt er haftig sein Werk mit dem Seufzer, doch wohl etwa nur von Dem verstanden zu werden, der mit ihm schon die gleiche künstlerische Anschauung theilt").

6. Wagner's new ideas about opera had received wide circulation, not only from those people who had read *Die Kunst und die Revolution* and *Das Kunstwerk der Zukunft* (both of which had appeared in 1849) but also from those who had read the many newspaper articles that discussed his theories. Theodor Uhlig and Hans von Bülow were particularly active on Wagner's behalf; Uhlig wrote several articles for the *Neue Zeitschrift für Musik* during 1850 and 1851. For a list of his articles, see Wagner, *Sämtliche Briefe,* 4:197 note; for a discussion of the publicity Wagner's writings received during this time, see Ernest Newman, *The Life of Richard Wagner,* 2:218–28.

7. Wagner, *A Communication to My Friends,* 1:284 (*Eine Mittheilung an meine Freunde,* 4:303).

8. Ibid., 1:283–84 (4:302–3).

9. Ibid., 1:362 (4:385—"meine musikalische Stimmung").

10. Wagner described this creative process as early as 1844 in a letter to the Berlin critic Karl Gaillard: "I cannot say that I have an over-high opinion of my *métier* as a poet and confess that I only took it up as a matter of necessity: no decent texts were offered to me, and so I had to write them myself. Now, however, it would be impossible for me to set someone else's libretto to music for the following simple reason: with me it is not the case that I pick on some subject or other, set it to verse and then start thinking about suitable music for it. In this type of procedure I would have to face the evil of having to get enraptured twice over, which is impossible. My way of creating is different: first of all no subject can attract me except one which immediately conjures up not only a poetic but also a musical vision within me. Before I start writing even the very first line I am already intoxicated with the musical aroma of my creation; all the sounds, all the characteristic motives are in my head so that, when the text is finished and the scenes are ordered, the actual opera is also completed, and the detailed musical treatment is more in the nature of a quiet and calm working-out process after the event, for the moment of real production is already past. But to this end one can choose only subjects which cannot be treated in any manner but a musical one: I would never choose a subject which, in the hands of a

well-versed dramatist, could just as easily be turned into spoken drama. But as a musician I can select subjects, I can invent situations and contrasts which must always remain a closed book to the dramatic author and to the spoken drama" (quoted in Hans Gal, *Richard Wagner*, p. 147; for the original German, see Wagner, letter to Karl Gaillard, 30 January 1844, *Sämtliche Briefe*, 2:357–58).

11. Wagner, *A Communication to My Friends*, 1:364 (*Eine Mittheilung an meine Freunde*, 4:387—"Das in der musikalischen Sprache Auszudrückende sind nun . . . einzig Gefühle und Empfindungen: sie drückt den von unserer, zum reinen Verstandesorgan gewordenen Wortsprache abgelösten Gefühlsinhalt der rein menschlichen Sprache überhaupt in vollendeter Fülle aus. Was somit der absoluten musikalischen Sprache für sich unausdrückbar bleibt, ist die genaue Bestimmung des Gegenstandes des Gefühles und der Empfindung, an welchem diese selbst zu sicherer Bestimmtheit gelangen").

12. Ibid., 1:364 (4:388).

13. Ibid., 1:367 (4:391).

14. Ibid., 1:372 (4:396). The section on melody in this essay should be read in conjunction with Wagner's remarks about Gluck in *Oper und Drama*. A comparison of the two shows that Wagner's description of his own melodic innovations resembles in many respects his description of Gluck's; and it suggests, consequently, that Wagner's own principal operatic innovation was not so much melodic as formal.

15. Ibid.

16. Ibid., 1:326 (4:346).

17. Wagner recorded his first reading of Schopenhauer in his annals for 1854 between the entries "Beginning September: Minna on visit to Saxony and Weimar. (also Waldheim: Röckel.)" and "26 September: complete fair copy of Rheingold score" (Wagner, *The Diary of Richard Wagner*, p. 104). Wagner noted in *Mein Leben* that it was the poet Georg Herwegh who introduced him to Schopenhauer's work (see idem, *My Life*, pp. 614–15).

18. Wagner, *My Life*, p. 616.

19. Cosima Wagner, *Cosima Wagner's Diaries*, 2:859. Gobineau is chiefly known today for the racial theories propounded in his *Essai sur l'inégalité des races humaines*.

20. The summary here is drawn from Ronald Gray, "The German Intellectual Background," pp. 39–51; Jack M. Stein, *Richard Wagner and the Synthesis of the Arts*, pp. 113–17; and William Ashton Ellis's introductory notes to Wagner, *Richard Wagner's Prose Works*, 5:x–xiv. Nietzsche's *Schopenhauer als Erzieher* is more about Nietzsche's growth as a philosopher than it is about Schopenhauer's philosophy as such; but it well illustrates how Nietzsche, at least, learned from Schopenhauer without copying him in all things (see Friedrich Nietzsche, *Schopenhauer as Educator*, trans. James W. Hillesheim and Malcolm R. Simpson [South Bend, Indiana: Regnery Gateway, 1965]), p. 26, for example).

21. Wagner, *My Life*, pp. 615–16.

22. For a discussion of Wagner's use of Schopenhauer's philosophy in his librettos, see Gray, "The German Intellectual Background," pp. 50–51. In his librettos, as in his

daily life, Wagner altered Schopenhauer's philosophy to meet his own immediate needs.

23. See Arthur Schopenhauer, *The World as Will and Representation,* trans. E. F. J. Payne (Indian Hills, Colorado: The Falcon's Wing Press, 1958; repr. New York: Dover Publications, 1969), 1:255–67 and 2:447–57. For two discussions of Schopenhauer's view of music, see Gray, "The German Intellectual Background," pp. 47–49; and L. Dunton Green, "Schopenhauer and Music," *The Musical Quarterly* 16 (1930): 199–206.

24. Schopenhauer, *The World as Will and Representation,* 2:448.

25. Ibid., 1:261.

26. Ibid., 2:448–49.

27. Cosima Wagner, *Cosima Wagner's Diaries,* 2:623–24.

28. Wagner, "On Franz Liszt's Symphonic Poems," 3:238 ("Über Franz Liszt's symphonische Dichtungen," 5:239). Wagner had earlier paid tribute to Liszt at the close of *Eine Mittheilung an meine Freunde.*

29. Ibid., 3:246 (5:247—"die Musik kann nie und in keiner Verbindung, die sie angeht, aufhören die höchste, die erlösende Kunst zu sein. Es ist diess ihr Wesen, dass, was alle anderen Künste nur andeuten, durch sie und in ihr zur unbezweifeltsten Gewissheit, zur allerunmittelbarst bestimmenden Wahrheit wird").

30. Ibid., 3:247 (5:248).

31. Ibid., 3:248 (5:249).

32. Ibid., 3:249 (5:250—"steht dem gemeinen Leben viel näher, und wird nun dann verständlich, wenn er seine Idee in einer Handlung uns vorführt, die in ihren mannigfaltig zusammengesetzten Momenten einem Vorgange dieses Lebens so gleicht, dass jeder Zuschauer sie mit zu erleben glaubt. Der Musiker dagegen sieht vom Vorgange des gemeinen Lebens gänzlich ab, heft die Zufälligkeiten und Einzelheiten desselben vollständig auf, und sublimirt dagegen alles in ihnen Liegende nach seinem konkreten Gefühlsinhalte, der sich einzig bestimmt eben nur in der Musik geben lässt").

33. Ibid., 3:251 (5:252). Although Wagner does not say so, the process he saw Liszt going through in writing his symphonic poems appears to be the ultimate refinement of the poetic intent at work.

34. Wagner, *Music of the Future,* 3:295 (*Zukunftsmusik,* 7:124—"konkreten Gehalt").

35. Ibid., 3:317–18 (7:149).

36. Ibid., 3:324 (7:156–57—"dass ich von einem richtigen Instinkte ausgegangen war, wenn ich in der gleichmässigen gegenseitigen Durchdringung der Poesie und der Musik dasjenige Kunstwerk mir als zu ermöglichen dachte, welches im Moment der scenischen Aufführung mit unwiderstehlich überzeugendem Eindrucke wirken müsste, und zwar in der Weise, dass alle willkürliche Reflexion vor ihm sich in das reine menschliche Gefühl auflöse. Dass ich diese Wirkung hier erreicht sah, . . . diess hat mich aber zu noch kühneren Ansichten von der all-ermöglichenden Wirksamkeit der Musik bestimmt").

37. Ibid., 3:326 (7:158).

38. Ibid., 3:327 (7:159—"die strengsten, aus meinen theoretischen Behauptungen flies-

senden Anforderungen zu stellen: nicht weil ich es nach meinem Systeme geformt hätte, denn alle Theorie war vollständig von mir vergessen; sondern weil ich hier endlich mit der vollsten Freiheit und mit der gänzlichsten Rücksichtslosigkeit gegen jedes theoretische Bedenken in einer Weise mich bewegte'').

39. Wagner, *Beethoven,* 5:83 (9:103).

40. Ibid., 5:85 (9:105).

41. Ibid., 5:100 (9:121—''betritt das lyrische Pathos fast schon den Boden einer idealen Dramatik im bestimmteren Sinne, und, wie es zweifelhaft dünken dürfte, ob auf diesem Wege die musikalische Konzeption nicht bereits in ihrer Reinheit getrübt werden möchte, weil sie zur Herbeiziehung von Vorstellungen verleiten müsste, welche an sich dem Geiste der Musik durchaus fremd erscheinen, so ist andererseits wiederum nicht zu verkennen, dass der Meister . . . durch einen dem eigensten Gebiete der Musik entkeimten, durchaus idealen Instinkt hierin geleitet wurde'').

42. Ibid., 5:101 (9:122).

43. Ibid., 5:101 (9:123).

44. Ibid., 5:104 (9:125—''nicht störend zu unserer musikalisch bestimmten Empfindung, weil er uns keinesweges Vernunftvorstellungen anregt''). In view of the confusion this assertion in *Beethoven* has sometimes caused, I would like to emphasize that Wagner was not speaking of words in general here but of the words in the Catholic mass, ''formulae of faith'' (ibid. [''Glaubensformeln'']), that through many years and repeated use had lost their individual, specific meanings.

45. This is another opinion, expressed in *Beethoven* and related to Wagner's reading of Schopenhauer, that is easy to misconstrue. Wagner had never failed to recognize music's power of expression. The point is that music can override the meaning of words, can be incompatible with that meaning, not that it should.

46. Wagner, *Beethoven,* 5:104–5 (9:126—''um der dichterischen Absicht einen sowohl präziseren, als tiefer dringenden Ausdruck zu geben'').

47. Ibid., 5:105 (9:126–27—''Dass weder für das eine noch für das andere Rezeptionsvermögen eine vollkommene ästhetische Befriedigung zu gewinnen war, erklärt sich offenbar daraus, dass . . . die Opernmusik nicht zu der, der Musik einzig entsprechenden Andacht umstimmte, in welcher das Gesicht derart depotenzirt wird, dass das Auge die Gegenstände nicht mehr mit der gewohnten Intensität wahrnimmt''). Wagner complained that in ordinary opera the alternating attractions of sight and sound so occupied the audience's attention that it was impossible for one to use the faculty of thought to discover what was happening on the stage.

48. Ibid., 5:106 (9:127—''dass die Musik auch das vollkommenste Drama in sich schliesse'').

49. Ibid., 5:106 (9:128).

50. Ibid., 5:112 (9:134—''ein gewisses Übermaass, eine gewaltsame Nöthigung zur Entladung nach aussen'').

51. Ibid., 5:112 (9:135—''nicht das dramatische Gedicht, sondern das wirklich vor unseren Augen sich bewegende Drama, als sichtbar gewordenes Gegenbild der Musik,

wo dann das Wort und die Rede einzig der Handlung, nicht aber dem dichterischen Gedanken mehr angehören'').

52. See Robert W. Gutman, *Richard Wagner: The Man, His Mind, and His Music,* pp. 319–20; and Stein, *Richard Wagner and the Synthesis of the Arts,* pp. 157–58.

53. Wagner, *Beethoven,* 5:121 (9:145).

54. Wagner, *The Destiny of Opera,* 5:129 (*Über die Bestimmung der Oper,* 9:155).

55. Ibid., 5:138 (9:166—''einer Unzulänglichkeit des dichterischen Wesens'').

56. Ibid., 5:142 (9:171).

57. Ibid., 5:144 (9:172—''eine fixirte mimische Improvisation von allerhöchstem dichterischem Werthe'').

58. Ibid., 5:148 (9:178).

59. Ibid., 5:149 (9:179—''erhabenen Unregelmässigkeit''). Wagner referred to these formal structures of classical music as ''cramped and sterile'' (ibid., 5:147 [9:177]), implying, of course, that not only were the forms confining to organic development but that they could not create new forms to alleviate that confinement.

60. See note 57 above.

61. Wagner noted that Wilhelmine Schröder-Devrient's dramatic ability could make even worthless music (Wagner's example of such music is Bellini's *I Capuleti ed i Montecchi*) seem great (see Wagner, *The Destiny of Opera,* 5:141 [*Über die Bestimmung der Oper,* 9:169]). The great singer was an early supporter of Wagner; he almost never tired of praising her dramatic ability or of singling her out as an example of what a singing actress should be.

62. One should remember, however, that the degree to which both gesture and tone were understandable in drama depended primarily on the degree to which each was conditioned by the libretto. Wagner discussed this point in *Oper und Drama,* part 3, chapter 7.

63. Wagner, *Actors and Singers,* 5:198 (*Über Schauspieler und Sänger,* 9:238).

64. Ibid., 5:198–99 (9:239—''hier das unermesslich vermögende Orchester, dort der dramatische Mime; hier der Mutterschooss des idealen Drama's, dort seine von jeder Seite her tönend getragene Erscheinung'').

65. Ibid., 5:203 (9:244).

66. Ibid.

67. Ibid., 5:204 (9:245—''durch Anschwellung und Accent nach dem Sinn der Rede'').

68. Ibid., 5:206 (9:248).

69. Ibid., 5:209 (9:251). Wagner considered Weber an excellent composer of lyric moments but one unequal to the demands of drama. Weber was an example of a composer who had proven barren when (as in the scene in *Der Freischütz* between Kaspar and Max) the poetic seed was offered to him.

70. Ibid., 5:209 (9:252—''einen bisher nicht gekannten ununterbrochenen musikalischen Fluss'').

71. Ibid., 5:213 (9:256).

72. Ibid.

73. Ibid.

74. Wagner, *A Glance at the German Operatic Stage of Today,* 5:275 (*Ein Einblick in das heutige deutsche Opernwesen,* 9:329). Considering the complexity of the libretto of *Tristan und Isolde,* this statement of Wagner's might seem somewhat disingenuous. But it is apparent from what follows that, in this case at least, Wagner was thinking of the *Meistersinger* performance to which he subsequently refers; *Tristan* is, for the moment, forgotten.

75. The composition sketches for *Götterdämmerung* occupied Wagner from 20 October 1869 to 22 July 1872; the autograph score, from 3 May 1873 to 21 November 1874.

76. Wagner, "Prologue to a Reading of *Götterdämmerung* before a Select Audience in Berlin," 5:305 ("Einleitung zu einer Vorlesung der *Götterdämmerung* vor einem ausgewählten Zuhörerkreise im Berlin," 9:366).

77. Ibid., 5:305 (9:366–67).

78. Ibid., 5:306 (9:367—"naive Präzision, welche das wahre Leben des Drama's ausmacht").

79. Wagner, "On the Name 'Musikdrama,' " 5:300–1 ("Über die Benennung 'Musikdrama,' " 9:361—"denn, man mochte es drehen und wenden wie man wollte, die 'Musik' blieb immer das eigentlich Störende für die Benennung, obwohl Jeder doch wiederum dunkel fühlte, dass sie trotz allem Anscheine die Hauptsache sei, und diess nur noch mehr, wenn ihr durch das ihr zugesellte wirkliche Drama die allerreichste Entwickelung und Kundgebung ihrer Fähigkeiten zugemuthet ward").

80. Ibid., 5:302 (9:362).

81. Ibid., 5:303 (9:365—"statt dessen geht nun in diesem Akte fast gar nichts wie Musik vor sich").

82. In this article, Wagner again tried to define the poet and the musician in terms derived from Schopenhauer's concept of the dream world (see Wagner, *On Poetry and Composition,* 6:137–42 [*Über das Dichten und Komponiren,* 10:188–94]).

83. Wagner, *On Operatic Poetry and Composition in Particular,* 6:154 (*Über das Opern-Dichten und Komponiren im Besonderen,* 10:206).

84. Ibid., 6:164 (10:218—"Stümperwerke").

85. Ibid.

86. Ibid., 6:170 (10:225—"vor Allem nie einen Text zu adoptiren, ehe sie in diesem nicht eine Handlung, und diese Handlung von Personen ausgeübt ersehen, welche den Musiker aus irgend einem Grunde lebhaft interessiren").

87. Ibid., 6:171 (10:227).

88. Wagner, *On the Application of Music to the Drama,* 6:176 (*Über die Anwendung der Musik auf das Drama,* 10:233).

89. Ibid., 6:179 (10:236).

90. Ibid., 6:182 (10:240).

91. Ibid., 6:183 (10:240).

92. Ibid., 6:183 (10:241—"Dennoch muss die neue Form der dramatischen Musik . . . die Einheit des Symphoniesatzes aufweisen, und diess erreicht sie, wenn sie, im innigsten Zusammenhange mit demselben, über das ganze Drama sich erstreckt, nicht nur über einzelne kleinere, willkürlich herausgehobene Theile desselben. Diese Einheit giebt sich dann in einem das ganze Kunstwerk durchziehenden Gewebe von Grundthemen, welche sich ähnlich wie im Symphoniesatze, gegenüber stehen, ergänzen, neu gestalten, trennen und verbinden; nur dass hier die ausgeführte und aufgeführte dramatische Handlung die Gesetze der Scheidungen und Verbindungen giebt, welche dort allerursprünglichst den Bewegungen des Tanzes entnommen waren").

93. Ibid., 6:184 (10:242).

94. Ibid., 6:185 (10:243).

95. Ibid., 6:186 (10:244).

96. Ibid., 6:187 (10:245).

97. Ibid., 6:189 (10:248).

98. Ibid., 6:188 (10:247—"ein gesuchter Effekt").

99. See Gutman, *Richard Wagner*, p. 322.

100. Wagner, *Religion and Art*, 6:223 (*Religion und Kunst*, 10:286).

101. Ibid. ("der lyrische Ausdruck entzückungsvoller Anbetung").

102. See Wagner, *The Destiny of Opera*, 5:129 (*Über die Bestimmung der Oper*, 9:155).

103. See Gutman, *Richard Wagner*, p. 321. Gutman attempts to show that Wagner vacillated from one point of view to another about what the relationship between words and music in opera should be. According to Gutman, not only could Wagner not make up his mind on this matter; he was too proud to admit that the theories in *Oper und Drama* could ever be out of date.

104. The first halves of these chapter titles are drawn from sentences in Ellis's translations of three of Wagner's essays: *Music of the Future* (3:331); *Actors and Singers* (5:213); and *Religion and Art* (6:244).

Chapter 5

1. Robert Bailey gives 19 December 1856 as the date of the earliest dated sketch for *Tristan und Isolde*. For this and a discussion of how Wagner's sketches from the time he was working on *Siegfried* reveal his increasing interest in *Tristan*, see Bailey, "The Method of Composition," pp. 308–27. Wagner recorded in the annals for 1857 his decision to take up *Tristan*: "About mid-June decide to break off 'Siegfried' for 'Tristan' " (Wagner, *The Diary of Richard Wagner*, p. 107).

2. Wagner, *A Communication to My Friends*, 1:375–76 (*Eine Mittheilung an meine Freunde*, 4:399).

3. In this study, generic pitch names are indicated by roman capitals (for example,

F major, A minor, a diminished-seventh chord on G). Specific pitch names are italicized. Lowercase letters are used for the octave beginning on middle c; lowercase letters followed by superscripts, for the octaves above that (c^1 and c^2, for example). Notes in the octave below middle c are indicated by capital letters; and notes in the octaves below that, by capital letters followed by subscripts (C_1 and C_2, for example).

4. These observations are, in general, equally true of the prelude to the opera, which the sailor's song recalls in more than its motivic associations. The prelude is harmonically ambiguous, to say the least (although it can be heard as though it were in A minor); it is rhythmically vague (especially at the beginning, where it is almost impossible to determine the meter except by looking at the score) and improvisatory in nature; and it extends itself over the dynamic gamut.

5. The musical ideas in the prelude to act 3 also figure in "Im Treibhaus," one of the two *Wesendonck Lieder* specifically designated by Wagner as a study for *Tristan und Isolde*. The five poems by Mathilde Wesendonck that Wagner set were written late in 1857, after the *Tristan* libretto and under the influence of its ideas. "Im Treibhaus," the last of the poems to be set, was composed in May 1858. (Wagner had completed the composition sketch for act 1 of *Tristan* near the beginning of January 1858.)

    Since Wagner was making use of musical ideas intended primarily for his *Tristan* libretto to set poetry written by another person, one can hardly expect to find parallel poetic situations between "Im Treibhaus" and the beginning of act 3 or a correspondence of musical and poetic thoughts in the two settings; and yet, there are similarities. The situation of the ailing Tristan, for example, corresponds to that of the sorrowing plants, surrounded by warmth and light but cut off from their true home, stretching their limbs wide in passionate longing only to embrace empty space. In both the song and the prelude, the same musical figure is associated with this idea of struggling against restraint. The second musical idea in the prelude, the ascending two-part line in the strings, is associated in the song with the "süsser Duft" that rises on the air, a "der Leiden stummer Sorge." The healing presence of Isolde finds its counterpart in the poem in the sympathy of the narrator for the plants and her feeling of kinship with them. Another similarity is the line from the poem "Öder Leere nicht' gen Grauss," which recalls the shepherd's response to Kurwenal: "Öd und leer das Meer!"

6. Ernest Newman, *The Wagner Operas*, p. 264.

7. The shepherd's first tune is "harmonically" reminiscent of the prelude to act 3: in both there is an alternation between F minor and D-flat major; there is whole-step and chromatic descent and a cadence in C minor with a return to F minor.

8. For a discussion of this aspect of Wagner's compositional procedure, see Bailey, "The Method of Composition," p. 270.

9. It was the appearance of growth that Wagner admired so much in Beethoven's development of the *Freude* melody in the Ninth Symphony. At the same time, however, Wagner recognized the compositional procedure for what it was and appears to have taken it for his model in general (see Wagner, *Opera and Drama*, 2:106–10 [*Oper und Drama*, 3:384–89]).

10. See Joseph Kerman, *Opera as Drama* (New York: Random House, Vintage Books, 1952), p. 201.

11. George Bernard Shaw, "The Tone Poet," p. 113.

12. For a discussion and assessment of the effect on his music of Wagner's tendency to explain and justify in his librettos, see Hans Gal, *Richard Wagner,* pp. 151–57.

13. See Wagner, "On the Name 'Musikdrama,' " 5:303–4 ("Über die Benennung 'Musikdrama,' " 9:365).

14. See Wagner, *Music of the Future,* 3:331 (*Zukunftsmusik,* 7:164—"in der musikalischen Ausführung des 'Tristan' gar keine Wortwiederholung mehr stattfindet").

15. In discussing Wagner's claims to being a poet, Hans Gal has written that "in *Tristan* the romantically emotional paroxysms lead to the most extravagant hypertrophy of lyrical metaphor." Gal goes on to speak specifically of the "Was wir dachten" section of the love duet, discussed here, in the following terms: "This pompous balderdash is completely submerged, dissolved, transmuted in the music. It offered singable words to the composer, and apparently that was all he needed for his purpose at the moment. His music took care of the poetic utterance, and his lyricism was in no way fettered by such verbal spaghetti" (Gal, *Richard Wagner,* pp. 155–56; compare Shaw, "The Tone Poet," p. 115).

16. One example of this view appears in Elliott Zuckermann, *The First Hundred Years of "Tristan,"* p. 22: "Of the two sexual climaxes that are unmistakably depicted in the orchestra, one is interrupted by the entry of Kurvenal on an unnamable discord, and the other occurs after Tristan has been dead for twenty minutes. The subject of *Tristan* is unconsummated passion." Another example that applies specifically to the end of the opera (as if the writer had somehow missed the second act) occurs in Jacques Barzun, *Berlioz and the Romantic Century,* 3rd ed., 2 vols. (New York: Columbia University Press, 1969), 2:202: "Wagner reinforced by his natural sensuality and by the rhythm and subject of his *Liebestod* the great movement for sexual liberation that began in the sixties. Now that the reform has been accepted we need not be so spellbound by a passionate act which requires one hundred and ten men to perform."

17. See the quotation from Zuckermann, *The First Hundred Years of "Tristan,"* in the preceding note.

18. Wagner, *Music of the Future,* 3:331 (*Zukunftsmusik,* 7:164).

19. See Donald Francis Tovey, *The Main Stream of Music and Other Essays* (New York: Oxford University Press, 1949), p. 171; and Kerman, *Opera as Drama,* p. 212. In an article on Beethoven, Tovey referred in passing to the Wagnerian motive labeller who analyzed the *Liebestod* "into a dozen one-bar themes, giving a psychological name to each, not noticing the psychologically and musically vastly more important fact that the dying Isolde (or rather the orchestra) is singing the whole last 100 bars of the great duet in the second act" (Tovey, *The Mainstream of Music and Other Essays,* pp. 278–79).

20. Wagner, "Prelude to *Tristan und Isolde,*" 8:387.

Chapter 6

1. It should be pointed out that, practically speaking, the historical setting of *Die Meistersinger* probably allowed for elements of comedy that might not have been available to Wagner in myth. The fact that Wagner dealt only peripherally with comedy in *Oper und Drama* is just one more indication of how specific its view of opera is.

2. Wagner, *A Communication to My Friends,* 1:329 (*Eine Mittheilung an meine Freunde,* 4:349).

3. Ibid., ("Spiessbürgerschaft").

4. There is an exception to this statement in Hans Sachs's final speech, particularly in the "Habt acht!" section. Wagner apparently had doubts about this speech and had to be persuaded to include it in the opera (see Richard Du Moulin-Eckart, *Cosima Wagner,* trans. Catherine Alison Phillips, 2 vols. [New York: Alfred A. Knopf, 1930], 1:255); possibly he did so against his better judgment.

5. There is an obvious similarity in Wagner's musical effects in *Die Meistersinger* and *Tristan und Isolde.* In both operas, the orchestra speaks prominently on behalf of the lovers. Tonality represents the outside world (sailors, shepherd, and hunters in one case; churchgoers and mastersingers in the other); and the lovers, in contrast, are characterized by lyric chromaticism *(Die Meistersinger)* or tonal ambiguity *(Tristan und Isolde).*

6. The first prose sketch for *Die Meistersinger* was written in July 1845; the second and third sketches in October-November 1861 and the libretto between the end of December 1861 and the end of January 1862. During all these years, Wagner had the opportunity to develop musical ideas for the opera and had early "with the utmost distinctness . . . composed the principal part of the Overture in C Major" (Wagner, *My Life,* p. 802). He actually sketched the beginning of the overture in November 1861 and wrote out the whole piece in February-March 1862. He then began work on the composition sketches for act 1 but did not complete the full score for the act until March 1866. He worked on the sketches for act 2 from May to September 1866 and for act 3 from October 1866 to March 1867. He completed the full score for act 2 in June 1867 and for act 3 in October 1867.

   One of the motives in the overture (the first five measures in E major) appears in the opening scene of the opera and is the melody that Wagner eventually used as the first third of the prize song's *Abgesang.* Since, however, almost five years lay between Wagner's first work on the overture and the beginning of his work on act 3 and since his original conception of the prize song was completely different from the song as it now stands (see Ernest Newman, *The Wagner Operas,* pp. 369–71), it is not likely that Wagner had decided when he wrote the overture to use this particular melody in the prize song. Nevertheless, it is clear from the context of the scene (if not from the overture) that, whether or not Wagner had thought of the ultimate use to which the motive would be put, he associated it with the lovers in an important way musically and dramatically.

7. In this study, the two versions of the prize song are not distinguished by different names as is sometimes done.

8. As an illustration of Wagner's esthetic belief that "art, in order to be art, must conceal itself and appear in the guise of nature," Carl Dahlhaus has pointed out that Walther's trial song is not an example of spontaneous creation or natural genius but "presupposes the most intense effort and application" (Dahlhaus, *Richard Wagner's Music Dramas,* p. 69). The point is probably worth making, but it has little, if anything, to do with the opera. Of course the spontaneity of the trial song is illusory: it is the business of theater to present illusions, not the hard work that goes into creating them.

9. See Dahlhaus, *Richard Wagner's Music Dramas,* pp. 75–77.

10. Needless to say, there are inconsistencies here in the libretto that, like those in *Oper und Drama,* Wagner did not trouble himself to reconcile. What matters in the theater, however, is that one has the illusion that Sachs in the third act is teaching Walther something he does not know. It is a case of *feeling* that the scene between Sachs and Walther is right rather than *knowing* that it is wrong.

    The trial scene as a whole, however, illustrates an important Wagnerian belief about musical composition in his time: the opposition between current practice and what Wagner would have considered to be "eternal" artistic truths. The reason Wagner's (like Walther's) music was so little understood and so endlessly criticized was that it ignored "conventional" rules and practices. This is what Beckmesser (Wagner's scarcely disguised caricature of the "unsympathetic" critic Eduard Hanslick) points out—although, ultimately, to no avail. In *Die Meistersinger,* at least, it is the eternal truths, rather than the accepted artistic practice, to which the folk respond.

11. I have borrowed this example, with slight alterations of my own, from Newman, *The Wagner Operas,* p. 345.

12. In part 1 of *Oper und Drama,* Wagner had criticized Meyerbeer for seeking to create musical effects first and dramatic reasons for the effects only after the effects themselves had been decided on. But Wagner did not accuse even Meyerbeer of violating opera's forms (as Beckmesser does) for the sake of effect.

13. In regard to the subject of inconsistency in Wagner's works, perhaps it should be mentioned that Sachs, while preserving the foundations of the mastersingers' art, is, for all practical purposes, destroying the superstructure of that art. Wagner offers little explanation, moreover, of how Sachs's instruction of David (if one can judge what David has been taught by what he teaches) can have been so very different from his instruction of Walther.

14. The words of the *Abgesang* may be a new creation on Walther's part; but he has already used at least three and a half measures of the melody that begins the *Abgesang* (as well as melodic fragments from the *Stollen*) at the end of act 1, scene 1, as he pledges his possessions, his blood, and his poet's sacred resolve to winning Eva ("Für euch Gut und Blut! / Für euch / Dichters heil'ger Mut!").

15. The melodic contours of the prize song are general and unrelated to specific words in the poem not only because the song is lyrical and strophic but also—and perhaps primarily—because Wagner wrote the song's melody before he wrote its words (see Newman, *The Wagner Operas,* pp. 369–71; see also Wagner, *The Diary of Richard Wagner,* p. 122).

16. Wagner, *Actors and Singers,* 5:213 (*Über Schauspieler und Sänger,* 9:256).

17. Ibid.

Chapter 7

1. See Wagner, *Opera and Drama,* 2:317 (*Oper und Drama,* 4:220–21).

2. Wagner, *Music of the Future,* 3:338 (*Zukunftsmusik,* 7:172).

3. See Stein, *Richard Wagner and the Synthesis of the Arts,* p. 213. Opposed to Stein's view is that of Hans Gal: "The musician Wagner had to have a poetical concept in

order to become productive, and without the poet the composer could never have existed. . . . There is no getting away from it: Wagner was only a musical dramatist, and only as a poet-composer could he rise to his full stature" (Gal, *Richard Wagner,* pp. 146–47).

4. See Wagner, *Opera and Drama,* 2:317–24 (*Oper und Drama,* 4:220–26).

5. See Wagner, *Beethoven,* 5:76 (9:95–96).

6. The music here, in the context of a Wagnerian opera, suggests a reference to Rossini; the flower maidens, moreover, recall one of Wagner's comments about Rossini in *Oper und Drama:* "the uncommonly handy modeler of artificial flowers, which he shaped from silk and satin and drenched their arid cups with that distilled substratum, till they began to smell like veritable blooms" (Wagner, *Opera and Drama,* 2:41 [*Oper und Drama,* 3:309–10]).

7. Cosima's diary entry for 26 March 1878 reads, in part: "R. continues working on his text and says he will have 18 maidens, no more. No one in the audience will take any notice of the text, he says, but the singers sing differently and feel like individuals if they do not just have to sing senseless repetitions in chorus, and this adds to the general effect, as, for instance, with the song of the Valkyries" (Cosima Wagner, *Cosima Wagner's Diaries,* 2:49–50).

8. Wagner, *Religion and Art,* 6:223 (*Religion und Kunst,* 10:286).

9. Cosima's diary entry for 11 August 1877 contains the following relevant remark: "Finally the revelation of 'Nehmt hin mein Blut' ['Take ye my blood']—R. tells me he wrote it down shortly before my return, with his hat and coat on, just as he was about to go out to meet me. He has had to alter the words to fit it, he says; . . . with the 'Prize Song' in *Die Meistersinger,* too, the melody came first, and he adapted the words to it. He had already told me yesterday that one must beware of having to extend the words for the sake of the melody" (Cosima Wagner, *Cosima Wagner's Diaries,* 1:977).

The editors of Cosima's diaries have altered her original words in the above passage from "extend the words for the sake of the melody" to "extend a melody for the sake of the words" in the belief that their alteration makes better sense (see ibid., 1:1154). This is clearly an error on the editors' part, however, and shows a complete misunderstanding not only of the passage but also of Wagner's entire operatic esthetic. Since Wagner was obviously warning against adopting as a common practice what he had just done ("He has had to alter the words to fit it") and since he had never recommended this procedure, I have restored the original words to the passage above. (In this regard, see also ibid., 2:216 and 2:268.)

10. The question of form that the lyric and declamatory aspects of music in opera bring up was, of course, the principal subject not only of *Oper und Drama* but of most of Wagner's later theoretical writings as well.

11. Paul Bekker attempted to show that a three-act formal structure—preparation, action, and fulfillment—was typical of Wagner's dramaturgy. According to Bekker, "the two outer acts are necessary to the form, but as far as the content is concerned they serve simply as preparation and conclusion to the action-carrying middle act" (Bekker, *The Changing Opera,* p. 185). Bekker felt that this framing aspect of the two outer acts was particularly apparent and significant in *Parsifal.*

12. See Rudolf Stephan, "Gibt es ein Geheimnis der Form bei Richard Wagner?" p. 11.

13. The ridicule Wagner heaped on iambic verse in *Oper und Drama* did not prevent him from using it, as in the case of Kundry's lullaby, when he deemed it dramatically appropriate. For the earlier view of iambic verse, see Wagner, *Opera and Drama*, 2:241 (*Oper und Drama*, 4:134).

14. The three descending half steps (and the inversion of this figure) that occur so frequently in this scene as Kundry tries to seduce Parsifal also appear prominently in the inner voices of the "Durch Mitleid wissend" motive (see, for example, the statements of the motive in act 1 before Parsifal's first entrance and at the end of the act; see also Kundry's paraphrase on the motive [example 7.14] at the beginning of the scene discussed here).

15. Wagner, *Religion and Art*, 6:224 (*Religion und Kunst*, 10:287).

Chapter 8

1. Wagner, *A Communication to My Friends*, 1:326 (*Eine Mittheilung an meine Freunde*, 4:346).

2. Robert W. Gutman, *Richard Wagner: The Man, His Mind, and His Music*, p. 320.

3. Cosima Wagner, *Cosima Wagner's Diaries*, 1:457. A few weeks later, on 8 March 1872, Cosima recorded the following related remark: "In general R. criticizes Schopenhauer for not having paid sufficient attention to the male and female elements" (ibid., 1:465).

4. Wagner, *Music of the Future*, 3:306 (*Zukunftsmusik*, 7:136).

5. It should be pointed out again that one of the major inconsistencies in *Oper und Drama* involves Wagner's attempt to reconcile his concept of the intellectual, explaining function of words with his belief in the all-pervading emotional power of music. In this regard, no matter how much a poet concentrates the words in his libretto, many nonlyrical (and therefore nonmusical) words must, of necessity, be retained in order to prepare the emotional situations upon which the power of music subsequently expands.

6. Wagner, "Prologue to a Reading of *Götterdämmerung* before a Select Audience in Berlin," 5:305 ("Einleitung zu einer Vorlesung der *Götterdämmerung* vor einem ausgewählten Zuhörerkreise im Berlin," 9:366).

7. Wagner, *The Artwork of the Future*, 1:134 (*Das Kunstwerk der Zukunft*, 3:123—"So vermag die Dichtkunst das wirkliche Kunstwerk—und diess ist nur das sinnlich unmittelbar dargestellte—gar nicht zu schaffen, ohne die Künste, denen die sinnliche Erscheinung unmittelbar angehört; der Gedanke, dieses blosse Bild der Erscheinung, ist an sich gestaltlos, und erst, wenn er den Weg wieder zurückgeht, auf dem er erzeugt wurde, kann er zur künstlerischen Wahrnehmbarkeit gelangen. In der Dichtkunst kommt die Absicht der Kunst sich überhaupt zum Bewusstsein: die anderen Kunstarten enthalten in sich aber die unbewusste Nothwendigkeit dieser Absicht. Die Dichtkunst ist der Schöpfungsprozess, durch den das Kunstwerk in das Leben tritt: aus Nichts vermag aber nur der Gott Jehova etwas zu machen,—der Dichter muss das Etwas haben, und dieses Etwas ist der ganze künstlerische Mensch, der in der Tanz- und Tonkunst das zum Seelenverlangen gewordene sinnliche Verlangen

kundgiebt, welches durch sich erst die dichterische Absicht erzeugt"). *Das Kunst-werk der Zukunft* offers substantial evidence that Wagner's emphasis on gestures and physical show in his later later writings grew out of his earlier writings, not out of his reading of Schopenhauer from 1854 on.

8. Wagner, "A Letter to Hector Berlioz," 3:290 ("Ein Brief an Hector Berlioz," 7:118— "durch eine innige Vereinigung beider Künste das jeder einzelnen Unausdrückbare mit überzeugendster Klarheit ausgedrückt werde"). The letter first appeared in the *Presse Théatrale* for 26 February 1860 in response to an earlier review of Wagner's music made by Berlioz in the *Journal des Débats* for 9 February 1860.

9. Christoph Willibald Gluck, "Dedication to *Alceste,*" trans. Eric Blom, in *Source Readings in Music History,* comp. and ed. Oliver Strunk (New York: W. W. Norton & Co., 1950), p. 674.

10. Idem, "Letter to M. de la Harpe," trans. Ulrich Weisstein, in *The Essence of Opera,* ed. and annotated by Ulrich Weisstein (New York: W. W. Norton & Co., 1969), p. 111. In the Gluck-Piccini quarrel, de la Harpe took the side of Piccini and the Italians.

11. Wagner, *The Artwork of the Future,* 1:191 (*Das Kunstwerk der Zukunft,* 3:187—"So, im wechselvollen Reigen sich ergänzend, werden die vereinigten Schwesterkünste bald gemeinsam, bald zu zweien, bald einzeln, je nach Bedürfniss der einzig Maass und Absicht gebenden dramatischen Handlung, sich zeigen und geltend machen. Bald wird die plastische Mimik dem leidenschaftslosen Erwägen des Gedankens lauschen; bald der Wille des entschlossenen Gedankens sich in den unmittelbaren Ausdruck der Gebärde ergiessen; bald die Tonkunst die Strömung des Gefühles, die Schauer der Ergriffenheit allein auszusprechen haben; bald aber werden in gemeinsamer Um-schlingung alle drei den Willen des Drama's zur unmittelbaren, könnenden That er-heben. Denn Eines giebt es für sie alle, die hier vereinigten Kunstarten, was sie wollen müssen, um im Können frei zu werden, und das ist eben das Drama: auf die Erreichung der Absicht des Drama's muss es ihnen daher allen ankommen").

12. Hans Gal has written that "there simply is no permanent equilibrium in the relation-ship between dramatist and composer: the one or the other occasionally has to make a sacrifice" (Gal, *Richard Wagner,* p. 154).

13. Wagner, *The Artwork of the Future,* 1:190–91 (*Das Kunstwerk der Zukunft,* 3:185–86— "Nicht eine reich entwickelte Fähigkeit der einzelnen Künste wird in dem Gesammt-kunstwerk der Zukunft unbenützt verbleiben, gerade in ihm erst wird sie zur vollen Geltung gelangen. So wird namentlich auch die in der Instrumentalmusik so eigen-thümlich mannigfaltig entwickelte Tonkunst nach ihrem reichsten Vermögen in die-sem Kunstwerke sich entfalten können, ja sie wird die mimische Tanzkunst wie-derum zu ganz neuen Erfindungen anregen, wie nicht minder den Athem der Dicht-kunst zu ungeahnter Fülle ausdehnen. In ihrer Einsamkeit hat die Musik sich aber ein Organ gebildet, welches des unermesslichsten Ausdruckes fähig ist, und diess ist das Orchester. . . . Das Orchester ist, so zu sagen, der Boden unendlichen, allge-meinsamen Gefühles, aus dem das individuelle Gefühl des einzelnen Darstellers zur höchsten Fülle herauszuwachsen vermag: es löst den starren, unbeweglichen Boden der wirklichen Scene gewissermassen in eine flüssigweich nachgiebige, eindruckemp-fängliche, ätherische Fläche auf, deren ungemessener Grund das Meer das Gefühles selbst ist").

14. Ibid., 1:193–94 note (3:189–90 note).

15. See note 3 above.

16. In this regard, it seems significant that Wagner sketched the choral scenes in the second acts of both *Die Meistersinger* and *Parsifal* independently of the words in his original librettos and then wrote new words to fit the music he had sketched (see Robert Bailey, "The Method of Composition," p. 278). Wagner had followed the same procedure earlier in *Lohengrin.*

17. "Ihr schlosset nicht in gleichen Ton: / das macht den Meistern Pein."

18. This E-major relationship in *Tristan* and other structural tonal devices in Wagner's operas are mentioned in Joseph Kerman, "Wagner: Thoughts in Season," *The Hudson Review 13* (1960–61): 329–49.

19. See Wagner, "On Franz Liszt's Symphonic Poems," 3:246 ("Über Franz Liszt's symphonische Dichtungen," 5:239).

20. The view expressed here is in opposition to that suggested in Jack M. Stein, *Richard Wagner and the Synthesis of the Arts*, pp. 211–13.

21. Wagner, *Religion and Art*, 6:223 (*Religion und Kunst*, 10:286).

22. Wagner, *On the Application of Music to the Drama*, 6:186 (*Über die Anwendung der Musik auf das Drama*, 10:244).

23. See Wagner, *A Communication to My Friends*, 1:362–67 (*Eine Mittheilung an meine Freunde*, 4:385–91).

24. See Wagner, *On the Application of Music to the Drama*, 6:185 (*Über die Anwendung der Musik auf das Drama*, 10:243). If the composer had been Meyerbeer, of course, Wagner, for one, would have insisted that the compositional process was the other way around.
     An excellent example of a musical effect that preceded its verse and suggested it comes from one of Mozart's letters written during the composition of *Die Entführung aus dem Serail*: "As we have given the part of Osmin to Herr Fischer, who certainly has an excellent bass voice . . . , we must take advantage of it. . . . But in the original libretto Osmin has only this short song and nothing else to sing, except in the trio and the finale; so he has been given an aria in Act I, and he is to have another in Act II. I have explained to Stephanie the words I require for this aria—indeed I had finished composing most of the music for it before Stephanie knew anything whatever about it. I am enclosing only the beginning and the end, which is bound to have a good effect. Osmin's rage is rendered comical by the use of Turkish music. . . . The passage 'Drum beim Barte des Propheten' is indeed in the same time, but with quick notes; but as Osmin's rage gradually increases, there comes (just when the aria seems to be at an end) the allegro assai, which is in a totally different tempo and in a different key; this is bound to be very effective. For just as a man in such a towering rage oversteps all the bounds of order, moderation and propriety and completely forgets himself, so must the music too forget itself" (Mozart, letter to Leopold Mozart, 26 September 1781, *The Letters of Mozart and His Family*, 2:768–69). This letter seems particularly relevant to Wagner's argument here, since it shows clearly that Mozart (the opera composer Wagner respected above all others) achieved at least one musical-dramatic effect by what at first appears to be the "reverse" creative procedure that Wagner criticized so severely in the works of composers like Meyerbeer. A closer reading of the letter, however, reveals a creative process much like Wagner's

concept of the poetic intent: the "poetic" idea of a man in a towering rage suggested to Mozart the means whereby that rage could be realized musically. Had Mozart been his own poet, he could at that point have written words to meet the requirements of both the idea and the musical realization of it. Since he was not a poet, he did the next best thing: he told the poet what words he required. The important point is that an idea that fit into a dramatic context occurred to a person who knew the expressive range of music and how to command it.

25. See Wagner, *On Operatic Poetry and Composition in Particular,* 6:172 (*Über das Opern-Dichten und Komponiren im Besonderen,* 10:228).

26. Ibid., 6:169 (10:224–25).

27. Ibid., 6:170 (10:225).

Bibliography

This study makes reference principally to Wagner's published essays and operas. The secondary sources cited which deal with Wagner form only a small part of the vast number of writings about Wagner and his work. More extensive bibliographies can be found in the following entries listed below: Robert W. Gutman, *Richard Wagner: The Man, His Mind, and His Music*; Jack M. Stein, *Richard Wagner and the Synthesis of the Arts*; Curt von Westernhagen, *Wagner: A Biography*; and the article on Wagner in *The New Grove Dictionary of Music and Musicians*.

Abraham, Gerald. *A Hundred Years of Music*. 3d ed. Chicago: Aldine Publishing Company, 1964.

Adler, Guido. *Richard Wagner: Vorlesungen gehalten an der Universität zu Wien*. 2d ed. Munich: Drei Masken Verlag, 1923.

Bailey, Robert. "The Genesis of *Tristan und Isolde* and a Study of Wagner's Sketches and Drafts for the First Act." Ph.D. dissertation, Princeton University, 1969.

_____. "The Method of Composition." In *The Wagner Companion*, pp. 269–338. Edited by Peter Burbidge and Richard Sutton. New York: Cambridge University Press, 1979.

Barth, Herbert; Mack, Dietrich; and Voss, Egon, comp. and ed. *Wagner: A Documentary Study*. Translated by P. R. J. Ford and Mary Whittall. New York: Oxford University Press, 1975.

Barzun, Jacques. *Berlioz and the Romantic Century*. 3d ed. 2 vols. New York: Columbia University Press, 1969.

Bekker, Paul. *The Changing Opera*. Translated by Arthur Mendel. New York: W. W. Norton, 1935.

_____. *Richard Wagner: His Life in His Work*. Translated by M. M. Bozman. London: J. M. Dent and Sons, 1931.

Black, Michael. "The Literary Background: Poetry, Poetic Drama and Music Drama." In *The Wagner Companion*, pp. 60–84. Edited by Peter Burbidge and Richard Sutton. New York: Cambridge University Press, 1979.

Chamberlain, Houston Stewart. "Notes chronologiques sur *L'Anneau de Nibelung*." *Revue wagnérienne* 3 (February 1888; reprint ed., Geneva: Stalkine Reprints, 1968):263–76.

Cooke, Deryck. *I Saw the World End: A Study of Wagner's "Ring."* New York: Oxford University Press, 1979.

_____. "Wagner's Musical Language." In *The Wagner Companion*, pp. 225–68. Edited by Peter Burbidge and Richard Sutton. New York: Cambridge University Press, 1979.

Dahlhaus, Carl. *Richard Wagner's Music Dramas*. Translated by Mary Whittall. Cambridge: Cambridge University Press, 1979.

_____. "Wagners dramatisch-musikalisches Formbegriff." In *Colloquium Verdi-Wagner (Rom 1969)*, pp. 290–303. Edited by Friedrich Lippmann. Analecta Musicologica, vol. 11. Cologne and Vienna: Böhlau Verlag, 1972.

David, Richard. "Wagner the Dramatist." In *The Wagner Companion*, pp. 115–39. Edited by Peter Burbidge and Richard Sutton. New York: Cambridge University Press, 1979.

Dent, Edward J. *The Rise of Romantic Opera*. Edited by Winton Dean. Cambridge: Cambridge University Press, 1976.

Du Moulin-Eckart, Richard. *Cosima Wagner*. Translated by Catherine Alison Phillips. 2 vols. New York: Alfred A. Knopf, 1930.

Flechsig, Irmtraud. "Beziehungen zwischen textlicher und musikalischer Struktur in Richard Wagners Tristan und Isolde." In *Das Drama Richard Wagners als musikalisches Kunstwerk*, pp. 239–56. Edited by Carl Dahlhaus. Studien zur Musikgeschichte des 19. Jahrhunderts, vol. 23. Regensburg: Gustav Bosse Verlag, 1970.

Gal, Hans. *Richard Wagner*. Translated by Hans-Hubert Schönzeler. New York: Stein and Day, 1976.

Glasenapp, Carl Friedrich. *Life of Richard Wagner*. Translated by William Ashton Ellis. 6 vols. London: Kegan Paul, Trench, Trübner & Co., 1900–1908.

Gluck, Christoph Willibald. "Dedication to *Alceste*." Translated by Eric Blom. In *Source Readings in Music History*, pp. 673–75. Compiled and edited by Oliver Strunk. New York: W. W. Norton & Co., 1950.

_____. "Letter to M. de la Harpe." Translated by Ulrich Weisstein. In *The Essence of Opera*, pp. 110–13. Edited and annotated by Ulrich Weisstein. New York: W. W. Norton & Co., 1969.

Gray, Ronald. "The German Intellectual Background." In *The Wagner Companion*, pp. 34–59. Edited by Peter Burbidge and Richard Sutton. New York: Cambridge University Press, 1979.

Green, L. Dunton. "Schopenhauer and Music." *The Musical Quarterly* 16 (1930):199–206.

Grout, Donald J. *A Short History of Opera*. 2d ed. New York: Columbia University Press, 1965.

Gutman, Robert W. *Richard Wagner: The Man, His Mind, and His Music*. New York: Harcourt Brace Jovanovich, 1968.

Halm, August. *Von Grenzen und Ländern der Musik*. Munich: G. Müller Verlag, 1916.

Kerman, Joseph. *Opera as Drama*. New York: Random House, Vintage Books, 1952.

_____. "Wagner: Thoughts in Season." *The Hudson Review* 13 (1960–61):329–49.

Laudon, Robert Tallant. "Sources of the Wagnerian Synthesis: A Study of the Franco-German Tradition in Nineteenth-Century Opera." Ph.D. dissertation, University of Illinois, Urbana, 1969.

Lippman, Edward Arthur. "The Esthetic Theories of Richard Wagner." *The Musical Quarterly* 44 (1958):209–20.

Lorenz, Alfred. *Das Geheimnis der Form bei Richard Wagner*. 4 vols. Berlin: Max Hesses Verlag, 1924–33.

Magee, Bryan. *Aspects of Wagner*. New York: Stein and Day, 1969.

Mozart, Wolfgang Amadeus. *The Letters of Mozart and His Family*. Translated and edited by Emily Anderson. 2d ed. Prepared by A. Hyatt King and Monica Carolan. 2 vols. New York: St. Martin's Press, 1966.

The New Grove Dictionary of Music and Musicians, 1980 ed. S.v. "Wagner, Richard," by Robert Bailey, Carl Dahlhaus, and Curt von Westernhagen.

Newman, Ernest. *The Life of Richard Wagner*. 4 vols. New York: Alfred A. Knopf, 1933–46.

_____. *The Wagner Operas*. New York: Alfred A. Knopf, 1949.

Nietzsche, Friedrich. *On the Genealogy of Morals.* Translated by Walter Kaufmann and R. J. Hollingdale. New York: Random House, Vintage Books, 1969.

_____. *Schopenhauer as Educator.* Translated by James W. Hillesheim and Malcolm R. Simpson. South Bend, Indiana: Regnery/Gateway, 1965.

Noufflard, Georges. *Richard Wagner d'après lui-même.* 2 vols. Paris: Librairie Fischbacher, 1885.

Schopenhauer, Arthur. *The World as Will and Representation.* Translated by E. F. J. Payne. Indian Hills, Colorado: The Falcon's Wing Press, 1958; reprint ed., New York: Dover Publications, 1969.

Shaw, George Bernard. "The Tone Poet." In *Shaw on Music*, pp. 110–16. Compiled by Eric Bentley. Garden City, New York: Doubleday & Company, Doubleday Anchor Books, 1956.

Stein, Jack M. *Richard Wagner and the Synthesis of the Arts.* Detroit: Wayne State University Press, 1960; reprint ed., Westport, Connecticut: Greenwood Press, 1973.

Stephan, Rudolf. "Gibt es ein Geheimnis der Form bei Richard Wagner?" In *Das Drama Richard Wagners als musikalisches Kunstwerk*, pp. 9–16. Edited by Carl Dahlhaus. Studien zur Musikgeschichte des 19. Jahrhunderts, vol. 23. Regensburg: Gustav Bosse Verlag, 1970.

Tanner, Michael. "The Total Work of Art." In *The Wagner Companion*, pp. 140–224. Edited by Peter Burbidge and Richard Sutton. New York: Cambridge University Press, 1979.

Tovey, Donald Francis. *The Main Stream of Music and Other Essays.* New York: Oxford University Press, 1949.

Wagner, Cosima. *Cosima Wagner's Diaries.* Edited by Martin Gregor-Dellin and Dietrich Mack. Translated by Geoffrey Skelton. 2 vols. New York: Harcourt Brace Jovanovich, 1978–80.

Wagner, Richard. *The Diary of Richard Wagner: 1865-1882.* Presented and annotated by Joachim Bergfield. Translated by George Bird. London: Cambridge University Press, 1980.

_____. *Gesammelte Schriften und Dichtungen.* 10 vols. Leipzig: E. W. Fritzsch, 1871–83.
    Works from the *Gesammelte Schriften und Dichtungen* cited in this study include: *Beethoven;* "Ein Brief an Hector Berlioz"; *Ein Einblick in das heutige deutsche Opernwesen;* "Einleitung zu einer Vorlesung der *Götterdämmerung* vor einem ausgewählten Zuhörerkreise im Berlin"; *Das Judenthum in der Musik; Die Kunst und die Revolution;* "Kunst und Klima"; *Das Kunstwerk der Zukunft; Eine Mittheilung an meine Freunde; Oper und Drama; Religion und Kunst; Über das Dichten und Komponiren; Über das Opern-Dichten und Komponiren im Besonderen; Über die Anwendung der Musik auf das Drama;* "Über die Benennung 'Musikdrama' "; *Über die Bestimmung der Oper;* "Über Franz Liszt's symphonische Dichtungen"; *Über Schauspieler und Sänger;* "Wieland der Schmiedt," *als Drama entworfen;* and *Zukunftsmusik.*

_____. *Die Meistersinger von Nürnberg.* Libretto. Translated by Peter Branscombe. In booklet accompanying Angel Records, SEL-3776, 1971.

_____. *Die Meistersinger von Nürnberg.* Piano-vocal score. New York: G. Schirmer, 1904.

_____. *My Life.* "Authorized" anonymous translation. 2d ed. New York: Tudor Publishing Company, 1936.

_____. *Parsifal.* Piano-vocal score. New York: G. Schirmer, 1962 [the copyright date given is for the English translation that appears in the score].

_____. *Richard Wagner's Prose Works.* Translated by William Ashton Ellis. 8 vols. London: Routledge & Kegan Paul, 1892–99; reprint ed., New York: Broude Brothers, 1966.

Works cited from *Richard Wagner's Prose Works* include all those listed above under the entry for the *Gesammelte Schriften* as well as five additional works that do not appear in the *Gesammelte Schriften*: "Man and Established Society"; "On E. Devrient's *History of German Acting*"; "Prelude to *Tristan und Isolde*"; "The Revolution"; and "Theater Reform."

_____. *Sämtliche Briefe*. Edited by Gertrud Strobel and Werner Wolf. 4 vols. to date. Leipzig: VEB Deutscher Verlag für Musik, 1967–.

_____. *Tristan und Isolde*. Orchestral score. Leipzig: C. F. Peters, n.d.; reprint ed., New York: Dover Publications, 1973.

_____. *Tristan und Isolde*. Piano-vocal score. New York: G. Schirmer, 1906.

Warrack, John. "The Musical Background." In *The Wagner Companion*, pp. 85–112. Edited by Peter Burbidge and Richard Sutton. New York: Cambridge University Press, 1979.

Westernhagen, Curt von. *Richard Wagners Dresdener Bibliothek: 1842–1849*. Wiesbaden: F. A. Brockhaus, 1966.

_____. *Wagner: A Biography*. Translated by Mary Whittall. 2 vols. Cambridge: Cambridge University Press, 1978.

Zukerman, Elliott. *The First Hundred Years of "Tristan."* New York: Columbia University Press, 1964.

Index